THE POLITICAL PROCESS AND ECONOMIC CHANGE

AUTHORS

BRUNO S. FREY
WILLIAM R. KEECH
DONALD R. KINDER
MAURICE D. LEVI
WALTER R. MEBANE, JR.
KRISTEN R. MONROE
MARTIN PALDAM
R. ROBERT RUSSELL
CARL P. SIMON
M. STEPHEN WEATHERFORD

THE
Political Process
AND
Economic Change

K R I S T E N R. M O N R O E, E D I T O R

AGATHON PRESS, INC.

New York

© 1983 Agathon Press, Inc.
15 East 26 St., New York, NY 10010

LIBRARY OF CONGRESS CATALOGING IN PUBLICATION DATA

Main entry under title:

The political process and economic change.

   Includes bibliographies and index.
   Contents: Introduction: The development of political
economy/Kristen Monroe—Politics, economics, and
the underground economy/Bruno Frey—The political
dimensions of wage dynamics/Martin Paldam—(etc.)
   1. Economics—Addresses, essays, lectures. 2. Political science—Addresses, essays, lectures. 3. Economic
policy—Addresses, essays, lectures.
HB73.P635   1983   338.9   83-11866
ISBN 0-87586-063-X
ISBN 0-87586-062-1 (pbk.)

Printed in U.S.A.

Contents

The Authors

BRUNO S. FREY is Professor of Economics and Director of the Institute for Empirical Economic Research at the University of Zurich. His visiting appointments have included Nuffield College, Oxford, The Institute for International Economic Studies at the University of Stockholm and, recently, All Souls College, Oxford. With his main research interest in the economics of nonmarket issues, Professor Frey has been a pioneer in developing the economic theory of politics. His publications include more than one hundred journal articles and three books: *Umweltokonomie*, *Modern Political Economy*, and *Democratic Economic Policy*.

WILLIAM R. KEECH is Professor of Political Science at the University of North Carolina at Chapel Hill. His main research interests concern the theory and practice of representative government and the politics of macroeconomic policy. In addition to many articles, he is the author of *The Impact of Negro Voting: The Role of the Vote in the Quest for Equality* and coauthor, with Donald R. Matthews, of *The Party's Choice*.

DONALD R. KINDER is Associate Professor at the University of Michigan's Department of Political Science and Center for Political Studies in the Institute of Social Research. He has written extensively on elections and public opinion. Currently, he is completing a book on the impact of television news on mass consciousness and on the political consequences of economic distress.

MAURICE D. LEVI is Bank of Montreal Professor of International Finance in the Faculty of Commerce and Business Administration of the University of British Columbia. He has held visiting appointments at Hebrew University of Jerusalem, the Massachusetts Institute of Technology, the National Bureau of Economic Research, and the University of California at Berkeley. He is widely published in economic journals and is the author of *International Finance* and *Economics Deciphered*.

WALTER R. MEBANE, JR. is a member of the Department of Political Science at the University of Michigan and a Ph.D. candidate in the Department of Political Science at Yale University. Taking cues from both the cognitive science movement and Husserlian phenomenology, he is currently studying how ordinary people understand economics, energy, and government, both in world affairs and as these matter in their daily lives.

KRISTEN R. MONROE, Assistant Professor in the Department of Politics at New York University, is currently Visiting Assistant Professor in the Department of Politics at Princeton University. Her primary research interests have been constructing econometric models of the economy's political importance. Her chapter with Maurice Levi is part of a broader research attempt to develop a microlevel theory of how expectations and uncertainty affect individual political behavior, a theory which weds the economists' emphasis on rationality as a conscious calculation of costs and benefits with the social psychological emphasis on behavior derived from preconscious and subconscious impulses. Her book *Presidential Popularity and the Economy* will be published early in 1984.

MARTIN PALDAM is Senior Lecturer in the Department of Economics at the University of Aarhus in Denmark. His interests in political economy focus on voting and popularity functions and the noneconomic components of business cycles. His economic research includes price-wage formation and development, labor, and international economics. Author of some 50 papers in macroeconomics and public choice, his recent book specified a quarterly econometric model of the Danish economy.

R. ROBERT RUSSELL is Professor of Economics and Director of the C. V. Starr Center for Applied Economics at New York University. His principal research interests are microeconomic theory and public policy. After teaching at the University of California at both Santa Barbara and San Diego, he served as Director of the Council on Wage and Price Stability under President Carter and was a Brookings Institute Visiting Scholar in 1981. His books include *Duality, Separability, and Functional Structure: Theory and Economic Applications* and *Microeconomics: A Synthesis of Modern and Neoclassical Theory.*

CARL P. SIMON is Associate Professor of Economics and Mathematics at the University of Michigan. His research interests are general equilibrium theory and dynamic economic models, especially those dealing with differential commodities. He is coauthor, with Ann D. Witte, of *Beating the System: The Underground Economy* and among his articles is "Effective Price Mechanisms," with Donald Saari, published in *Econometrica.*

M. STEPHEN WEATHERFORD is Associate Professor of Political Science at the University of California at Santa Barbara. His research is concerned with the process through which economic interests are mobilized into political demands and expressed in political participation. His contribution to this book is part of a larger project on economic conditions and economic voting, themes also discussed in his 1983 article in the *American Political Science Review.*

Foreword

What is meant by contemporary political economy? Because this is the first in a series of works in contemporary political economy and because the area of study itself is becoming increasingly important in both political science and economics, the concept of contemporary political economy as a field should be addressed directly.

A subject with a long and varied past, political economy originally referred to classical economic theory as developed by Adam Smith, David Ricardo, and the Parson Malthus. Since then, the intellectual and political upheavals in social science have greatly distorted political economy as a discipline separate from political science and economics. Few schools in the United States offer separate PhDs in political economy. There is no one journal of political economy accepted as the definitive one in the field. The subject evokes much emotion but little agreement concerning the proper nature of the study of political economy.

The unifying concept in this series is political economy as the systematic analysis of the interaction between the political and economic systems. It is a nonideological concept, one which includes analysis of theories of political economy ranging from the Marxist to the public choice orientation. The method of analysis, however, is that of the exact sciences rather than the Marxist concept of science.[1] The emphasis is on systematic works of both a theoretical nature and those which model and empirically examine theoretical concepts, especially in cross-cultural and cross-national comparisons. To provide adequate understanding of the field for the undergraduate or nonprofessional student of political economy and to introduce the professional reader to the concept of this particular series, the introductory chapter of this volume traces the development of political economy as a discipline and discusses the particular contribution of the work offered in the following chapters.

Acknowledgments. All but one of the chapters in this volume were presented at an international conference supported by the National Science Foundation, the Exxon Educational Foundation, and New York University. While individual authors have acknowledged special debts in their chapters, the authors as a group would like to acknowledge the generous comments of the other conference participants: James Alt, Jean Blondel, Richard Brody, Eli Ginzberg, Bernard Grofman, Douglas A. Hibbs, Jr., Samuel Kernell, C. Duncan MacRae, Edward Nell, and Paul Whitely. None of the participants or the funding agencies are responsible for any of the interpretations or conclusions offered in this book.

I would like also to thank Fernando Viana, Johanna Cowie, Beatrice Lewis, George Sharrard, and Karen Dalton for their administrative, computational, and secretarial assistance in organizing the conference and preparing the conference volume. A special thanks are due two young scholars, Dona Metcalf Laughlin and Laura J. Scalia, for their editorial assistance in the manuscript preparation. Finally, I would like to thank Paul B. Hoeber, a most generous and scholarly publisher, who patiently and with great care put together the final volume.

Kristen R. Monroe

NOTE

1. Henry W. Spiegel in *The Growth of Economic Thought* (1971) discusses the alternative scientific methods employed in different schools of political economy.

THE POLITICAL PROCESS AND ECONOMIC CHANGE

1: Introduction: The Development of Political Economy

Kristen R. Monroe

The founders of political economy were philosophers sharing common assumptions concerning the political setting and the analytical method most conducive to economic well-being. Concerned with the individual's welfare within a prospering economic system and reacting against the state's role in mercantilism, these early writers nevertheless set their microlevel analyses firmly within a particular institutional and political setting, one free of state monopoly and interference. This institutional framework was believed necessary for the free enterprise system to operate in accordance with the natural laws of economics.

Within this system, Smith claimed the natural laws of economics would provide economic welfare for society. Scarcity would be eliminated through the efforts of free men pursuing their individual well-being. Malthus and Ricardo accepted Smith's view, although Ricardo's analysis of the distribution process suggests he was cognizant of political problems affecting economic growth. All three founders of classical political economy, however, assumed the economic system would be able to dispose of its output unfettered by political distortions. All three also accepted an economic approach that stressed an abstract-generalizing method of analysis. Later schools of political economy disagreed with these views and, because of these disagreements, important breaks occurred among the historicists, socialists, Marxists, and eventually, among members of the Austrian and the Lausanne schools.[2]

The first break with the Classical School was the minor one by early 19th century economists, who divided over the proper method of analysis. The historians stressed an inductive empirical approach, while the theoreticians preferred the inductive method. John Stuart Mill subsequently reconciled British historians and theoreticians. No such reconciliation took place on the Continent, however, largely because of personalities and historical events. Here the split between historians and theoreticians was much graver.

The center of debate was Germany. The central component of this split was 19th century German romanticism's denigration of the value of reason and natural order. Classical economists had advocated a scientific method of wringing general rules of human behavior from reason; under Hegel's influence, German economists rejected this in favor of an alternate scientific approach emphasizing the observation of the unique in its endless historical variation. This German historicism acquired international importance when German universities became centers of world learning in the late 19th century. As a method of analysis, German historicism was hostile to the secularized natural law tradition of Adam Smith and the later English political economists. It rejected utilitarianism in favor of an almost secular idolatry of the state and nation, occasionally to the point of advocating unquestioning obedience of the people to governmental authority.[3]

Socialist critics of classical political economy emanated from a different ideological tradition, one that stressed class rather than national or individual aspirations. Socialist critics argued that existing economic arrangements systematically excluded the poorest class. They rejected the institutional framework of laissez-faire economics and advocated substantive rather than merely legal equality. All socialist political economists shared a dissatisfaction with a social order in which the competition for private profit led to poverty and insecurity for so many.

Despite common roots, the socialist thinkers offered a wide variety of alternatives to classical political economy. Some opposed all private property. Others were antistate. Some, like Proudhon, rejected both the state and private property. Some proposed cooperative movements to replace competition as the guiding force of society, while others saw the trade union movement as the vehicle for shifting the balance of economic bargaining power to the worker. Some socialists even suggested monetary reforms to give producers purchasing power commensurate with their productive capacity. Finally, some argued that moral suasion was the way to effect change, while others advocated force.

Despite their international overtones, the early pre-Marxist socialist movements split along national lines. English socialists advocated gradualism, accomodationism, libertarianism, and voluntarism. French socialists tended to follow a mass revolutionary tradition, although some did advocate state-induced socialism. The German socialists relied heavily on the state as the impetus for change. Because many of the early socialists were involved in day-to-day politics, all tended toward pragmatic responses to specific events rather than to academic theories. Despite this, these pre-Marxist socialists left an important legacy of political ideas to mainstream practictioners of political economy: the promotion of industrial development; government by a managerial elite; making work more attractive for workers; educational reform; the social responsibility of property; and the idea of state management of the money supply.

Karl Marx inherited much from his socialist predecessors: the emphasis on class, the rejection of reason as a touchstone of human behavior, and the acceptance of the Germanic historical method of scientific analysis. Marx rejected the peaceful means of change advocated by the majority of socialists, however, because he believed these too idealistic in trusting the state as an instrument of social transformation. The prime mover in Marx's thought is not reasoned discourse but the inevitable evolution of history, which eventually will result in so much misery for the masses that they will rebel, overthrow their capitalist oppressors, and found a new classless society.[4]

Because of Marx's importance, socialists after Marx have to be divided into two general camps: Marxists and nationalistic Marxist socialists. The country that was most influenced politically by Marxism, of course, was Russia. Even before the revolution, czarist Russia shared Marx's rejection of the classical economists' methodological commitment to reason in favor of the laws of history and the will of the state. Because later Soviet economics developed in isolation from Western political economic thought, which it considered bourgeois or revisionist, Soviet political economy remained based on the Germanic and premarginalist concepts repudiated by most Western economists nearly 50 years before the Russian Revolution.[5] Later, a less ideological strand of Russian economic thought developed, one that had much in common with mainstream Western economics in its mathematical orientation.[6] All of the 20th century Soviet economic plans were based on input-output analysis, heavily mathematical and deductive in approach.[7] It is ironic that orthodox Soviet public policy thus has incorporated techniques based on rationality and the natural laws of mathematical economics; indeed, it is totally dependent on these techniques, and yet nevertheless continues to reject these concepts at the ideological level.

While these events were occurring in Russia, other Marxist socialist thought was dividing along national lines. The French Marxists, for example, leaned toward a radical syndicalism that rejected both political compromise and political reason. British Marxism-Socialism, influenced by the Fabian Society and Henry George, tended to be gradualist, pragmatic, and democratic.[8] Many non-Russian Socialist thinkers reentered mainstream economics after World War II via the Keynesian theories of the welfare state. This merger of separate ideological traditions was aided by the work of Leon Walras, whose general equilibrium system was abstract enough to cut across the diversity of institutions and include socialist variants, and by the work of Vilfredo Pareto and Enrico Barone, whose adaptation of Walras's system to allow for socialist planning merged with Keynesian macroeconomics and fiscal policy, drawing the state heavily into the regulation of the economy.

MAINSTREAM POLITICAL ECONOMY AND THE MARGINALIST REVOLUTION

The historicist, socialist, and Marxist schisms within political economy were heavily political in nature. A more crucial schism within the discipline took place along more technical, mathematical lines. This schism is referred to as the marginalist revolution. The theoretical origin was the late 19th century rejection of the labor theory of value in favor of utility theory. This marked a revolutionary departure from classical political economy. Political economy's traditional concern with general welfare and the state's role in ensuring that welfare now became secondary to a concern with microeconomic movements in which the economic variables were not political but rather mathematical or functional, and the interest was in relating change in one variable to change in another. Concerns with economic growth became less important than the attempts to locate equilibrium positions within a framework in which the total quantity of resources was given. The consumer and the firm, rather than national income or economic growth and development, became the central focus of mainstream economic analysis until the 1930s and the advent of Keynesian economics.

The intellectual fathers of the marginalist transformation were Malthus and Bentham.[9] Building on works by these men and on later works by Cournot,[10] Von Thünen, and Gossen, the marginalist transformation began in full force in the 1870s with the publication of works by W. Stanley Jevons, Carl Menger, and Leon Walras.[11] Coming from different traditions, these three authors eventually founded separate schools that arrived at similar conclusions concerning marginalism. The Austrian school embraced utility theory. The Lausanne school emphasized more abstract general equilibrium analysis. The Cambridge economists followed Alfred Marshall, whose work not only encompassed utility theory and equilibrium analysis, but also included the seeds of the later debate between contemporary monetary and fiscal theorists.

The Austrian school, begun by Carl Menger, Friedrich von Wieser, and Eugen Von Böhm-Bawerk, is noted politically for its strong emphasis on political individualism and economic noninterventionism and its emphatic rejection of Marx and socialism. Methodologically, the Austrian school is noted for its purely theoretical analysis, free of empirical tests. While it had much in common with English marginalism, the Austrian school eventually went in a different direction. This separatism was partly the result of a language barrier which resulted in many early Austrian works not being translated into English until 80 years after their German publication. But the break was also caused by important national political differences.[12]

Menger interpreted economic relationships in terms of causes and effects rather than in terms of mutual interdependence, the technique used in most modern economics.[13] Menger's work was anti-Marxist, a trait shared by the other two early Austrians, Friedrich von Wieser and Eugen Von Böhm-Bawerk. Both of these men were strongly critical of Marx, the interventionist socialist state, and German historicism. Böhm-Bawerk expanded his criticism to include reform socialism and economic intervention. The Austrian tradition was thus identified with laissez-faire principles and anti-Marxism.

This tradition was carried on by two important later Austrians: Ludwig von Mises and Friedrich von Hayek. Mises criticized socialism for lacking a rational method of pricing. He opposed economic interventionism strongly enough to deny the government a role even in setting monetary policy. Mises's extreme antigovernment views, especially after Keynes, isolated him from contemporary economics. Hayek, 20 years Mises's junior, was more tolerant of mathematical economics and mainstream economic views. Hayek was also a strong advocate of individualism and libertarianism, however, and a staunch opponent of state intervention, which he saw as leading to totalitarianism and serfdom. His tolerance of mathematics was tempered by his criticism of "Scientism," which he referred to as the application of controls suitable for the inanimate objects of natural science but not for human beings.

The Lausanne school of economics adopted essentially the same methodological orientation as the English marginalists. Influenced by both Cournot and Auguste Walras, Leon Walras developed a mathematical equilibrium model largely ignored until Leontief's development of input-output analysis fused Walras's general equilibrium economy with modern matrix algebra. Only then did Walras's work enter mainstream econometrics.[14]

The contribution of Walras's successor at Lausanne, Vilfredo Pareto, is greater, but mixed. Pareto's economic analysis constructed a world ordered by rational behavior. The concept of Pareto optimum, the point at which no action can be taken to benefit one member of society without hurting another member, underlies much of contemporary welfare economics.

While the Austrian and Lausanne schools made important contributions to political economy, by far the most important marginalist influence on mainstream economics came from Alfred Marshall and his followers. A mathematician, Marshall intended to study economics only long enough to answer certain ethical questions that troubled him.[15] His study changed the direction of contemporary economics and synthesized classical and marginalist economics. Marshall's marginal productivity theory of distribution, his concept of rising and falling long-run cost, internal and external economies of scale, the concept of the representative firm, and his use of partial equilibrium analysis and the *ceteris paribus* assumption accelerated the movement to the microeconomic and mathematically orientated analysis which characterizes contemporary economics, shifting it away from the political economy of its earlier practictioners.

The break between economists and political economists resulting from the marginalist revolution was nearly complete by the early part of the 20th century. The Depression returned attention to the political components of economic policy. Politically, Keynes advocated heavy government involvement in the economy. Methodologically, he argued strongly in favor of reasoned discourse as a way of achieving economic consensus and well-being. His emphasis on aggregates assumes there is a common good. His emphasis on empirical verification, including his rejection of the *ex ante* notions of microeconomics which reflect subjective estimates of the future, in favor of the *ex post* aggregate welfare of macroeconomics, assumes that people can see and appreciate this good and that it is a phenomenon understandable to the common man and not just to a few mathematically trained economists. In essence, Keynes's strong political economy orientation is reflected in his belief that the government should intervene to prevent human suffering while the market mechanisms slowly sort themselves out.

ECONOMIC ANALYSIS IN CONTEMPORARY POLITICAL ECONOMY

A key development in 20th century economics is the use of the econometric method. Under this method, assumptions are stated carefully and concepts defined in terms both concise and consistent. Models are constructed and tested using empirical data, much as in biometrics or statistics. As a result of the widespread use of this statistical methodology within social science, the gap between the social and the natural sciences seemed to narrow. Although econometrics fused French mathematical economics with English statistics, the major work was done in the United States, particularly after the influx of European scholars during World War II. American economics came to be dominated by econometric analysis. As the method spread to political science and sociology, political scientists became more technical and scientific in their examination of such concepts as class, voting, or political attitudes. At the same time, many economists were increasingly recognizing the critical role the government played in economic policy making and in establishing economic conditions. They began to include political factors in their models of the economy. The time had come for a new political economy. The contributions in this volume exemplify this.

The first three chapters in this volume deal with political business cycles and public policy. The first chapter, by Frey, proposes a broad theoretical framework useful for understanding short-term politico-economic interactions ranging from political business cycles to voting functions. Paldam's chapter is an explicit expansion of previous work discussing political business cycles. The chapters by Keech and Simon and by Russell indirectly consider such cycles, although their emphasis is on public policy. The remaining chapters all concern the economy's direct political impact. Weatherford refines our understanding of class. Kinder and Mebane focus on the sociotropic voter. Finally, Monroe and Levi alert us to the political importance of economic expectations and uncertainty.

Paldam's work harkens back to the kind of broad macroanalysis of interest to the original founders of political economy. His concern with political business cycles reflects that of Ricardo, Smith, and Mathus. His work also reflects a Marxist orientation to business cycles emanating from Kalecki's original work in this area. This reflects a central European tradition, an almost Hegelian view of cycles as part of an historical movement. One is reminded of the ill-fated Kondratieff, a Russian economist whose work on business cycles showed a revitalized Western economy, a conclusion which led to his incarceration in a Stalinist labor camp.

Paldam's concern with political business cycles grows out of a happier scholarly tradition, beginning with the important theoretical works by Nordhaus and MacRae and with Tufte's widely circulated book, which drew public attention to political business cycles. Essentially, the theory explaining such cycles argues that in democratically elected governments, incumbents follow macroeconomic policies that place good economic times just before elections and the hard times after elections. Paldam examines the main theories on political business cycles and expands the theory to explain labor market activity. An empirical examination of wage patterns and strikes in 17 Western democracies finds strong international components in such labor activities. Paldam concludes that examinations of political business cycles which omit such factors from their analysis provide inadequate explanations of both labor market activity and business cycles.

The chapter by Keech and Simon also assumes that governmental economic decisions are influenced by the prospect of electoral advantage. Their work combines the normative and the mathematical approach to understanding public policy. This chapter is concerned with practical reforms that will make political institutions more democratic and more responsive to the needs and wishes of a populace. Their consideration of proposed reforms in the length of presidential terms leads to an examination of how the length of the presidential term might affect economic outcomes. They assume, as Paldam did, a political business cycle in which incumbents manipulate the economy for short-term political advantage. Rather than an empirical cross-national examination, however, their approach is a mathematical one. By distilling complex politico-economic problems to their essence and putting them into clearly specified mathematical terminology, Keech and Simon are able to consider the different proposed changes in term length and follow the consequences of each more clearly.

Using Nordhaus's model of political business cycles, Keech and Simon make several assumptions regarding the motivations of politicians, the measurement of the quality of economic policy, and the set of feasible policies over time. These assumptions are combined in a mathematical model of policy making where political behavior is affected by the length of electoral terms. Traditionally, a single six-year presidential term has been advocated because it is believed to remove politics from presidential behavior, thereby elevating policy outcomes from politics to statesmanship. An alternate view suggests this will also remove accountability, and thereby produce inferior policy outcomes. Restricting their analysis to the examination of specific economic outcomes, Keech and Simon find the term length that maximizes economic welfare depends on the parameters of the model, especially the parameter that represents the voters' memory. Although Keech and Simon concede that politicians eligible for reelection do not necessarily maximize votes, and that those who are ineligible do not necessarily maximize welfare, the most significant finding of their analysis suggests there is no one single best term length for all conditions.

Russell's chapter on income policy also concerns public policy. Russell's underlying concern is the one that troubled Keynes: how does government intervention in the economy affect those long range economic processes which are part of a natural economic order? In this, both Keynes and Russell are heirs of the Adam Smith who argued against mercantilism and for a more limited governmental intervention. This question of governmental interference or intervention is a central question in the political economy of all contemporary schools, from the Keynesians to the Austrians and the American supply side economists.

Russell is concerned with the incomes policies which are part of governmental efforts to insure economic well-being by controlling wages and prices. Russell first asks: "Do incomes policies work?" After outlining the arguments on both sides of the debate, Russell builds on his administrative experience in the Carter administration to construct a sophisticated econometric model to test the usefulness of incomes policies as supplements to fiscal and monetary policies. He examines the evidence on three incomes policies adopted in recent U.S. experience: the Kennedy/Johnson guideposts, the Nixon administration's economic stabilization program and Carter's pay and price standards program.

Russell concludes that these programs have an ameliorative effect which can be useful primarily to buy time for the government to take the institutional actions which will effect more lasting change.

Despite its heavy empirical orientation and absence of explicit discussion of any "best" economic policy, Russell's work also reflects the normative tradition in political economy which believes government should be more responsive to the needs and wishes of its people. (Russell notes that the U.S. public prefers wage and price controls 2 : 1 in most polls, despite most professional economists' cautions against them.) Russell's work is an important example of how the government can take decisive action to rebuild public confidence while the government makes more extensive institutional economic changes.

Kinder and Mebane accept as given the economy's effect on politics, especially on voting and popular support for incumbents and political parties. Their concern is to determine how the voter decides whether the incumbent did a good job in managing the economy. Kinder and Mebane make the sociotropic voter their theoretical foundation. This theory suggests people vote not on the basis of their individual economic situation so much as on a consideration of overall economic conditions. In other words, voters ask not "What have you done for me lately?" but "What have you done for the country?" Their work, suggesting that political preferences originate in the voter's estimate of overall economic well-being rather than in his own economic situation, touches on one of the most important current debates concerning the economy's impact on voting and political attitudes.

This work is important, however, not just for the significant theoretical formulation of the sociotropic voter or even for reintroducing the concept of a public interest into analysis, but also for its careful microlevel analysis and for providing the linkage between microlevel and macrolevel behavior. The work weds the microlevel concerns of contemporary economists and psychologists with the political scientist's concerns with macrolevel outcomes.

Like Kinder and Mebane, Weatherford also assumes the economy's importance for voting is well accepted and that the next step in the analysis is to examine the process by which the economy affects the vote choice. Weatherford points to political parties and socioeconomic class as two important mediating influences whose role is more complex than has been thought. Weatherford's contribution here is twofold. First, his review of previous studies demonstrates the need for proper specification of both party and class in models of short-term politico-economic interaction. In particular, he argues that lagged indicators are necessary to detect the public's economic memory. Beyond this, however, Weatherford juxtaposes two traditional explanations of class: the Marx/Dahrendorf focus on the physical and social relations of production and the Blau/Duncan paradigm of status attainment. These alternate explanations produce different substantive findings when class is included in empirical analyses of the economy's political impact. Weatherford's reformulation of class categories makes important strides in capturing the process by which socioeconomic inequality affects politics and will doubtless influence later empirical examinations of the political importance of class.

Frey's work on the underground economy also originates in a tradition which examines the economy's impact on votes and incumbent popularity. Frey's extensive work in this area has always demonstrated an exceptional sensitivity to what econometric modelling can and cannot reveal about political behavior. This particular work, however, reveals a creativity which is extraordinary even for Frey. Still concerned with explaining voting and incumbent popularity, Frey draws attention to an increasingly important sector usually omitted from analysis: the underground economy. This sector includes unrecorded economic transactions which remain outside government restrictions or levies and which range from the black market and organized crime to tax evasion and barter exchanges. The extent of the economic activities occurring within this underground economy demonstrates the importance of including it in analysis: for the United States, estimates of the amount of the underground economy range from the 1981 Organization for Economic Cooperation and Development estimates of 1.5% of GNP in the 1970s, to the 1980 Internal Revenue Service estimates of between 5.9 and 7.9% of GNP for 1976, to Feige's 1980 estimates of 27% and Tanzi's 1980 estimates of 8.1 to 11.7% of GNP.[16]

To follow up on the importance of this underground economy, Frey develops a four-sector model to explain vote and popularity. His model includes (1) the official private economy, (2) the underground economy, (3) the public sector's political sector, i.e., people in the government, and (4) the public sector's administrative/bureaucratic sector. In this theoretical treatment, Frey develops the logic explaining how the economy affects individuals in each of these sectors when they make their decision on whether to support the government or opposition. This theoretical work can be used as the basis of later empirical examinations of the government's support function, the underground economy, and the Laffer curve. Its theoretical breadth makes it applicable to cross-national comparisons of both democratic and nondemocratic societies.

The Monroe and Levi chapter is the last of the three selections in this book which are directly concerned with the economy's political impact. An empirical examination of American presidential popularity from 1950 to 1975, it resembles the Kinder and Mebane effort to move beyond the aggregate economic predictors traditionally employed in this area. The emphasis here, however, is on economic expectations and economic uncertainty. The authors test two alternative theories of short-term political-economic interaction. The first theory is the traditional revolution of rising expectations, arguing that political change results not so much from actual economic conditions as from the gap between actual and expected economic conditions. The second theory stresses the political consequences of uncertainty concerning future economic conditions; rather than arguing that the popularity of incumbents rises and falls when the economy performs better or worse than expected, it suggests that popularity increases when there is certainty about the economic future and falls when there is uncertainty. The authors find that economic expectations have political significance, but that the psychological process by which economic expectations are translated into political response is more complex than earlier analysts have realized. When changes in a key economic variable remain fairly steady or constant, the expected rate of change becomes politically relevant. In this case the gap between the expected and the actual growth rate was politically significant. In other instances where the long-term pattern of change in economic fluctuations is more erratic, as was the case with inflation in the late 1960s and 1970s, then the public seems to be troubled merely by the existence of uncertainty. Public uneasiness over the government's inability to control the economy appears to offset any pleasure at doing better than had been expected in the inflation gamble. Like Kinder and Mebane, the authors draw on microlevel work stressing social psychological theories. Methodologically, their work should also draw attention to the needs of political economy to forge links with other disciplines.

All of the essays in this volume build on past works of political economists. It is hoped that they will provide both new theoretical foundations and substantive empirical findings which will benefit scholars in this exciting field.

NOTES

1. Deleted.

2. There were other minor schisms; these are only the main divisions.

3. See Spiegel (1971) for a discussion of this.

4. For a fuller discussion of how contemporary Marxist analysis differs from the marginalist approach to economic issues, see Nell (1973).

5. For example, Nikolai Bukharin rejected the idea of a natural law of economics that existed independently of the will of individuals or groups. Steeped in the German historicist tradition, he argued for substituting a state-planned economy for the traditional one regulated by markets and competition.

6. The experience of N. D. Kondratieff, however, indicates how risky even such technical work could be, if it touched on Soviet orthodoxy concerning rationality and the natural laws of economics. When his work on long-range economic cycles suggested that capitalism would experience a period of renewed prosperity, Kondratieff was removed from his research position, arrested for conspiracy, deported to Siberia in 1930, and never heard from again (see Spiegel, 1971, pp. 486–487).

7. Perhaps the Soviets considered input-output analysis a legitimate form of analysis because it is derived from politically neutral mathematics; perhaps it was because its originator, Wassily Leontief, was born and educated in Russia.

8. This is reflected in the British Fabian Society's taking its name from the Roman General Quintus Fabius Maximus Cuncutor, who was known for his holding tactics.

9. Malthus suggested using differential calculus as a method of analysis, and Bentham developed the concept of diminishing marginal utility, suggesting societies should seek to maximize pleasure and to minimize pain.

10. Augustine Cournot (1801–1877) was a French mathematical economist whose work (1838) on the mathematical principles of the theory of wealth was the first systematic application of marginal principles to the theory of a firm. Cournot did not base his work on utilitarianism, however; he looked instead to the philosophy of Descartes and the French rationalists, who argued that reason would reveal a mathematically ordered world. This reliance on reason rather than experience put

the French economic tradition at odds with the British theorists, especially those who did empirical econometric work.

11. In Germany, Johan Heinrich von Thunen (1783–1850) applied marginal principles to the theory of production, and Hermann Heinrich Gossen (1810–1858) developed a comprehensive, though almost entirely neglected, marginal utility theory of consumption. Because the works of Cournot, Gossen, and Von Thunen were of little contemporary consequence, however, these men are remembered primarily for their influence on Marshall.

12. It is no accident that the Austrian school of economics developed in Austria rather than in Germany. The intellectual and political climate in Austria differed greatly in critical ways from that of Germany. First of all, the natural law tradition had remained more influential in Catholic Austria than in Protestant Germany. This meant that Austria retained more of the Kantian legacy. Secondly, Joseph Von Sonnenfels (1732–1817), holder of the first Chair of Economics at the University of Vienna and a scholar who made a tremendous impact on Austrian economics, was a humanist and a follower of the Enlightenment. Von Sonnenfels's textbook on economics, widely used until 1848 in Austrian universities, provided a formulation of liberal thought that emphasized the rule of reason and a method of analysis that postulated general principles valid for all mankind. Finally, politically Austria was more fertile ground than Germany for economic theories that accentuated reason and natural law. A historicism that stressed the movement of history and the glorification of a national past was conducive to national unity in Germany, where a single ethnic group aspired to nationhood, but it would hardly have been prudent in the Austro-Hungarian empire, made up as it was of several national cultures.

13. Menger's later work (*Problems of Economics*, published in Germany in 1883 but not translated into English until 1963) further elaborated on his methodology of social science, which was a methodological individualism in which microeconomic phenomena are the focus of analysis. For this reason, and also because his works did not appear in English until after the Keynesian revolution and because he was hostile to mathematical economics, which he felt was an inadequate tool for exploring the "essence" of economic phenomena, Menger's work has had limited impact on the discipline at large. The language barrier and World War II isolated the Austrian school from American academics.

14. At the time of its publication, Walras's work was ignored by all the major centers of political economy. The Germans preferred pure historicism. The Austrians were hostile to mathematical expositions, and in England, Marshall judged Walras's work too exclusively mathematical.

15. Since Marshall influenced Keynes and Pigou, who in turn influenced most later mainstream political economists, contemporary political economy thus

inherited the classical humanistic tenets concerning natural law, rationality, and democratic institutions.

16. See the chapter by Frey for full details and citations.

REFERENCES

Nell, Edward (1973). "Economics: The Revival of Political Economy." In Robin Blackburn (ed.), *Ideology in Social Science*. New York: Vintage Books.

Spiegel, Henry William (1971). *The Growth of Economic Thought*. Durham, N.C.: Duke University Press.

Tufte, Edward R. (1978). *Political Control of the Economy*. Princeton, N.J.: Princeton University Press.

2: Politics, Economics, and the Underground Economy

Bruno S. Frey

WHY CONSTRUCT POLITICO-ECONOMIC MODELS?

Over the last few years many countries have paid increasing attention to the so-called "underground" or "hidden" economy. The expansion of the underground economy is commonly attributed to an increasing tax burden, which induces people to leave the official economy and take up work in the untaxed underground economy.[1] Another relationship which has attracted great attention in the atmosphere of tax revolt in the United States and some other countries is the so-called *Laffer curve*,[2] which suggests that a decrease in the tax rate leads to an increase in tax receipts because at lower tax rates people are motivated to work and invest more, thus raising the tax base.

Both the underground economy and the Laffer curve are important parts of politico-economic interaction. Indeed, the interrelationships between the economic and political sectors of society can more adequately be dealt with if the underground economy is integrated into politico-economic analysis. Politico-economic models[3] composed of the private and government sectors have so far failed to do this. There have been only a few attempts to take into account additional sectors, such as defense,[4] the central bank,[5] and the labor market.[6]

In this chapter, a four-sector model of political economy is developed consisting of (1) the official private economy, (2) the underground economy, and the public sector, which is split into (3) a political (government) sector and (4) an administrative bureaucratic sector. The government sector depends on the political support of other sectors—in particular, the voters. The bureaucratic sector, on the other hand, does not need to be reelected, but it depends on the tax receipts extracted from the official private economy.

The integration of the underground economy and the stress on taxation lead to a shift in emphasis from business cycle movements to allocation and distribution.[7] The model considered here studies in what sectors goods are produced and for what purposes the inputs are used. It deals in particular with the allocation of the work force between the private and the public sectors, and between the official and the underground private economies.

This study has a threefold aim: (1) to develop an outline of the theoretical relationships among the four sectors identified, (2) to introduce the available empirical evidence referring to these relationships, and (3) to show how the econometric estimation of such central aspects as the vote and popularity functions, the size of the underground economy, and the Laffer curve can be improved using the theoretical model developed.

First, we deal with the three kinds of actors (government, public bureaucracy, and private individuals) in the four sectors of society. They are all assumed to maximize their utility, subject to specific constraints, by using the instruments available to them. It turns out that the behavior of individuals in the private sector (their decisions to support the government or the opposition, and to work in the official or the underground economy) can be modeled without any major problems. Much more difficult is capturing the behavior of the aggregate entities called "the government" and the "public bureaucracy."

In order to derive results relevant for the estimation problems considered here, specific behavioral assumptions are made that serve to describe the government's and the bureaucracy's actions in a particular historical period and country, and with respect to a particular problem. These "scenarios" make it possible to informally derive policy functions that are of crucial importance for econometric testing.

Next, the theoretical model is used to suggest how to improve the estimation of vote and popularity functions, the size of the underground economy, and the Laffer curve. Finally, some concluding remarks are offered.

THE POLITICAL SECTOR: GOVERNMENT

The government is taken to be a homogeneous actor. Previous politico-economic models of representative democracies (Frey and Schneider 1978a, b) have assumed that government gains utility from putting its ideological goals into action. The main constraint on its actions is the need to receive sufficient political support. Because of the complexity of the task and limited knowledge, the government is not supposed to perform a formal maximization of its utility subject to the political support constraint, but rather to grope toward a sufficing solution, concentrating on whether its prospects of staying in power are good or not and how close the next election is. In a representative democracy, the government can usually stay in office if it receives a sufficient share of votes at election time. (Government popularity serves as a convenient indicator of reelection prospects in the period between elections.) Although necessary for political survival, an election victory is not a sufficient condition for retaining power because major interest groups may force a government to resign between elections. One of the most important of these interest groups is the public bureaucracy, on whose support the government depends for a great many reasons, not the least of which is that the government is unable to act if its bureaucracy refuses to collaborate.

Thus the overall support enjoyed by the government depends on its popularity with the public and its acceptance by the government bureaucracy. The government's support from the population at large is influenced by the following factors:

1. The size of the groups supporting it. The number of workers in the private economy,[8] L_p, is the sum of the official, L_o, and the underground, L_u, work force:

$$L_p = L_o + L_u \tag{1}$$

The other group distinguished here, the public bureaucrats, number B. Thus we have

$$L = L_p + B \tag{2}$$

where L is the total labor force (and population) that is exogenously given.

2. The political participation rates π_p and π_B, respectively.

3. The probability that a randomly chosen person supports the government, σ_p and σ_B, for the populace and the bureaucrats, respectively.

Thus the total support received by the government is

$$S = \frac{L_p}{L} \cdot \pi_p \cdot \sigma_p + \frac{B}{L} \cdot \pi_B \cdot \sigma_B \tag{3}$$

There is considerable empirical evidence on the relative size of the two groups' political participation and support propensity. A wealth of data[9] strongly suggests that public bureaucrats have a considerably higher voting participation than other groups in society ($\pi_B > \pi_p$).[10] Wolfinger and Rosenstone (1980) find, for example, that in the 1974 U.S. national elections, state public employees' voting participation was 13 percentage points, and local public employees' participation was 17 percentage points *higher* than that of the rest of the population, with all other influences kept constant.[11]

There is also evidence that bureaucrats more often make their influence felt on government beyond the simple act of voting. This is to be expected because they often have superior information and knowledge, which gives them a relative advantage in using other avenues of influence. Several studies (e.g., see Rubinfeld, 1977; Courant, Gramlich, and Rubinfeld, 1979) also indicate that bureaucratic voters' revealed preferences are different from those of the rest of the population. In particular, bureaucrats favor higher public expenditures, which suggests that they consistently differ from the general populace in their evaluation of the government's actions, and therefore in their support ($\sigma_B \neq \sigma_p$). The government's need to cover its expenditures by tax receipts will be discussed in the next section.

THE ADMINISTRATIVE SECTOR: PUBLIC BUREAUCRACY

The utility of the people who work in the bureaucracy and of a homogeneous bureaucracy as a whole is assumed to depend on bureaucrats' income and "power." No definition of power will be attempted here: suffice it to note that power has both an internal and an external aspect. The larger a public bureaucracy is in terms of the number of people it employs (B), the better are an individual bureaucrat's chances of rising in the hierarchy, and therefore of gaining influence.[12] The external aspect relates to the domain of bureaucratic influence, which is the official private economy (and the bureaucratic sector itself). The greater the share of the population active in the underground economy (L_u/L), the smaller the bureaucrats' influence because this sector is, by definition, outside their control.[13] This is one reason that bureaucrats abhor the unofficial economy. Another is that they are convinced that "laws must be obeyed."

Bureaucratic support of the government, then, tends to increase the larger the wage rate of the bureaucrats, w_B, the larger the number of bureaucrats, B, and the smaller the relative size of the uncontrolled underground sector, L_u/L:

$$\sigma_B = \sigma_B\left(w_B; B, \frac{L_u}{L}\right) \tag{4}$$

with

$$\frac{\partial \sigma_B}{\partial w_B} > 0, \quad \frac{\partial \sigma_B}{\partial B} > 0, \quad \frac{\partial \sigma_B}{\partial (L_u/L)} < 0$$

The main constraint on the bureaucracy's actions is the need to finance the expenditures to pay for its members (bureaucratic wage sum):

$$W_B = w_B \cdot B \tag{5}$$

Since bureaucratic wages are not set according to competitive conditions, it is possible that they are higher than wages for similar work in the official economy ($w_B > w_o^B$).[14] Bureaucrats are able to achieve this advantage by restricting entry into the bureaucratic sector (the number of bureaucrats, B, is used as an instrument).

Tax income, T, is not only used by the bureaucracy to cover its wage bill but also by government to finance its expenditures for public goods:

$$T = W_B + G \tag{6}$$

In this simple model, G is assumed to be given.[15] Neither politicians nor bureaucrats can determine tax income, only tax rates.

PRIVATE ECONOMIES: OFFICIAL AND UNDERGROUND

The utility of the individuals in the private economy is derived from their command over (1) private goods (per capita or net wage rate) disposable in both the official (w_o^n) and the underground economy (w_u^n), and (2) publicly supplied (indivisible) goods, G. Thus, the higher the per capita incomes in the two sectors and the larger the supply of public goods, the greater the support for government:

$$\sigma_p = \sigma_p \left(w_o^n, w_u^n; G \right) \tag{7}$$

all derivatives being positive.[16]

The Official Private Economy

Disposable income in the regular nonpublic sector is defined by

$$w_o^n = \left(1 - \tau \right) w_o \tag{8}$$

where $0 \leq \tau \leq 1$ is the (average and marginal) tax rate (minus the rate of transfers). The gross wage rate, w_o, is assumed to depend on marginal (labor) productivity in the official private economy:

$$w_o = P_o' \tag{9}$$

Both average (P_o) and marginal productivity (P_o') depend on the number of workers in the official economy (L_o) and the amount of regulation

(R):

$$P_o = P_o(L_o, R) \qquad (10)$$

with

$$\partial P_o / \partial L_o < 0$$

Although an increase in regulation may increase or decrease productivity ($\partial P_o / \partial R \gtrless 0$), recent American research suggests that under present conditions, productivity is negatively affected by government regulations for the following reasons:

1. Government regulations hamper technical progress because an increasing share of expenditures for research and development is siphoned off to meet safety and environmental standards.[17] Denison (1979a, b) suggests that the average annual impact of environmental regulations imposed after 1967 on the rate of productivity growth was -0.05% in 1967–1969, -0.1% in 1969–1973, -0.22% in 1973–1975, and -0.08% in 1975–1978. Christainsen and Haveman (1981) have found that federal regulations were responsible for between 12 and 21% of the slowdown in the growth of labor productivity in U.S. manufacturing during 1973–1977 as compared to 1958–1965.

2. Government regulations lead to inefficiencies in sectoral allocations (e.g., see Posner, 1975, or Hamer, 1979).

3. The whole private official economy is strongly burdened. According to a well-known estimate by Weidenbaum (1979), the direct and indirect costs of federal regulations alone in the United States amounted to 3.6% of the gross national product (GNP) in 1976; another estimate (Downing and Lawson, 1979) that included state regulations concluded that the figure was 9.4% of the GNP for the same year. One hastens to add that these studies look only at the costs imposed by government regulations; if the benefit side had also been considered, the overall effect might well have been positive.[18]

The issue of whether government regulations in effect today benefit or hamper productivity in the official private economy is thus unresolved; the answer depends on the specific conditions of the country and the period examined. Following the bulk of contemporary American studies, we will assume here that the overall effect of such regulation is negative, $\partial P_o / \partial R < 0$.

The Underground Economy

The "hidden" or "underground" sector is that part of the private economy that evades taxation and regulation.[19] Since both tax evasion and disregard of regulations are prohibited, those who choose to be active in the underground economy have to take into account the expected costs of being caught. In analogy to the burden of taxation (tax rate), the expected cost is formulated as a rate per dollar earned in the unofficial economy, c. The net wage rate in the hidden economy is

$$w_u^n = (1 - c)w_u \tag{11}$$

with $0 \le c \le 1$.

The expected cost, c, is the probability of being detected multiplied by the effective size of the punishment. Cross-section and time-series studies of the economics of crime provide ample evidence that an increase in expected punishment has a deterrent effect on (potential) offenders,[20] that is, it is indeed perceived as a reduction in the (expected) returns (wage rate) of working in the irregular sector. Here, the expected cost of punishment is treated as if it were an implicit tax on activities in the underground economy.

Work in the hidden economy is probably quite close to the economists' model of perfect competition: there is free entry (except possibly into activities that are criminal in and of themselves, e.g., heroin dealing) and there are no governmental restrictions or levies. It therefore can be assumed that the gross wage rate equals marginal productivity:

$$w_u = P_u' \tag{12}$$

Marginal (P_u') and average productivity (P_u) depend only on the number of people employed:

$$P_u = P_u(L_u) \tag{13}$$

with

$$\partial P_u / \partial L_u < 0$$

It is theoretically uncertain whether productivity is higher or lower in the underground economy as compared to the private official economy. On the other hand, since there is no intervention or regulation by government—for example, no health provisions and no restrictions on hiring and firing[21]—one would expect that $P_u > P_o$. On the other hand, there are the costs of producing clandestinely and evading detection and punishment by the public authorities. Moreover, no legally enforceable contracts are possible, and it is likely that private enforcement (of the Mafia type) leads to considerable cost. These factors suggest a lower productivity in the underground economy ($P_u < P_o$).

The Distribution of Labor

People are assumed to (marginally) choose to work in the official economy or in the hidden private economy according to where the net wage rate is higher. An equilibrium distribution of labor is reached when the net wage rates are equalized:

$$w_o^n = w_u^n \tag{14}$$

Combining Eqs. (9)–(14) yields

$$(1 - \tau) \cdot P_o(L_o, R) = (1 - c) \cdot P_u(L_u) \tag{15}$$

This equation is very useful for purposes of estimation. If one of the five explanatory variables is unknown, it may, under appropriate data conditions, be inferred from the other variables by one of the following methods:

1. If the instruments τ, c, R and labor productivity, P_o, in the official private economy are known (which may well be the case), it is possible to compute productivity in the underground economy, P_u.
2. If the instruments τ and c as well as the two labor productivities, P_o and P_u, are known, it is possible to estimate the output side of regulation, R (compared to the input side).
3. If the instruments τ and R as well as the two labor productivities, P_o and P_u, are known, the expected cost of punishment, c, may be inferred.

Equation (15) is graphically illustrated in Fig. 1, which shows how the equality of net wage rates determines the distribution of labor between the official and underground sectors, and how changes in the tax rate, regulation, and expected costs affect the outcome.

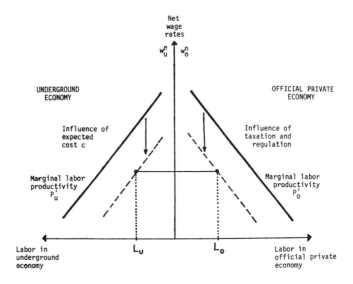

FIG. 1.   Determination of the distribution of labor between the official and underground sectors.

Equation (15) may be transformed into

$$\frac{L_u}{L_o} = \phi(\tau, R, c) \tag{16}$$

with

$$\frac{\partial \phi}{\partial \tau} > 0, \quad \frac{\partial \phi}{\partial R} \gtrless 0, \quad \frac{\partial \phi}{\partial c} < 0$$

The higher the rate of taxation and the intensity of regulation (assuming that $\partial P_o / \partial R < 0$), and the lower the expected cost imposed by the authorities for illegal work, the higher the number of workers in the underground as compared to the official private economy.

CLOSING THE MODEL

In our four-sector politico-economic model, labor is the only scarce resource, being constrained by the total labor force, L. Total labor is distributed among the private official and underground economies and the bureaucratic sector.[22]

Combining Eqs. (1), (2), and (16) leads to

$$L_o = L_o(\tau, R, c; B) \tag{17}$$

Occupation in the private official economy is determined by the instruments given at the right-hand side of (17): the higher the tax rate and the intensity of regulation, the lower the expected costs of working in the underground economy; and the higher the number of employees in the public bureaucracy, B, the lower the number of workers (or hours worked) in the private official economy.

The relevant taxes are imposed only on the private official economy; they are the financial counterpart of the goods and services that the public sector (bureaucracy) needs in order to function. The tax base thus consists of the total output, X_o, and therefore, the total wage income, in the private official sector:

$$T = \tau \cdot X_o \tag{18}$$

Private official output is defined as

$$X_o = P_o \cdot L_o \tag{19}$$

which, taking into account Eqs. (10) and (17), is equal to

$$X_o = X_o(\tau, R, c; B) \tag{20}$$

with

$$\frac{\partial X_o}{\partial \tau} < 0, \frac{\partial X_o}{\partial R} < 0 \quad \text{given} \quad \frac{\partial P_o}{\partial R} < 0$$

$$\frac{\partial X_o}{\partial c} > 0, \frac{\partial X_o}{\partial B} < 0$$

Combining Eqs. (18) and (20) yields

$$T = T(\tau, R, c; B) \tag{21}$$

An increase in the tax rates, of course, does not necessarily result in an increase in tax receipts ($\partial T/\partial \tau \gtrless 0$), because the fall in the tax base (if $\partial X_o/\partial \tau < 0$) can negate any positive effects of an increase in rates. An increase in regulation causes tax receipts to fall ($\partial T/\partial R < 0$) if the regulation affects productivity negatively ($\partial P_o/\partial R < 0$). The higher the expected costs of working in the underground economy, the higher the tax receipts will be ($\partial T/\partial c > 0$). An increase in the number of bureaucrats depresses tax receipts ($\partial T/\partial B < 0$) because fewer people are available for work in the private economy.

GOVERNMENT SUPPORT FUNCTION

This and the next two sections of this chapter discuss how the theoretical model developed can be used to improve the econometric (politometric) estimation of some central topics in political economy.

The government support function has often been estimated in the form of vote and popularity functions. There now exists a great many estimates for different countries and periods (for surveys, see, e.g., Monroe, 1979; Paldam, 1981; and for examples, see the studies contained in Whiteley, 1980, or in Hibbs and Fassbender, 1981). Most approaches use all or part of the main macroeconomic measures of the state of the economy; that is, the unemployment and inflation rates, and the growth of real disposable per capita income. Only a few studies, for example, that of Schneider and Pommerehne (1980), explicitly consider the effect of taxes and/or public expenditures on government support.

The theoretical model developed here suggests two major extensions of the empirical estimation of support functions:

1. It may be worthwhile to differentiate between (at least) two groups of supporters, the general population and the bureaucrats, because they are likely to differ strongly from each other.
2. In addition to income gained in the official sector, that is, income that is reported in official statistics, income received from underground activities[23] should also be taken into account, as shown in Eq. (7). Including income not reported to tax and statistical offices may be of great relevance. Feige (1979), for example, estimates that while the official economy grew by 23% over the 2-year period 1976–1978, the underground economy grew by 91% in terms of (nominal) GNP. If the growth of irregular income[24] is indeed sizable, its inclusion in a support function is required to correctly specify that function and to avoid biased estimates of the influence of *all* explanatory variables.

ESTIMATING THE SIZE OF THE UNDERGROUND ECONOMY

The Present State

There are at least five distinct approaches to measuring the size of the underground economy that go beyond pure speculation and guesstimates[25]:

1. Surveys based on samples of voluntary replies of individuals who are directly or indirectly asked to reveal their participation in the hidden sector.
2. Tax auditing and other compliance methods that force individuals to state their overall income.
3. The discrepancy between income (which is measured mainly from tax statistics) and expenditures (if they are independently measured). This method can be used at both the individual and the national levels.
4. The difference between the officially measured and the actual participation rates.
5. The observed additional demand for currency and/or money beyond that needed to fuel the official economy.

Each of these approaches yields quite different results, which is not surprising since each includes different aspects and sections of the overall underground economy.[26] However, even when the same approach is applied to the same country and period, estimates can differ strongly. For the United States, for example, the tax auditing method suggests that the underground sector is rather small, but while the OECD (1981) estimated it was around 1.5% of the official GNP in the 1970s, the U.S. Internal Revenue Service (1980) reported it was between 5.9% and 7.9% of the GNP in 1976. The initial discrepancy approach yielded a share of 9.4% of the GNP in 1948, which decreased to 4.0% in 1977 (Park, 1979). The currency demand deposit ratio approach, which assumes that all underground activities are undertaken in cash, gave a "conservative" estimate of 10% of the official GNP for 1976, and a more "realistic" estimate of 13–14 for both 1976 and 1979 (Gutmann, 1977, 1979b). The effect attributed to taxation alone was estimated to be an underground economy of 8.1–11.7% of the GNP for 1976 (Tanzi, 1980). When the "excess" demand for money was taken as an indicator of the underground economy, its size was estimated to be as large as 33% of the GNP in 1979 (Feige, 1979), which was later modified downward to 27% by the same author (Feige, 1980).

Using the stated approaches, the following estimates of the size of the underground economy in terms of official GNP were reached for other countries (around 1978): Canada, 3–12%, United Kingdom, 7%; Sweden, 7–17%; Norway, 6–16%; Federal Republic of Germany, 6–13%; Spain, 23%; and Italy, 30% (see Frey and Pommerehne, 1982b).

Most of these studies (and others) do not explicitly consider the *causes* leading to an underground economy (e.g., see Gutmann 1977, 1979b). Only a few authors have made an effort to at least quantify the influence of *one* causal variable, taxation, mainly in the context of the "excess" currency approach. It turns out that the influence of tax rate increases on the demand for currency (which should be positive because people are driven underground where they need more cash for payments) is rather unstable (Tanzi, 1980), and may produce statistically significant wrong signs (Klovland, 1980). Similar problems were encountered by Feige (1980) when he tried to relate taxation to the size of his estimate of the hidden economy.

The wide variance in results of the five approaches to measuring the underground economy and the instability and wrong signs that appear when the influence of taxation is taken into account suggest that the functions used to estimate the size of the underground economy are badly specified and that, indeed, *a theoretical basis is lacking*.

Approach Suggested by Our Model

The theoretical model of politico-economic interdependence that we have developed points to two aspects that should be taken into account when estimating the size of the hidden economy:

1. The existence of an underground economy is due to *various important determinants*. Besides taxation, we have identified the extent and intensity of regulation of the official economy, and the effort of public agencies to punish working in the illegal economy. Using Eq. (16),

$$\frac{L_u}{L_o} = \phi(\tau, R, c) \tag{16}$$

and taking account of the definition of output in the underground economy,

$$X_u = P_u \cdot L_u \qquad (22)$$

as well as of Eq. (20), the relationship of underground to official income follows immediately:

$$\frac{X_u}{X_o} = \Psi(\tau, R, c) \qquad (23)$$

It is expected that $\partial\Psi/\partial\tau > 0$, $\partial\Psi/\partial R > 0$, and $\partial\Psi/\partial c < 0$. It should be remembered that Eq. (16) and, therefore, Eq. (23) are derived from an equilibrium relationship, and that at a given point in time the net wage rates w_u^n and w_o^n may be unequal, and that a *movement* of labor between the two sectors may take place. This may be accounted for by explicitly modeling an adjustment process to the distribution of labor desired by the individuals. The desired (equilibrium) relationships shown in Eqs. (16) and (23) may be estimated by using four different approaches:

(i) The distribution of labor (L_u/L_o) can be evaluated on the basis of surveys or the analysis of official and actual participation rates. The size of the underground economy compared to the official GNP (X_u/X_o) may then be derived by estimating the productivity functions:

$$P_o = P_o(L_o, R) \qquad (10)$$

$$P_u = P_u(L_u) \qquad (13)$$

(ii) The use of currency, the total supply of money, the decline in the official participation rate, and the fall in working hours can be taken as (partial) indicators of the existence and development of the underground economy. It is of the utmost importance to take into account *only that part* of the change in these indicators, I, that can be attributed to the underground economy (e.g., working hours also tend to fall because people want more leisure). Therefore it is necessary to separate the two influences by estimating the equation

$$I = I\left(\underbrace{\tau, R, c}; \text{other determinants}\right) \qquad (24)$$

due to the underground economy

(iii) If the relative size of the underground economy (X_u/X_o) is considered unmeasurable even by indirect indicators, yet another procedure may be envisaged. The *weights* attached to the causal factors (τ, R, c) may be introduced on the basis of outside information, and the change in the size of the hidden economy over time or across regions may then be derived:

$$\frac{X_u}{X_o} = \alpha_1 \tau + \alpha_2 R - \alpha_3 c \tag{25}$$

If no reliable outside information on the size of the weights (α_1, α_2, α_3) is available, one may use "unit weighting"; that is, one may attribute the same influence to each (suitably normalized) factor. This procedure[27] may seem naive, but empirical research has shown that it yields quite good *ex ante* forecasts, under appropriate conditions.[28]

(iv) Approaches (ii) and (iii) may be combined. The fall in the participation rate and in working hours and the increased use of currency (compared to "normal use") may be taken as indicators of the *effect* of the unobserved variable underground economy, and the (suitably normalized) variables (τ, R, c) may be taken as the *causes*. This approach yields the equations

$$
\begin{array}{c}
\tau \\
R \\
c
\end{array}
\Longrightarrow
\left(\frac{X_u}{X_o} \right)
\begin{array}{l}
\nearrow \text{fall in participation rate} \\
\longrightarrow \text{fall in working hours} \\
\searrow \text{increased use of currency}
\end{array}
\tag{26}
$$

This set of equations may be estimated by econometric methods developed for the analysis of unobserved variables.[29]

2. The theoretical model also suggests that the *interdependence* among the various sectors must be taken into account. This interdependence has been completely neglected by all approaches so far. In particular, in addition to the "causal" equations (16) and/or (20), the *reaction* of the political and administrative sectors to the existence and expansion of an underground economy must be introduced. As has been pointed out, it is quite difficult to derive a behavioral equation for government and bureaucracy that would be specific enough for the problem considered here. For that reason, we will develop two behavioral scenarios which show both the estimation problems created by interdependence and the difficulties arising for the statistical identification of the relationships.

SCENARIO A   The government notices that its support from the bureaucracy is falling (Eq. 3). It attributes the bureaucrats' dissatisfaction to the fact that their power declines as people shift to the underground sector (Eq. 4). In order to restore its bureaucratic support to the level needed for reelection, the government decides to attack the underground economy by increasing controls and the severity of punishment for illegal work. The government's policy function is

$$c = c\left(\frac{L_u}{L_o}\right), \qquad c' > 0 \tag{27}$$

The empirically observed relationship between the expected punishment, c, and the (relative) size of the shadow economy (in terms of labor), L_u/L_c, or of an indicator thereof, depends on two quite different influences: the cost effect of punishment,

$$\left(\frac{L_u}{L_o}\right) = \phi(c, \ldots), \qquad \partial\phi/\partial c < 0 \tag{16}$$

and, in the opposite direction, the governmental policy function:

$$c = c\left(\frac{L_u}{L_o}\right) \tag{27}$$

The problem consists in separating these two influences. Generally, this is possible by explicitly and simultaneously estimating a *set* of equations containing Eqs. (16) and (27).

SCENARIO B   The government notes a decrease in its support and decides to shore it up by increasing taxation[30] in order to satisfy the population with a higher supply of public goods (Equation 7) and/or to satisfy the bureaucracy by granting higher wages (Eq. 4). Provided the fall in support is due to an increase in the underground economy, L_u/L_o, the (implicit) governmental policy function appears to be

$$\tau = \tau\left(\frac{L_u}{L_o}\right), \qquad \tau' > 0 \tag{28}$$

Behind an empirically observed relationship between the tax rate, τ, and the size of the hidden economy, L_u/L_o,[31] there are two quite distinct relationships: the cost effect of taxation,

$$\left(\frac{L_u}{L_o}\right) = \phi(\tau, \ldots), \qquad \frac{\partial \phi}{\partial \tau} > 0 \qquad (16)$$

and the policy equation (28) describing a causation in the opposite direction. Again, the problem is to clearly identify each of these equations.

The two scenarios are intended to illustrate the premise that it is important to consider not only the factors causing the existence and expansion of the underground economy, but also the likely reactions of public decision makers. The scenarios have dealt with likely policies undertaken by the government, but they can also be applied to the bureaucracy's policy. In any case, the conclusion is that the interdependence among the various sectors of the economy must be explicitly modeled in order to allow a sound empirical estimate of the size of the shadow economy.

ESTIMATING THE LAFFER CURVE

Figure 2 shows the general idea of the Laffer curve: Increasing the tax rate, τ, first increases tax receipts. But at $\tau = \tau^*$, a maximum is reached,

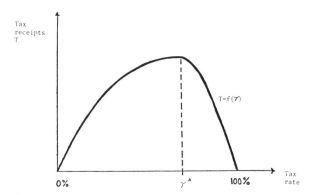

FIG. 2. The relationship between tax receipts and the tax rate according to Laffer.

and further tax increases will cause a decrease in tax receipts. Laffer's own interpretation of reality (for the United States) is that $\tau > \tau^*$, and that, therefore, a reduction in the tax rate raises tax receipts because it increases work incentives. The empirical studies undertaken seek to estimate the tax function,

$$T = f(\tau) \tag{29}$$

with the help of survey methods or formal econometric techniques. The results show a mixed picture. In Sweden, where the marginal tax rate on earned labor income is around 80%, it has been calculated (Stuart, 1981) that the revenue-maximizing tax rate would be approximately 70%. Sweden is thus on the downward sloping portion of its Laffer curve. Studies for the United States using three major macroeconometric models (Data Resources, Wharton, Chase Econometrics) suggest that a decrease in taxes would substantially increase the federal deficit in the forseeable future, and that tax cuts certainly do not pay for themselves (see Kiefer, 1979). An OECD report (1975) that surveyed all studies available at that time found that "variations in taxes do not cause important changes in the supply of work effort" (p. 6). Hemming and Kay (1980) state even more clearly that "the evidence runs strongly against the argument that tax rates in Britain, or any other country, are at levels such that the maximum available tax revenue is close to being obtained" (p. 85). As with estimates of the size of the underground economy, these studies can be criticized on two grounds:

1. Tax receipts depend not only on the tax rate, but also on other determinants, as shown in Eq. (21):

$$T = T(\tau, R, c; B)$$

In particular, the ease with which individuals can switch to the hidden economy and the punishment they expect to incur by doing so (given by τ, R, and c), as well as the labor constraint behind this switch (given by B), must be considered. The problem is not so much whether people stop working when tax rates rise, as Laffer and others argue, but whether they continue working in the official economy or switch to the underground sector.

2. The interdependence between the tax equation (18) and the possible policy reaction by government and bureaucracy must be included in the

estimation model. The scenarios developed in the preceding section apply fully here.

CONCLUDING REMARKS

This chapter seeks to integrate the underground economy into politico-economic relationships. Beyond the intrinsic interest such an integrated model of the political economy may have, the main purpose is to improve the theoretical basis for the empirical estimation of three important and much-discussed topics: the government's support function, the size of the underground economy, and the Laffer curve. It turns out that in all three cases the theoretical background developed helps to identify the multitude of factors determining the phenomena observed, and the links of their interdependence.

Acknowledgments. An earlier version of this chapter was presented at the Seminar in Modern Economic Analysis held in Disentis, Switzerland, October 9–11, 1981. I am grateful for helpful comments to Pierre Allan, Gebhard Kirchgässner, Werner W. Pommerehne, Friedrich Schneider, Hannelore Weck, and to the participants at the New York conference, especially Kristen Monroe.

NOTES

1. See, for example, the popular accounts in *Business Week* (1978) and the *Economist* (1979), and the scientific studies by Gutmann (1977), Feige (1979), de Grazia (1980), and Isachsen and Strom (1981).

2. This relationship has been rediscovered by American economists not terribly well versed in the history of doctrines. It was discussed as early as the fourteenth century by the Arabic philosopher Ibn Khaldun in his *Muqaddimah*, and in the second half of the fifteenth century (but not published until 1668) by the Italian economist D. Caraffa. It is known in German-speaking public finance circles as *Swiftsches Steuereinmaleins* (see Lotz, 1916). For a modern discussion, see, for example, Wanniski (1978) and various articles in the reader by Laffer and Seymour (1979).

3. Politico-economic models are theoretically based on econometric or polito-metric estimates of the relationships between the economy and the polity. The present state of research is well documented by the articles contained in the volumes edited by Whiteley (1980) and by Hibbs and Fassbender (1981); a survey is given in Frey (1978, 1979). It should be noted that politico-economic models have yielded superior *ex ante* and *ex post* forecasts when compared with "pure economic" models; they use the *same* data for estimation. The author's model for Germany (created jointly with Friedrich Schneider) has in this way been compared with the one by Krelle; the German politico-economic model (including central bank behavior) with the ones by Fair and by Cowart, and the United Kingdom model with the one by Chrystal and Alt. (See Frey and Schneider, 1979, 1981a, 1981b.)

4. See, for example, Lambelet (1973) and Luterbacher and Imhoff (1980).

5. See Frey and Schneider (1981a).

6. See Gärtner (1981).

7. The often-used identification of politico-economic models with "political business cycles" is therefore inadequate.

8. For the sake of simplicity, no differentiation is made between the labor force and population in each sector.

9. The data refer, however, almost exclusively to voting. The concept of support used here is wider; it includes other types of activities that improve the government's position relative to the opposition.

10. See Tingsten (1937). The following section is based on the survey by Frey and Pommerehne (1982a).

11. The figures quoted thus indicate what changes in voting participation are to be expected when somebody of a given sex, education, and social background switches from the private to the bureaucratic sector, or vice versa.

12. This idea lies behind many economic theories of bureaucracy; for an example, see Niskanen (1971, 1975).

13. In the discussion, it is argued that the bureaucracy may be better off with some percentage of underground activity than with a zero amount.

14. For empirical analyses of this proposition, see, for example, Smith (1977), Quinn (1979, 1980), and Bartel and Lewin (1981).

15. In this simplified model, there is no need to take account of the bureaucrats' taxes because they constitute a flow that stays *within* the public sector. If bureaucrats' income is taxed more, tax income rises, which, according to Equation (6), increases the bureaucrats' wage sum, W_B, by exactly the same amount

(given G). Thus, the taxation of bureaucrats does not change the relationship between the sectors as a whole.

16. It may be that those workers remaining in the official sector become dissatisfied with the government when the share of workers in the unofficial sector rises. This possibility is disregarded here.

17. The share may amount to 20% of total R & D and may be as high as 40% with the proposed federal fuel economy rules, according to a popular textbook (Gordon 1978: 534).

18. This is, in fact, argued by Tabb (1980) in a reply to Weidenbaum's study.

19. Most people active in the underground economy also hold a job in the official sector, usually to benefit from the social insurance system and to mislead tax authorities. The division of work between the two sectors should therefore be thought of in terms of hours worked.

20. See, for example, Carr-Hill and Stern (1973), Ehrlich (1973, 1979), Heineke (1978), and Goldberg and Nold (1980).

21. This may be unimportant for the United States, but it is of crucial importance for almost all other industrial countries, and many developing countries as well, where it is extremely difficult, or virtually impossible, to dismiss anybody in the official economy, except in cases of bankruptcy.

22. It is assumed that only a negligible number of people are active as professional politicians.

23. The same is true for employment and price developments in the hidden economy that may sizably affect the official data reported. Gutmann (1979a) estimates that the overall official unemployment rate in the United States is overstated by 1.5 percentage points when the official unemployment rate is about 6%.

24. It should be pointed out that other studies find a much smaller increase in the United States hidden economy, and some even note a decrease. For a survey of the results, see Frey and Pommerehne (1982b).

25. The following discussion draws on material contained in Frey and Pommerehne (1982b).

26. Though the concept "underground economy" may be defined in various ways, there is a growing consensus that it includes activities in terms of GNP that are not presently captured by official statistics.

27. See Dawes and Corrigan (1974), Wainer (1976), Dawes (1979), and Einhorn and Hogarth (1979).

28. It has been used to estimate the comparative size of the underground economies of 17 OECD countries; see Frey and Weck (1983).

29. See, for example, Jöreskog and Sorbom (1977).

30. Such a policy function was described as early as the fourteenth century by Ibn Khaldun: "Often, when the decrease in support of the reigning dynasty is noted, the amounts of the individual imposts are increased:" (Cited in Laffer and Seymour, 1979: p. 5).

31. As noted, for example, by Feige (1980), Klovland (1980), and Tanzi (1980).

REFERENCES

Bartel, A., and D. Lewin (1981). "Wages and Unionism in the Public Sector: The Case of Police." *Review of Economics and Statistics* 63:53–59.
Business Week (1978). "The Fast Growth of the Underground Economy." March 13:73–77.
Carr-Hill, R. A., and N. H. Stern (1973). "An Econometric Model of the Supply and Control of Recorded Offences in England and Wales." *Journal of Public Economics* 2:289–318.
Christainsen, G. B., and R. T. Haveman (1981). "Public Regulations and the Slowdown in Productivity Growth." *American Economic Review, Papers and Proceedings* 71:320–325.
Courant, P. N., E. M. Gramlich, and D. L. Rubinfeld (1979). "Public Employment Market Power and the Level of Government Spending." *American Economic Review* 69:806–807.
Dawes, R. M. (1979). "The Robust Beauty of Improper Linear Models in Decision-Making." *American Psychologist* 34:571–582.
_____, and B. Corrigan (1974). "Linear Models in Decision Making." *Psychological Bulletin* 81:95–106.
De Grazia, R. (1980). "Clandestine Employment: A Problem of Our Time." *International Labour Review* 119:549–563.
Denison, E. F. (1979a). *Accounting for Slower Economic Growth*. Washington, D.C.: Brookings.
_____ (1979b). "Pollution Abatement Programs: Estimates of Their Effect upon Output Per Unit of Input, 1975–1978." *Survey of Current Business*, Part 1; 59:58–59.
Downing, P. B., and A. Lawson (1979). *Policy Consequences of Regulatory Cost Measurements*. Department of Economics, Virginia Polytechnic Institute and State University (mimeographed).
Economist. 1979. "Exploring the Underground Economy." Sept. 22:106–107.
Ehrlich, I. (1973). "Participation in Illegitimate Activities: A Theoretical and

Empirical Investigation." *Journal of Political Economy* 81:521–565.

Einhorn, H. J., and R. M. Hogarth (1979). "Unit Weighting Schemes for Decision Making." *Organizational Behavior and Human Performance* 13:171–192.

Feige, E. L. (1979). "How Big Is the Irregular Economy?" *Challenge* 22:5–13.

_____ (1980). "A New Perspective on Macroeconomic Phenomena. The Theory and Measurement of the Unobserved Sector of the United States Economy: Causes, Consequences and Implications." Wassenaar: Netherlands Institute for Advanced Study.

Frey, B. S. (1978). *Modern Political Economy*. London: Martin Robertson.

_____ (1979). "Politometrics of Government Behavior." *Scandinavian Journal of Economics* 81:308–322.

_____, and W. W. Pommerehne (1982a). "How Powerful Are Public Bureaucrats as Voters?" *Public Choice* 38:253–262.

_____, and W. W. Pommerehne (1982b). "Measuring the Hidden Economy: Though This Be Madness, Yet There Is Method in It?" In V. Tanzi (ed.), *The Underground Economy in the United States and Abroad*, Lexington, Mass.: Heath, pp. 3–27.

_____, and F. Schneider (1978a). "An Empirical Study of Politico-Economic Interaction in the United States." *Review of Economics and Statistics* 60:174–183.

_____, and F. Schneider (1978b). "A Politico-Economic Model of the United Kingdom." *Economic Journal* 88:243–253.

_____, and F. Schneider (1979). "An Econometric Model with an Endogenous Government Sector." *Public Choice* 34:29–34.

_____, and F. Schneider (1981a). "Central Bank Behavior: A Positive Empirical Analysis." *Journal of Monetary Economics* 7:291–315.

_____, and F. Schneider, (1981b). "A Politico-economic Model for the United Kingdom: New Estimates and Predictions." *Economic Journal* 91:737–740.

_____, and H. Weck (1983). "Estimating the Shadow Economy: A 'Naive' Approach." *Oxford Economic Papers* 35:23–44.

Gärtner, M. 1981. "Politik und Arbeitsmarkt. Ein Uebersicht über ausgewählte Makrotheorien." *Zeitschrift für die Gesamte Staatswissenschaft* 137:252–283.

Goldberg, I., and F. D. Nold (1980). "Does Reporting Deter Burglars? An Empirical Analysis of Risk and Return in Crime." *Review of Economics and Statistics* 62:424–431.

Gordon, R. J. (1978). *Macroeconomics*. Boston: Little, Brown.

Gutmann, P. M. (1977). "The Subterranean Economy." *Financial Analysts Journal* 34:26–27.

_____ (1979a). "The Grand Unemployment Illusion." *Journal of the Institute of Socioeconomic Studies* 4:20–29.

_____ (1979b). "Statistical Illusions, Mistaken Policies." *Challenge* 22:14–17.

Hamer, E. (1979). *Bürokratieüberwälzung auf die Wirtschaft*. Hannover: Schlütersche Verlagsanstalt.

Heinecke, J. M. (1978). *Economic Models of Criminal Behavior*. Amsterdam:

North-Holland.

Hemming, R., and J. A. Kay (1980). "The Laffer Curve." *Fiscal Studies* 1:83–90.

Hibbs, D. A., and H. Fassbender (Eds.) (1981). *Contemporary Political Economy*. Amsterdam: North-Holland.

Isachsen, A. J., and S. Strom (1981). *Skattefritt. Svart Sektor I Vekst*. Oslo: Universitetsforlaget.

Jöreskog, K. G., and D. Sorbom (1977). "Statistical Models for Analysis of Longitudinal Data." In D. J. Aigner and A. S. Goldberg (eds.), *Latent Variables in Socio-economic Models*. Amsterdam: North-Holland.

Kiefer, D. W. (1979). "An Economic Analysis of the Kemp/Roth Tax Cut Bill." In A. B. Laffer and J. P. Seymour (eds.), *The Economics of the Tax Revolt: A Reader*. New York: Harcourt Brace Jovanovich.

Klovland, J. T. (1980). "In Search of the Hidden Economy: Tax Evasion and the Demand for Currency in Norway and Sweden." Discussion Paper, 18/80. Bergen: Norwegian School of Economics and Business Administration.

Laffer, A. B., and J. P. Seymour, (eds.) (1979). *The Economics of the Tax Revolt: A Reader*. New York: Harcourt Brace Jovanovich.

Lambelet, J. C. (1973). "Towards a Dynamic Two-Theater Model of the East-West Arms Race." *Journal of Peace Science* 1:1–38.

Lotz, W. (1916). "Zur Lehre vom Steuereinmaleins" In *Festschrift für Lujo Brentano*. Munich and Leipzig.

Luterbacher, U., and A. Imhoff (1980). "The U.S. Politico-Economic System: An Analysis of Interactions between Popularity and Governmental Military and Civilian Expenditures." Working Paper No. 3. Geneva-Center for Empirical Research in International Relations, The Graduate Institute of International Studies.

Monroe, K. R. (1979). "Econometric Analysis of Electoral Behavior: A Critical Review." *Political Behavior* 1:137–175.

Niskanen, W. A. (1971). *Bureaucracy and Representative Government*. Chicago: Aldine-Atherton.

————— (1975). "Bureaucrats and Politicians." *Journal of Law and Economics* 18:617–643.

Organization for Economic Cooperation and Development (1981). "The Hidden Economy in the Context of the National Accounts." Paris: DES/NI/81.3.

Paldam, (1981). "A Preliminary Survey of the Theories and Findings on Vote and Popularity Functions." *European Journal of Political Research* 9:181–199.

Park, T. (1979). "Reconciliation between Personal Income and Taxable Income, 1947–1977." Washington, D.C.: Bureau of Economic Analysis. (Mimeographed).

Posner, R. A. (1975). "The Social Cost of Monopoly and Regulation." *Journal of Political Economy* 83:807–827.

Quinn, J. F. (1979). "Wage Differentials among Older Workers in the Public and Private Sectors." *Journal of Human Resources* 14:41–62.

————— (1980). "Compensation in the Public Sector: Are Civil Servants Overpaid?" Paper read at Meeting of the International Institute of Public

Finance, Jerusalem.

Rubinfeld, D. L. (1977). "Voting in a Local School Election: A Micro Analysis." *Review of Economic and Statistics* 59:30–42.

Schneider, F., and W. W. Pommerehne (1980). "Politico-Economic Interactions in Australia: Some Empirical Evidence." *Economic Record* 56:113–131.

Smith, S. P. (1977). *Equal Pay in the Public Sector: Fact and Fantasy*. Princeton, NJ: Princeton University Press.

Stuart, C. E. (1981). "Swedish Tax Rates, Labor Supply and Tax Revenues." *Journal of Political Economy* 89:1020–1038.

Tabb, W. K. (1980). "Government Regulation: Two Sides to the Story." *Challenge* 23:40–48.

Tanzi, V. (1980). "The Underground Economy in the United States: Estimates and Implications." *Banca Nazionale del Lavoro Quarterly Review* 135:427–453.

Tingsten, H. (1937). *Political Behavior: Studies in Election Statistics*. New York: Arno Press.

U.S. Internal Revenue Service (1979). *A General Opinion Survey*. Washington, D.C.: Office of Planning and Research.

Wainer, H. (1974). "Predicting the Outcome of the Senate Trial of Richard M. Nixon." *Behavioral Science* 19:404–406.

_____ (1976). "Estimating Coefficients in Linear Models: It Don't Make No Nevermind." *Psychological Bulletin* 83:213–217.

Wanniski, J. (1978). "Taxes, Revenues and the Laffer Curve." *Public Interest* 50:3–16.

Weidenbaum, M. L. (1979). "The High Cost of Government Regulation." *Challenge* 22:32–39.

Whiteley, P. (ed.) (1980). *Models of Political Economy*. Beverly Hills, CA: Sage.

Wolfinger, R. E., and S. J. Rosenstone (1980). *Who Votes?* New Haven and London: Yale University Press.

3: The Political Dimensions
of Wage Dynamics

Martin Paldam

This chapter examines the political business cycle in relation to the labor market, giving special emphasis to the dynamic wage relation. The first section of the chapter consists of an introduction to the political dimensions of wage dynamics. Two major weaknesses found in earlier works on the macro wage relation are discussed: aggregation problems and the neglect of political factors. This section concludes with an identification of the main types of political business cycles.

We then discuss the dynamic wage relation. The simple static Phillips curve is summarized, and the expectations-augmented dynamization and some micro-macro discussions of the rationality complex are outlined. We conclude with a review of the controversy concerning the concepts of long-run acceleration versus short-run myopia in political business cycles, and a presentation of empirical evidence pointing to the inadequacy of price expectations in explaining wage dynamics.

The logic of one of the two main sets of theories of political business cycles, the Nordhaus-MacRae theory, is taken up next. Applying this theory to the labor market, it demonstrates that the cycles in labor market activities are the opposite of the ones predicted by Nordhaus and MacRae. The empirical examination thus points to weaknesses in this key theory of political business cycles, and it is suggested that these weaknesses can be overcome by reference to the second set of theories concerning long-run problems resulting from sustained full employment: the Friedman-Phelps theory of the dynamic Phillips curve, the Kalecki theory of labor market discipline, and the neo-Kaleckian theory of the wage share. The similarities of these theories are discussed, and empirical evidence for industrial conflicts in 17 countries is examined. The conclusion is that wage patterns and industrial conflicts have strong international components and that theories of political business cycles which omit such considerations will fail to adequately explain political influence on labor markets.

THE POLITICAL DIMENSIONS OF WAGE DYNAMICS

It is an old tradition to study labor markets from a macroeconomic perspective, but since the advent of the Phillips curve (see Phillips, 1958; Lipsey, 1960), there has been a huge research effort whose main endeavor has been to explore the dynamics of the wage relation. After the introduction of the basic expectations-augmented Phillips curve (see Phelps, 1967; Friedman, 1968); a large number of dynamic wage relations appeared, with the concept of expected inflation ($\dot{p}_e$) as the dynamic element.

Still, there is much that we do not understand. The behavior of aggregate wage rises ($\dot{w}$) often surprises most observers, even though we are quite good at predicting the rate of unemployment (u). Two main explanations have been offered for our limited understanding of these things:

1. *The wrong level of aggregation is considered.* A few researchers have argued that the national market is too small a domain for analysis. (This, incidentally, is the author's view; see Paldam, 1980.) The great majority, however, contend that the problem is too much aggregation.

2. *Since labor markets are highly politicized, they are inadequately understood when only economic variables are considered.* This is the explanation we shall concentrate on in this chapter. Even though it is commonly found in the literature, it has been the subject of remarkably little research at the aggregate level, probably because of the *political data availability problem*: it has proved very difficult to find an adequate aggregate measure for the political factor in the labor market.[1] This chapter discusses two sets of theories known as *the political business cycle theories*. They are developed as macro labor market theories and they claim to catch the aggregate political impact and to do so in a way that sidesteps the political data availability problem.

The two sets of theories have two things in common: they both claim that the aggregate political impact operates to generate (fairly regular) economic fluctuations; and each uses a version of the dynamic Phillips curve (or some formal equivalent of the curve). The connection to the Phillips theory is so close that our discussion raises two central questions about that theory:

1. Is the wage relation manipulable?
2. Can price expectations, $\dot{p}_e$, account for the dynamics of the wage relation?

While the first question deals with stability and with the orders of magnitude in certain trade-offs, the second points to the heart of our wage relation discussion. For, although the $\dot{p}_e$ variable is often expected to carry all the dynamic adjustments, few researchers ask whether this variable *can* carry such a heavy weight. We shall take up several aspects of both questions as we proceed with our discussion, and by the end of the chapter we shall have reached a rather negative answer to both questions.

The political business cycle theories differ in several ways, but the central differences concern the very way in which they are "political": alpha (α)-cycles are deliberately created by the government (or some other dominating decision maker) for its own advantage; while beta (β)-cycles are involuntarily generated by political pressures, or appear as secondary effects of policies with other aims.[2]

The main example of an α-cycle is the Nordhaus-MacRae electoral cycle (see Nordhaus, 1975; MacRae, 1977),[2a] which is the result of governmental manipulation of the economy for electoral gain. We discuss the Nordhaus-MacRae electoral cycle below. Since we are dealing here with the 3–5 years of an election period, we are concerned only with the manipulability of the dynamic Phillips curve in the medium term.

The β-type of political cycle has the same basic endogenous character as the traditional business cycle, even though it emerges from policy making itself, whereas the traditional business cycle presumes no (or a neutral) policy. The main example of a β-cycle is the one briefly sketched by Kalecki (1943). We shall interpret this theory as dealing with the longer-run consequences of following a short-run (Keynesian) full-employment policy.[3] Kalecki's sketch thus constitutes an early or pre-Phillips analysis of the same problem, which caused Phelps (1967) and Friedman (1968) to propose the expectations-augmented Phillips curve. Phelps and Friedman are obviously dealing with the longer-run trade-offs, but their analyses also turn on the weight that price expectations ($\dot{p}_e$) are supposed to carry. While the $\dot{p}_e$ adjustments carry the entire dynamics in the Phelps-Friedman theory, Kalecki argues for much broader socioeconomic adjustments. In this chapter we introduce a labor market climate variable, ϕ, to account for the Kalecki dynamics, and we discuss longer-run political cycles.

Before turning to the theories, the various political "levels" should be introduced. When dealing with labor markets, it is important to distinguish among three levels:

1. The level of political parties and government. Parties often express their main policy targets in the aggregate labor market variables; they have policies aiming at reaching these targets.
2. The level of the labor market organizations. Both workers and employers formed organizations whose explicit purpose is to influence wage rates, and these organizations have considerable monopoly power. But despite the extensive literature (see Parsley, 1980) dealing with the effects of unions on wages, it has so far proved impossible to find an adequate macro expression for union power.
3. The level of mass politics. When people are asked about their main worries in public opinion polls, unemployment, inflation, and real

income trends emerge rather prominently in the aggregated answers. These trends affect political behavior, such as voting, and the propensity of workers to engage in strikes (see discussion below).

At none of these levels does a clear one-way causality appear, and no pair of levels is independent. Furthermore, some intermediate levels are often important. Nevertheless, the distinction among these three levels is important to any consideration of the dynamic wage relation—for when we speak of adjusting expectations, in the labor market, we need to know who is adjusting their expectations. The answer to this question is especially important to the theory of the rational formation of expectations.

A DISCUSSION OF THE DYNAMIC WAGE RELATION

In the original article by A. W. Phillips (1958), the wage rate already showed some dynamics; but in elementary textbooks the Phillips curve is depicted as a simple static relation:

$$\dot{w} = \pi_w^*(u, \ldots) \tag{1a}$$

or

$$\dot{p} = \pi_p^*(u, \ldots) \tag{1b}$$

where either wage rises ($\dot{w}$) or price rises ($\dot{p}$) are explained by the unemployment rate (u) and related variables ($\ldots$), such as the vacancy rate, adjustment terms for regional or structural imbalances in the unemployment rate, and so on.[4]

Figure 1 illustrates the significance and stability of the two π^*'s by calculating the two correlations, $c_w = c(u, \dot{w})$ and $c_p = c(u, \dot{p})$, for all intervals between 1948 and 1975. The calculations are made for our sample of 17 OECD countries, listed in Table 1, and the results shown are the averages over all these countries. Figure 1 thus constitutes a veritable Phillips map covering almost three decades and 17 countries.

In both Figures 1 and 2, and in subsequent empirical demonstrations in this chapter, we present unweighted averages of data or coefficients for

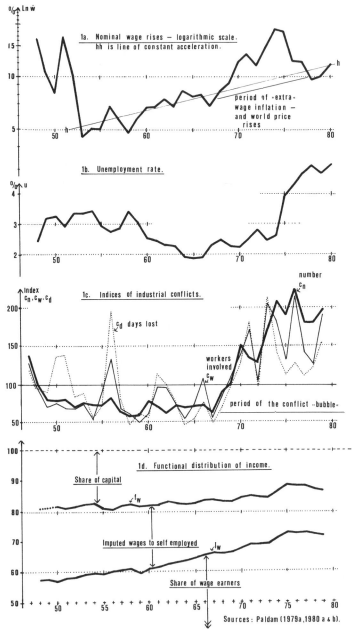

FIG. 1. Main labor market trends in 17 OECD countries (see Table 1).

Note: Unweighted averages of national data.

48

TABLE 1. Variables, Functions, Terms, and OECD Countries Discussed

Variables		Countries providing data (17)[f]
c_n, c_w, c_d	Indices for industrial conflict (number, workers involved, days lost)	Australia
		Belgium
		Canada
$e,$	Expectations; see also $\dot{p}_e$	Denmark
f_w	Wage share for factor of production[a]	Eire
l_w	Wage share for laboring class	Finland
g	Productivity	France
M	Money stock	Germany
		The Netherlands
$\dot{p}, \dot{p}_w, \dot{p}_y,$	Price rises, for goods and services,	Italy
$\dot{p}_e, \dot{p}_e^*$	expected price rises, synthetic series[b]	Japan
T	Time horizon for adjustment process	New Zealand
u	Unemployment rate	Norway
V_g	Vote for or popularity of government; hence a VP function is a function explaining v_g by (economic) variables	Austria
		Sweden
		United Kingdom
$\dot{w}$	Wage rises[c]	United States
y	GDP, total production	
$\dot{z}$	Wage rises abroad[d]	
ϕ	Labor market climate[e]	

Function terms	
π	Phillips terms in price-wage models
ψ	Wage-push terms in price-wage models
R	Cross-terms between wages and prices
λ_g	Target function for government

[a] Both F_w and l_w are defined in percentage points of net national income: f_w is greater than l_w, with imputed wages to self-employed persons, using average wages $\dot{w}$ as the accountancy wage.
[b] When we do not distinguish between price and wage inflation (i.e., when $l_w + \dot{g}$ are assumed constant), $\dot{p} = \dot{p}_y = \dot{p}_w$. A synthetic series, $\dot{p}_e^*$, is obtained for $\dot{p}_e$ when a certain formula for $\dot{p}_e$ is presumed, allowing us to calculate $\dot{p}_e$ from $\dot{p}, \dot{p} - 1$, etc.
[c] In empirical applications, $\dot{w}$ covers manufacturing only.
[d] When $\dot{z}$ is calculated for country i, $\dot{z}(i)$ is calculated as the average of the 16 $\dot{w}$'s for the other countries.
[e] Defined in text—an alternative to expectations in the push terms in price-wage equations.
[f] The data from these countries form the basis of the graphs in the figures. Since they have been independently compiled, we use unweighted averages of the results for each country.

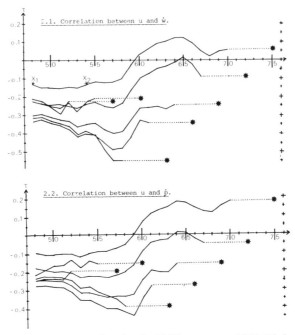

FIG. 2.   The dynamics of the simple Phillips curves 1948–75 in the average OECD country.

Note: Each curve connects a set of average correlations with different starting points and the same ending point as indicated with the *. The averages are over the countries listed in Table 1. Hence x_1 is the average of the correlations between unemployment and nominal wage rises calculated for the 28 annual observations from 1948 to 1975; x_2 is the similar average over the 22 years from 1954 to 1975. To allow us to disregard the possible nonlinearities of the two simple Phillips curves, a distribution free coefficient of correlation is used, Kendall's τ.

the different countries. How the best averages can be obtained is a debated point. In averaging across countries, a weight is often attached to each country to represent some relevant measure of its importance—for example, Americans often give the United States the weight of 50% (for country size) in country samples like the one considered. The main point of view here is that since we are dealing with cases that each represent an "experience," all cases are equally interesting—what really counts are phenomena that generalize across different sets of experience.

Figure 1 shows that until the late 1960s there was a fairly stable negative correlation of 0.3–0.4 between $\dot{w}$ and u, and a slightly smaller and less stable negative correlation between $\dot{p}$ and u. As we include more recent years and omit more of the earlier years, the correlations become positive.[5] What happens is evident from Figure 2. It is the phenomenon known as "stagflation"–the breakdown or the shift of the Phillips curve.

We shall follow the main tradition and take the Phillips curve to represent the reactions of prices to relative scarcities; that is, π_w is the relation in the labor market where w is the price, and π_p is the relation in the market for goods and services where p is the price. Obviously, u is the better proxy in the labor market; we also note that π_p is much the same as Keynes's *gab*. Surely we can assume there are many links between the two markets and we know that we lack something to account for the dynamics, so from the simple Phillips curve we reach the following more general, if still very aggregated price-wage model:

$$\dot{p} = \pi_p(u, \ldots) + \psi_p(e_p, \ldots) + R_p(\dot{w}, \ldots) + \varepsilon_p \qquad (2a)$$

$$\dot{w} = \pi_w(u, \ldots) + \psi_w(e_w, \ldots) + R_w(\dot{p}, \ldots) + \varepsilon_w \qquad (2b)$$

$$\dot{w} = \dot{p} + \dot{g} + \dot{l}_w \qquad (2c)$$

Here R_p and R_w are the two *cross-terms*. The price and wage equations are further tied together by Equation (2c), which contains productivity growth, $\dot{g}$, and changes in the wage share, $\dot{l}_w$. The π's now appear as two Phillips terms, presumed to be stable. To account for the dynamics, we have added the two *push terms*, ψ_p and ψ_w, where e indicates that the push is normally taken to be a function of some sort of expectations.

The model presented in Equation (2) is developed, operationalized, and estimated in Paldam (1980, 1983).[6] The main result in the first of these articles is the international character of the ψ's, while the second demonstrates that an index, c_n, for the number of industrial conflicts works rather well as ψ_w. We shall return to these results later, but first we shall look at the standard theory.

The models presented in Equations (2a) and (2b) are symmetrically formulated, and if we (somewhat unreasonably) assume that $\dot{g}$ and $\dot{l}_w$ are exogenous, then Equations (2a) and (2b) become very similar indeed. This argues for using an abbreviated formulation containing only one π and one ψ. The usual thing to do is to insert expected inflation, $\dot{p}_e$, as the

e_p. Then $\dot{p}$ and $\dot{w}$ become highly correlated, which suggests that R_p may be deleted. Thus we obtain the price version of the basic expectations-augmented Phillips curve:[8]

$$\dot{p} = \pi\gamma(u, \ldots) + \psi(\dot{p}_e) + \varepsilon \qquad (3a)$$

$$\dot{w} = \dot{p} + k \qquad (3b)$$

where k is constant. In principle, $\dot{p}_e$ is a straightforward concept, perfectly measurable by well-known polling techniques. When Eq. (3) was introduced by Phelps and Friedman, however, no such measures were available, so they proposed, as a first approximation, a simple adaptive mechanism that generated a synthetic series, $\dot{p}_e^*$ for $\dot{p}_e$:

$$\dot{p}_e^*(t) = \sum_{i=1, T_p} \gamma_i \dot{p}(t - i) \qquad (4)$$

where t is time and the γ's sum to 1 and decline regularly as we proceed backward in time to the horizon T_p.

With the large number of related formulas subsequently suggested (see Chan-Lee, 1980), we had a whole family of such artificial $\dot{p}_e^*$'s. Then, finally, sets of directly measured values of $\dot{p}_e$ were proposed, causing confidence in Equation (3) to decline. With sets of $\dot{p}_e$, two types of studies became possible: those inquiring into how $\dot{p}_e$ actually works in Eq. (3), and those seeking to determine how much of $\dot{p}_e$ is explained by $\dot{p}$, $\dot{p} - 1$, $\dot{p} - 2$, and so forth. Many studies of both types have been published in the last few years, but much remains hotly debated. One of the major puzzles concerns the size of T_p, about which two very different views persist.

Friedman (1968) originally proposed a very slow adjustment, so that T_p extends over a couple of decades; he based his supposition on older studies of the slow adjustment of interest rates to changing levels of inflation. Most later studies, starting with that of Solow (1969), have shown that to the extent that Eq. (4) works at all, it does so quite fast, so that T_p extends only over a couple of years. We shall call this the "expectation myopia result"; it will recur throughout this chapter.

The main evidence for slow adjustments comes from data such as those in Figure 2 for the average course of wages in the OECD area. As indicated (and further analyzed in Paldam 1980), this curve may be interpreted as showing a slow, steady acceleration in the wage and price levels throughout the OECD area ever since the Korea commodity price wave in the early 1950s. The average annual increase in the inflation rate is only 5% for the last three decades. That is, if $\dot{w}(t) = 10\%$, we get $\dot{w}(t + 1) = 10.5\%$ from the acceleration. No wonder the process remained inconspicuous for 15 years after 1953, when it started.

As long as we stick to model-generated expectations $\dot{p}_e^*$, we need not specify who is supposed to form these expectations; but as soon as we attempt to measure actual expectations, this question becomes crucial. Here some theoretical arguments should be mentioned. In the last decade a whole theoretical school has emerged out of the effort to deduce from basic axioms regarding rationality how $\dot{p}_e$ is formed. The key concept is the level of information for those forming $\dot{p}_e$. Here the logic behind the push term ψ comes into play, for the push clearly implies a group of "pushers" G.[8] This brings us back to the three political levels discussed in the introductory section of this chapter.

If the push occurs at the mass level, G must be a very large group, G_m, whose individual members have only a marginal influence, and hence no incentive to become well-informed. The adaptive process shown in Eq. (4) is likely to be the limiting case when people have no other information but their own experience. Thus, at the mass level, Eq. (4) is likely to have a relatively great weight and we may even expect the process to be fairly myopic. This, in fact, is what is found by Jonung (1981) in the latest—and largest—study of $\dot{p}_e$ at the mass level (covering a total of 10,000 Swedes).

At the core of business and labor organizations and political parties, G is a small group, G_c, of full-time professionals, most of whom are provided with staffs to collect, analyze, and assess all relevant information, including the thinking and intentions of the other actors in G_c.[9] Here adjustments are likely to be fast and irregular and Eq. (4) must play a small role. Still, there are pressures from the mass level, which we shall discuss above.

Actually, most wage increases and almost all price increases take place at the intermediate level of the individual firm or plant, and involve management, shop stewards, local trade union branch offices, and so forth. This intermediate level is rather susceptible to mass pressures, but it also receives a lot of information from the top.

Most attempts to measure expected inflation, $\dot{e}_p$, try to catch $\dot{e}_p$ at this intermediate level, especially on the managerial side. The best known of these attempts is a bit closer to the top than actual price and wage fixing. It is the index for U.S. price forecasts collected by Joseph A. Livingston from 30 to 40 independent experts over more than three decades. There have been many studies of these expert expectations, and disagreements as to what they tell persist. A recent report (Figlewski and Wachtel, 1981) concludes that even in these expert expectations there is myopia, and Eq. (4) plays a great role.[10]

Thus the studies point rather strongly to both expectation myopia and adaptive mechanisms. There are, however, some bits of information supporting the slow-adjustment view. Several of the Livingston series studies have pointed to systematic long-run biases in $\dot{p}_e$ compared to $\dot{p}$; but the most recent study (Brown and Maital, 1981) concludes that the series is largely unbiased.

By and large, then, $\dot{p}_e$ is a much more straightforward variable than often presumed, but it is highly doubtful that it can explain all the short-term dynamics of the wage relation, and even more doubtful that it can explain the long-run dynamics. Therefore at least, one more variable should be entered into the ψ terms. In the last section of this chapter, we shall argue that a concept of "labor market climate" ϕ makes sense (as was argued in Paldam 1980, 1983, and we shall provide a couple of proxies for ϕ which are actually available and work well in price-wage models.

THE DEVIOUS BUT EMPTY LOGIC OF THE NORDHAUS - MACRAE ELECTORAL CYCLE

If an economic variable displays a systematic variation over the electoral period, we say that there is an electoral cycle for this variable. The author (Paldam, 1979a) has previously shown that most larger national accounts aggregates contain weak but highly significant electoral cycles—the main pattern found is depicted in Figure 3.

The *empirical* literature (recently surveyed in Paldam, 1981a) dealing with electoral cycles is rather limited, coming to about only 20 titles. A major problem is the great variation in the path of events under different governments. Hence one has to analyze data for about 30 governments in

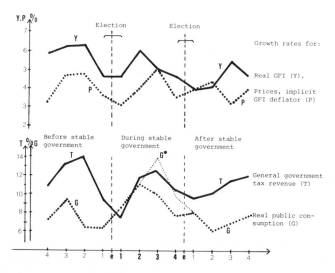

FIG. 3. The electoral cycle in real gross factor income (Y), prices (P), total tax revenue (T), and real government expenditure (G).

Note: Figures are from Paldam (1981b), with statistical tests, etc., in Paldam (1979a). The averages cover 35 stable governments, as in Figure 4. The thin dotted line (to G^*) includes the extreme values for the USA and Canada in 1951/52, during the Korean war.

order to establish the statistical significance of the average electoral pattern for a given series. To obtain the necessary amount of data is very time-consuming, and most studies have either taken short-cuts or included too few observations, with the result that their conclusions are either debatable or insignificant.

On the other hand, we do have a well-known and rather convincing *theory* of electoral cycles (developed by Nordhaus, 1975; and MacRae, 1977; and elaborated by many others). Our aim for now is to determine whether this theory can explain the cycles observed. As we have already seen, the Nordhaus-MacRae theory is an α-type political business cycle theory—that is, it results from the maximizing behavior of governments.

The starting point for the Nordhaus-MacRae theory is the seemingly reasonable assumption that, whatever divides the target functions λ_g of different governments, they all want to be reelected. Many studies have shown that the popularity and hence the vote for the government (V_g) is influenced by economic conditions. Therefore:

$$\lambda_g \sim V_g \qquad (5a)$$

Obviously, Eq. (5a) is not strictly fulfilled, as we shall discuss below (see problems 1 and 2), but first we shall look at the V_g function as analyzed in the literature. Since it has been discussed elsewhere at length,[11] here we shall only make eight points:

1. Changing economic conditions normally explain 20–40% of V_g, the vote for the government. Ordinarily, popularity indices (Gallup Polls) can be explained somewhat better than actual vote results, but we shall not distinguish between the two in this brief survey.
2. Clear results appear only when we are dealing with stable political systems, systems in which people choose between clearly differentiated alternative parties that can actually rule if elected. In complex multi-party systems with minority governments and frequent elections, the coefficients disappear or turn signs.
3. In stable systems the main result is the responsibility pattern; that is, people hold the government responsible for national economic conditions. If economic conditions improve, V_g goes up and vice versa.
4. Some studies indicate an asymmetrical pattern in which V_g goes down more easily than it goes up. In addition, all governments seem to encounter a general depreciation of popularity—a cost of ruling amounting to 1.6–1.7% of the vote.
5. The variables most frequently significant in vote and popularity functions are unemployment, u, price rises, $\dot{p}$, and the growth rate for real income, $\dot{y}$. Because of multicollinearity problems, it is still debatable whether u and $\dot{y}$ should enter at the same time, but they probably should.
6. Voters are normally found to be myopic: their time horizon, T_V, is rarely found to exceed 1 year.
7. The main problem with vote and popularity functions is their instability, even in the most stable two-party systems. We are beginning to understand when these functions change and also when a dynamic

model formulation appears (see problem 4 below), but even so, vote functions are poor predictors.

8. Finally, there is the unexplained 60–80% of the vote, that portion not accounted for by item (1) above. Different systems of trends and dummies can often account for a remarkably high fraction of this residual, but surely it is an uncomfortably large fraction to leave unexplained or to explain in a purely formal way. Sometimes this residual is termed the "political" fraction of the vote, and a few attempts have been made to use political variables to explain at least some of it, but much remains to be done.

All of these points lead us to write the following target function for the government:

$$\lambda_g \sim V_g = V_g(u, u_{-1}, \ldots, \dot{p}, \dot{p}_{-1}, \ldots, T_V) \tag{5b}$$

where if $T_V = 1$, we delete $u_{-1}, \ldots, \dot{p}_{-1}, \ldots$; if $T_V = 2$, we delete the ellipses after u_{-1} and after $\dot{p}_{-1}$; and so on.

From Equations (3) and (4) above, we derive a dynamic model between the variables in (5) which may be written as:

$$\dot{p} = \dot{p}(u, \dot{p}_{-1}, \dot{p}_{-2}, \ldots, \phi, T_p) \tag{6}$$

The Nordhaus-MacRae problem is to maximize the target function (V_g) subject to the dynamic model (for $\dot{p}$) at certain points (elections) separated by an interval (the election period). In general, the solution to this type of problem is a path where the variables contain cycles, with the interval as the period,—that is, the problem generates Nordhaus-MacRae electoral cycles.

To solve the problem, we have to have a control variable.[12] The obvious choice is u, which seems to be the variable closest to our actual instruments. Hence a policy for the 4-year election period is a set of four u's: $U^4 = (u_{+1}, \ldots u_{+4})$. The symbol ϕ is a typical uncontrolled variable to be forecast, giving the set ϕ^4. From equation (6), we get the central forecast:

$$\dot{P}^4 = \dot{P}^4(U^4, \phi^4) = (\dot{p}_{+1}, \ldots, \dot{p}_{+4}) \tag{7}$$

In addition to $\dot{P}^4$, we need a set of security intervals, $S^4(\dot{P}^4, \alpha)$, around the central forecast, assuming a certain security percentage, α.

Thus for any α, α percent of all $\dot{p}_{+t}$ is found in the interval $s(\dot{p}_{+t}, \alpha)$. Obviously the s's grow with t and α and depend on the stability of function (6) and the forecast error in ϕ. When planning policy, we look at

$$V_g = V_g(U^4, \dot{P}^4) \tag{8}$$

In addition, $s(V_g, \alpha)$ is relevant, and for this, we must also include the instability of the V_g function [see Eq. (5)].

The main part of the Nordhaus-MacRae theory deals with the central forecast. Here the presumption of voters' myopia (i.e., $T_v = 1$–2 years) means that the party in power must generate the most favorable economic conditions possible just before the election. Thus the solution to the Nordhaus-MacRae problem is to use high values of u early in the election period to reduce the medium-term element in $\dot{p}$ so that we can have both a low u and a relatively low $\dot{p}$ just before the election.

The exact distribution of $(U^4_{max}, \dot{P}^4_{max})$ depends on the weight of $\dot{p}$ and u in V_g and on the trade-offs possible during the 4 years of the election period. The main differences between Nordhaus (1975) and MacRae (1977) is that the former presumes that u has a greater weight in V_g than $\dot{p}$. Hence, Nordhaus gets a weak cycle in $\dot{p}$—the reverse of the one in u. MacRae gives equal weight to u and $\dot{p}$ in V_g, and he finds in $\dot{p}$ a cycle parallel to the one in u, so that $\dot{p}$ peaks when u is highest and vice versa.

In passing, we note that while the Nordhaus version of the Nordhaus-MacRae cycle only weakens the fit of the simple Phillips curve, the MacRae version turns the signs positive. Thus the Nordhaus-MacRae theory offers a possible explanation of the dynamics of the π^*'s as depicted in Figure 2—although, as we shall see, this possibility soon evaporates.

Table 2 shows the main test results for cyclicality in seven main labor market series over the 49 stable governments found in the 17 democratic countries analyzed. Our null hypothesis is that the series are random over the election period, and our tests are three fairly standard two-way analysis-of-variance tests. (The tests are explained in the notes to the table and in more detail in Paldam 1979a.)

The first interesting point to note is that when the results in Table 2 are compared with the corresponding results for the national accounts series (see Tables 2 and 3 in Paldam, 1979a), the cycles turn out to be *weaker* in the labor market series. This runs counter to the Nordhaus-MacRae

TABLE 2. Tests for Electoral Cycles in the Labor Market Series

Series as defined in Table 1	Tests based on normalization				Distribution-free test	
	Method A P%	Comment	Method M P%	Comment	Friedman's P%	Electoral reference cycle
A: 35 4-year governments						
(1) u, Unemployment	1	l.s.	3	s.o.(1)	6	
(2) i_w, Change of wage share[a]	12	n.s.	22	n.s.	52	
(3) $\dot{w}$, Growth of wages	99	n.s.	61	s.o.(3)	4	
(4) $\dot{p}$, Price increases	49	s.o.(2)	21	s.o.(2)	12	
(5) c_n, Number of conflicts[b]	45	n.s.	79	n.s.	10	
B: 14 3-year governments						
(1) u, Unemployment	50	s.o.(2)	26	s.o.(2)	68	1 2 3
(2) i_w, Change of wage share	12	s.o.(3)	32	n.s.	40	
(3) $\dot{w}$, Growth of wages	83	n.s.	72	n.s.	7	
(4) $\dot{p}$, Price increases	39	l.s.	35	l.s.	53	

Notes: The tests made follow the (cumbersome) procedure developed in Paldam (1979b). It is a fairly straightforward application of the standard two-way analysis of variance testing for randomness of the observations across the election period. The three results given are the probabilities ($P\%$) that the observations (or something skewed in the same direction) could be generated randomly. The three results are from three versions of the test. The standard test used is based on the normal distribution, and the series analyzed are very nonnormal—hence two methods for "normalization" are applied to the data before the test is made. The abbreviated comment says whether normalization is successful (l.s.), successful with n outlying observations [s.o.(n)], not successful (n.s.). In the latter case the test result is unreliable. The third row gives the results of the distribution free two-way analysis of variance, known as the Friedman test.

[a]Based on 34 governments only.

[b]Based on 28 governments only. The results for c_w and c_d are less significant (even) than the ones for c_n.

59

theory. For the 3-year governments, there are barely significant cycles in u and $\dot{w}$, looking almost as predicted by Nordhaus—in fact, our test results are almost the same as the ones reached by Nordhaus with a different technique. How these data look when depicted as averages is shown in Figure 4. Once more, we note that the cycle in u is much weaker than the corresponding cycles in the GNP series.

Figure 4, however, contains two rather strong pieces of evidence against the Nordhaus-MacRae cycle. The first follows from the often-made observation that unemployment is a very slow variable to turn. Thus, if a new government started by increasing unemployment, we should see unemployment peak in the second year. But here the greatest decrease in unemployment takes place in the second year. This finding corresponds nicely to the findings in Figure 3.

The second bit of evidence against the Nordhaus-MacRae theory emerges from the isolation of the 14 governments where the average trend is strongest. Here the main observations are that a policy to reduce unemployment is carried out as soon as possible by the new stable government, that the policy is pursued through the election period, and that the resulting lower level of unemployment persists after the election. Thus it seems that stable governments are relatively good at reducing unemployment—in fact, their success might be one reason for their stability.

Two more empirical points are worth making. First, when the shapes of all the U^4's and P^4's found are confronted, only one clear example of

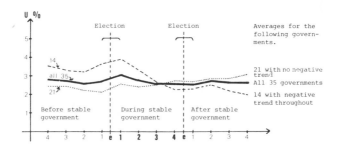

FIG. 4.   The average path of unemployment over the election period.

Note: Constructed as in Figure 3 covering the same 35 stable governments. *Source:* Paldam (1981b).

the MacRae possibility is found—the government in Eire in 1957 to 1960 —and even here the possibility is weaker than it should be, given the stochastic elements in Equations (5) and (6). Second, most of the stable governments, especially the ones that show a clear trend, are concentrated in the years 1955 to 1965, when unemployment was falling throughout the OECD area, as is seen in Figure 3.[13] Thus one could argue that the governments that happened to rule at a time when international conditions were most favorable were the governments that turned out to be the most stable.

We conclude, therefore, that there are no Nordhaus-MacRae cycles in the economy. We have found no evidence of the MacRae version, and what at first looked like evidence of the Nordhaus version disappeared on closer inspection. Thus we can say that any electoral business cycles that are discovered must have another explanation—that is, they must emerge from outside the labor market. In Paldam (1981a) an alternative theory of the β-type of political business cycle is proposed. The main thrust of the alternative theory is that the pressures operating on governments are so strong that they can not really plan four years ahead for their reelection. Instead, when they assume power they simply try to implement their policy—that is, they attempt to redeem their campaign promises. This effort creates an expenditure boom which leads to relatively large economic growth in the year after the election, which is the first year to be influenced by the new government. The boom causes prices to escalate in the third year; and to regain control of the economy, the government tightens up expenditures somewhat toward the end of that year. The pattern that results is almost the reverse of the optimal one.

This alternative theory will not be elaborated here. Instead, we shall concentrate on the following question: What is wrong with the Nordhaus-MacRae theory? We already have some notion from the preceding analysis, and now we shall become more specific. There are six main problems with the theory. The first two concern the behavior of governments, or rather the short-cut the theory takes when setting the preference function of the government, λ_g, equal to the maximizing of V_g on election day.

Problem 1. All governments (and all individuals ministers as well[14]) have other aims besides being reelected. The stronger these other aims are, the greater the variation becomes. This possibility is analyzed with great effect by Kirchgässner (1981) whose results generate all kinds of cycles. The cycles are very sensitive to the function maximized.

Problem 2. It is quite possible that λ_g is asymmetrical in a risk-averse way that dampens the propensity of governments to generate cycles. This may happen for two reasons. The first is the possible asymmetry of V_g, as mentioned under the fourth point in the vote function summary above. The second is that there is likely to be a rather sharp kink in λ_g where V_g shifts from majority to minority: the V_g^m point. The longer the security interval, $s(V)$, the greater the possibility that V_g^m is included; and obviously the larger the cycle the government tries to generate the longer $s(V)$ is.[15] The next two problems concern the two time horizons, T_v and T_p.

Problem 3. The formulation of Eqs. (5) and (6) points to the very symmetrical way in which T_v and T_p enter into the theory—this also applies to the expectation terms. If the proper expression of $\dot{p}$, $\dot{p}_{-1}, \ldots$, to be inserted in (6) is $\dot{p}_e$, then it seems reasonable that $\dot{p}_e$ should replace $\dot{p}$, $\dot{p}_{-1}, \ldots$, in Eq. (5) also. Some evidence that this is actually the case has been provided (see Schneider, 1978, pp. 54–60; and Monroe and Levi, 1983).[16] If Equations (5) and (6) contain the very same adaptive mechanisms, people will remember the previous bad times clearly only if they have an effect on the inflation rate at election time. It might be adduced from the above that T_v could be slightly shorter that T_p, and also that the weight of current unemployment might be different in the two functions; but clearly the near-symmetry of Eqs. (5) and (6) indicates small net gains by any government that manages to create Nordhaus-MacRae cycles.

Problem 4. Strong evidence that voters are less myopic than hitherto believed has recently emerged from a major dynamic reformulation of the vote function (see Hibbs, 1982, and four subsequent papers) but even so, four-fifths of the adjustment occurs within 2 years. T_v is found to be around 4 to 6 years. The longer T_v is, the harder it is to manipulate the functions.

Problems 5 and 6 follow from the text above and suggest that governmental manipulation of the economy for political gain may be counter-productive.

Problem 5. It follows from all the arguments above that the processes that form the pushing element in ψ (whatever they are and however they work) are hard to predict. We can predict some of the push, but any prediction 4 years in advance is likely to be very uncertain. Also, the V's are rather unstable. Hence the security intervals, $s(V)$, are certain to be rather large, even if the government can change the instruments as it goes along, and even if, as in parliamentary systems, it can call an early election when the economic conditions are favorable.[17] In summary, if it is impossible to predict the results of governmental manipulation of the economy for political gain, such manipulation is not worthwhile.

Problem 6 illustrates all the other problems. Of the four recent studies that try to model or analyze an economy for Nordhaus-MacRae cycles, that of Breuss (1980) is the most ambitious. He attempts to build a 24-equation model for Austria for the generation of Nordhaus-MacRae cycles, but can find no such cycles. Goldman and Poterba (1980) analyze the payoff to a U.S. government from cycles created by a set of estimated equations for Eqs. (5) and (6). They find the potential gain to be very small. Lecaillon (1981) discusses French fiscal policy in a Nordhaus-MacRae perspective and reaches similarly negative conclusions. Finally, Chrystal and Alt (1979) can find no Nordhaus-MacRae cycles in the United Kingdom.

LONG - RUN POLITICAL CYCLES—HOW GREAT ARE THE DYNAMICS?

In the late 1930s it was demonstrated that it is possible to do a great deal to counteract the slump of the old business cycle by simple fiscal means. Since then there have been a number of discussions about the long-run consequences of such Keynesian policies. A subset of these discussions centers on the labor market. We shall deal only with this subset.[18]

Kalecki (1943) and later Phelps (1967) and Friedman (1968) entered into the discussion by way of considering the consequences of sustained full employment.[19] These consequences, they thought, were a new kind of "political" business cycle which appears only after the old cycle has been mastered. It must follow, then, that we are dealing with mechanisms which work more slowly than those of the old cycle. In other words, we are talking of long-run political cycles.

The theories to be discussed have a lot in common. Not only do they start with the presumption that the economy can be steered to control a key target variable (here taken to be unemployment), but they also assume, at a certain level of generality, the same basic mechanism. This mechanism is as follows: When u is kept low, a problem (such as inflation) keeps accumulating. When x becomes sufficiently high, policy has to be changed to keep the target variable (u) high for a while as x is brought down.

The basic mechanism is a cyclical one because it has a symmetrical character over the cycle period, that is, from the time x starts to grow until it has been brought down again. In particular, we note that u is symmetrical around a level that is sustainable in the long run—the so-called natural level of unemployment, u_p.[20] For the cycle to be regular, x must be the type of problem that tends to be disregarded as it is building up, but has a rather forceful presence once it reaches a certain size. This is strongly consistent with our knowledge of the vote and popularity functions: for example, inflation is a problem which disappears from the functions when its rate is low, but becomes important (even dominating) once it really gets going. The same seems to be true of balance-of-payment deficits: they can be ignored until they accumulate into an accelerating debt burden. Thus it is likely that mass political pressures operate to enhance long-run cyclicality.

The basic mechanism is also a political one where the actions emerge from decision making itself. The kinks at the peak and the trough are due to changes in policy. The reaction point is at the level of x where events force the government to reverse policies. When the problem has disappeared, the government is not content to sustain the natural level (u_p) of unemployment, but rather seeks to reduce it to an unsustainable low level. Whether or not the government recognizes that this will make problems for some future government is not important for the mechanism, so long as the government feels forced by political pressures to follow policies that bring unemployment down below u_p.[21]

Not only is the basic mechanism the same in all the theories of long-run political cycles, but also the problem x, which is taken to be the rate of inflation ($\dot{p}$). The difference emerges in the way x accumulates. We shall look at four theories:

1. The Friedman-Phelps dynamics, where the only things adjusting to u are $\dot{p}$ and M, the stock of money. The accumulation process is formulated as an adjustment of inflationary expectations, $\dot{p}_e$.
2. The Kalecki dynamics, where the central phenomenon adjusting is the "discipline" of the labor market. Lower discipline leads to increasing inflation and—thanks to falling confidence among investors—falling investment.
3. The neo-Kaleckian dynamics,[22] where full employment leads to shrinking profits and hence to decreased investment in the framework of an accumulation theory of investment.

The fourth is not a theory in the same sense as the other three, but a very important aspect that must be taken into account by the other theories:

4. The processes discussed have strong international ramifications, so that no country is able to pass through a long-run political business cycle independently. The rate of inflation, in particular—but also the other main series to be discussed—contains large international elements.

The Friedman-Phelps dynamics was discussed above, where the main conclusion was the inadequacy of $\dot{p}_e$—expected inflation—to fill the role assigned to it by the theory.[23]

Kalecki's discipline—our ϕ variable[24]—is an attempt to find something more powerful than $\dot{p}_e$ to account for the price-wage dynamics. The most direct measure for this variable must be the frequency of industrial conflict, and we shall briefly discuss the connection between industrial conflict and the price-wage dynamics. The discussion will rely heavily on two recent articles by the author (Paldam, 1983; and Paldam and Pedersen, 1982) analyzing the relationship between the main labor market series and industrial conflicts in 15 to 17 countries from 1948 to 1975.

Three series are available for this variable—c_n, c_w, and c_d. These series have their main weight at different political levels: c_n, the number of

conflicts, is closest to the mass level. The other two series contain size
dimensions—c_w, the number of workers involved; and c_d, the number of
days lost. Since large industrial conflicts always involve labor unions, the
c_w and c_d series have their main weight at the level of labor market
organizations. The fact that c_n *always* gives the best fits in short-term
macroeconomic models points to the crucial importance of mass political
pressures.

The conflict series are notoriously poorly measured and, for a number
of reasons, are interesting economically as macro series only. Hence c_n is
only a proxy for ϕ. In some low-conflict countries, c_n turns out to be so
small as to be dominated by noise, so that c_n in these countries becomes a
poor proxy.

The main hypothesis of the Kalecki model is that c_n should be
negatively correlated with u. This negative correlation has, in fact, often
appeared, even as a short-run result, in the literature. But, as demonstrated in Figure 5a and analyzed in considerable detail in the two
articles by the author referred to above, this result is not a reliable one.
There is, however, a strong positive correlation between nominal wage
rises ($\dot{w}$) and the number of conflicts (c_n).[25]

It should come as no surprise (except perhaps to readers familiar with
the literature on the macroeconomic strike model) that the main connec-

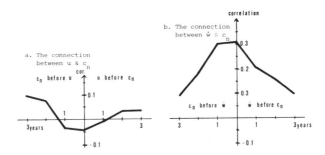

FIG. 5. Correlograms between industrial conflicts (c_n),
unemployment (u), and wage rises ($\dot{w}$). Results from 15
countries, 1948–75.

Note: The two curves are averages from Figures 3a and 4a in
Paldam (1980), where a much more thorough discussion is found
applying multivariate techniques.

tions between industrial conflicts and the economy are nominal wage rises; that, in fact, is what most conflicts are about. The interesting point is that the correlation is positive with all lags. Taking the lags as an indication of causality, we note that the strongest effects are those from the labor market climate (c_n) on wage rises $(\dot{w})$, indicating that the c_n series works well as explanatory variables in the wage relation. However, greater wage inflation clearly leads to more conflicts.[26]

The positive impact of c_n on $\dot{w}$ and of $\dot{w}$ on c_n explains the phenomenon of conflict inflation waves that is sometimes observed. In our terminology, it points to a cumulative effect of wage inflation and a deteriorating labor market climate. Thanks to the lags, such a wave may be of considerable duration. When Figure 2 is compared with Figure 5b, it seems highly probable that the extra inflation wave [over the h line of constant acceleration] noted after 1967 is such a conflict inflation wave throughout the OECD area.

The crucial point here is the international character of the process—it appears in both wage rises and the rise in the conflict levels. This may be demonstrated by calculating the intercorrelation in the series or by returning to the three equations of model (2). The model may be operationalized as follows[27]:

$$\dot{w} = \alpha_0 + \alpha_1 u + \alpha_2 \dot{p}_M + \alpha_3 \dot{p} \tag{9a}$$

$$\dot{p} = \beta_0 + \beta_1 u_{-1} + \beta_2 \phi + \beta_3 \dot{w} \tag{9b}$$

$$\dot{w} = \dot{p} + \dot{g} + \dot{l}_w \tag{9c}$$

For the unobserved ϕ, we use c_n or $\dot{z}$, as discussed below.

From what has been said already, it is not surprising that c_n works rather well as a proxy for ϕ, except in the low-conflict countries. The standard way to enter the international element is through import prices, $\dot{p}_M$, but the troublesome fact is that this is insufficient by far. To account for the remaining interdependence, the z variable is used. For each of the 17 countries, $\dot{z}$ is formed as the simple average of wage rises, $\dot{w}$, in the other 16 countries. When $\dot{z}$ is inserted for ϕ in (9a), it also works rather well, giving extremely significant and very stable coefficients both over time and across countries.

The really fascinating point, however, is that $\dot{z}$ and c_n explain almost exactly the same part of $\dot{w}$. In the low-conflict countries $\dot{z}$, of course, is much better than c_n, but in the other countries c_n is only slightly better than $\dot{z}$, and the multicollinearity between the two variables is very high. The interdependence is *not* generated by a similar development in the rate of unemployment: until the great downturn in 1974–1975 the countries had remarkably different unemployment histories. One of the big problems with the Friedman-Phelps theory is the fact that there seems to be no connection between the size and distribution over time of the wage acceleration and the unemployment histories of the different countries.[28]

The last mechanism to be discussed is that whereby the wage share, l_w, is thought to be one of the central quantities adjusting. To see what may happen, model (2) could be slightly reformulated as:

$$\dot{p}_y = \pi_p + \psi_p + R_p + \varepsilon_p \tag{10a}$$

$$\dot{p}_w = \dot{w} - \dot{g} = \pi_w + \psi_w + R_w - \dot{g} + \varepsilon_w \tag{10b}$$

$$\dot{p}_w - \dot{p}_y = \dot{l}_w \tag{10c}$$

Here Eq. (10a) determines the rate of price inflation, $\dot{p}_y$, and Eq. (10b) determines the rate of wage inflation, $\dot{p}_w$, where productivity growth, $\dot{g}$, is still presumed to be exogenous. It is now clear why economists like to presume that l_w is constant—this makes $\dot{p}_w = \dot{p}_y$ and gives us only one rate of inflation. This presumption has an old history, going back to the great studies of Arthur Bowley and Paul H. Douglas in the 1920s.[29]

From Figure 2, it appears that the two main shares, l_w and f_w, have shifted rather dramatically over the last three decades. In particular, the share of capital $(100 - f_w)$ has decreased by no less than 40% in the average OECD country since the mid-1950s. The strongest development has occurred in some of the smaller countries, while trends have been relatively weak in the largest country (the United States). The short-run fluctuations in l_w for the individual countries are even larger. The average numerical annual charge (in percentage points of net national income) of the almost 500 observations discussed in Paldam (1979b) comes to no less than 1.25%. Since the average inflation rate corresponding to these data is about 5%, we find that $\dot{p}_w$ and $\dot{p}_y$ differ by 25% on average. As may be inferred from the figures, half of this difference is of a long-run nature. So in spite of all links between the labor market and the market for goods and services, the data forcefully emphasize that we are dealing with two different markets.

Once the difference between $\dot{p}_w$ and $\dot{p}_y$ is recognized, the question arises: What decides the relative speed of inflation in the two markets? Because unemployment is a measure of tightness in the labor market and hence closest to $\dot{p}_w$, it appears likely that $\dot{p}_w$ will be larger than $\dot{p}_y$ if u is low. Since it is surely harmful to capital formation if the share of capital falls, in principle the x of the basic mechanism may be $x = 100 - f_w$, the share of capital.

The theory outlined here suffers from much the same problem as the Friedman-Phelps theory. It becomes extremely involved once the international linkage of both $\dot{p}_y$ and $\dot{p}_w$ is taken into consideration, and it is hard to relate the growth of l_w in the individual countries to their unemployment history.

If no sharp conclusions emerge from this discussion of the long-run political cycles, it is chiefly because we are dealing with very complex phenomena that have thus far managed to defy all the simple formulations proposed to contain them. We do, however, have a couple of main clues as to how the entire adjustment process should look. These clues are the theme of our concluding comments.

CONCLUSIONS

Our analysis so far has dealt with three closely related topics: (1) the theory of the electoral cycle, (2) the theories of long-run political cycles, and (3) the dynamics of the macro wage relation.[30]

Under the first topic, we discussed the Nordhaus-MacRae theory, which proposes that the dynamic wage relation is manipulated for electoral gains by the government. We concluded that this appears not to be the case, even when there are significant electoral cycles in the main national accounts aggregates, and that an alternative explanation of the electoral cycle is needed. It was proposed that this theory should be of a more endogenous nature where the short-term political pressures—especially mass political pressures—dominate the medium-term planning.

Under the second topic, a less homogeneous set of theories analyzing the longer-run consequences of sustained full employment was discussed. Once again, the discussion hinged on the adjustments of the wage relation. Two main points were argued: first, that we are dealing with rather complex adjustment processes within each country, involving the crucial factor of the labor market climate, the functional distribution of income, and so on; and second, that the adjustments have large international elements, which turn the entire adjustment process into a veritable wage tangle.

This goes a long way toward explaining why the third topic, the dynamic wage relation, has proved so extraordinarily difficult to handle. In the numerous attempts to dynamize the wage relation in the literature, the major effort has been to model the dynamics as a process adjusting inflationary expectations, $\dot{p}_e$. When this effort began, there were no data on $\dot{p}_e$, but now, with evidence on $\dot{p}_e$ rapidly accumulating, it appears that this modest variable is unable to carry the entire adjustment. Here the sociopolitical conflict variable (c_n equals the number of conflicts) and the international wage-push variable ($\dot{z}$ equals average wage rises abroad) both appear superior.

NOTES

1. The typical hard-headed economist dislikes the inclusion of political factors in the wage relation because the data availability problem makes them vague and unsubstantiated. It is one thing to state that wages are set by a "power relation," and quite another to demonstrate what a power relation is and how it actually works.

2. We shall discuss only one set of theories belonging to each of the two types. Though other possibilities could be mentioned, they are minor.

2a. The author wishes to note that in earlier works he has drawn a distinction between "electoral" and "electional" cycles, with electoral cycles referring to the cycles in party popularity over the election period and electional cycles denoting the economic cycles in an election period. However, such terminology has not been adopted in this chapter; instead, the Editor has followed the more common practice of defining economic electoral cycles as an umbrella term denoting economic fluctuations generated from political considerations.

3. Kalecki's brief analysis was written in connection with the discussion of the Beveridge Plan for full employment after World War II (see Kowalik, 1964). Remarks by Joan Robinson (1943)—using many of the same formulations and

arguments—also refer to the Beveridge Plan. Neither of these authors developed the theory.

4. Phillip's main contribution was the empirical demonstration of the long-run stability, as shown in Figure 1a—a finding which has withstood all subsequent analyses. The wage rate dynamics appear in the form of the loops over the business cycle (cf. Grossman, 1974). The idea behind the simple Phillips curve is an old one, and many are credited with originating it. There are also numerous explanations of the curve, but we prefer the simple one first proposed by Lipsey (1960).

5. The simple Phillips curve had its heyday in the 1960s, when the average OECD country had well-behaved π^*'s. The Phelps-Friedman formulation was proposed just when the π^*'s started to move upward, so it is no wonder that this formulation came to enjoy widespread popularity.

6. For this expositional short-cut, all terms in Eq. (2) are presumed to be additive. Also, we are forced to delete most of the refinements hidden in the " ... " because we are working with comparative data for 17 countries. For most countries, some fine-tuning of the data and a couple of dummies would probably lift the R^2 score by 0.1–0.3.

7. Rational expectations have been analyzed on both the macro and the micro level, and there is already substantial literature on the subject, though it is unevenly distributed on both sides of the Atlantic. Two very useful surveys are those of Shiller (1978) and Chan-Lee (1980).

8. In this group we include both those who push more or less aggressively, and those who resist the push more or less adamantly.

9. If the formula shown in Eq. (4) defines the no-information extreme in the rational expectations range (the limiting case for G_m where $m \to \infty$), then $\dot{p}_e$ of G_c should be the full-information extreme at the other end of the range. Also, we can speak of pure backward- and pure forward-generated expectations. In the later case, the actions of the agents become draws in a typical game situation.

10. The different sets of measurements for $\dot{p}_e$ are somewhat hard to compare owing to different techniques of measurement, length of the series, and the like. Despite all the problems of comparability, however, the two studies by Jonung (1981) and Figlewski and Wachtel (1981) reach remarkably similar conclusions.

11. The literature on vote and popularity functions now comes to about 100 items, as surveyed by Schneider (1978), Monroe (1979), and Paldam (1981b). Two surveys cover the electoral cycle literature: Frey (1976) and Paldam (1981a).

12. The optimal control mathematics necessary for solving this problem are a bit cumbersome to handle, but the mathematics are about the only part of the Nordhaus-MacRae theory where the problems are satisfactorily solved. The

reader is referred to the studies of Nordhaus (1975) and Kirchgassner (1981) for a discussion of these technicalities.

13. Tables and figures illustrating these two points are available from the author.

14. Often a minister is better viewed as the head of a certain administration than as a member of a certain government. Also, many governments are coalitions, so policy is set by consensus, not by a consistent common purpose.

15. The argument concerning the asymmetry of λ_g around V_g^m is from Frey and Ramser (1976), but in connection with the central forecast only. Their discussion deals with the steady state properties of the Nordhaus-MacRae cycle.

16. These two independent studies replace the $\dot{p}$'s with the Livingston index for $\dot{p}_e$ in functions of the popularity of the U.S. president. Both studies find a clearly significant, but rather limited improvement, which is consistent with voters' myopia.

17. One point in connection with problem 5 was recently illustrated by Ginsburgh and Michel (1983). They show how a Nordhaus-MacRae cycle weakens when an uncontrolled risk of an early election is introduced. To this we have to add that if the possibility for an early election is a control variable for the government, it enhances the possibility for the Nordhaus-MacRae cycle.

18. Another subset concentrates on the budget balance. Most of the issues in these (largely American) discussion have been covered in a symposium (see Brunner, 1978). Since the subsets are aspects of the same general question, one wonders why they have been discussed separately. However, we cannot try to integrate them here.

19. Kalecki's laconic note reappeared in the discussion in the early 1970s; see, for example, the work of Feiwel (1974) and the survey in Sherman (1979). Neither Friedman nor Phelps refers to Kalecki's analysis, but the parallel is obvious, as we shall see. The greatest problem in interpreting Kalecki's article is that it hardly mentions the time dimension—a strange omission by one of the pioneers of dynamic theory.

20. Empirically, we are dealing here with very elusive phenomena, for reasons that will shortly become obvious. This elusiveness applies to the arithmetic of the symmetries, to the exact location of u_p, and to the possible movements of u_p in the (very) long run.

21. The cycle is thus of the endogenous type described under β above. Also, the basic mechanism includes the cycles known as "planning cycles" or "infrastructure cycles," as described in the literature (see, e.g., Frey, 1978, Chaps. 8 and 9). It should be noted that this type of cycle depends much less on the institutional setup than the electoral cycles do.

22. This has been the point of view of a number of neo-Marxists, as surveyed by Sherman (1979). The theory exists both in a short-run version (see Boddy and Crotty 1975) and in a more relevant long-run version (see Glyn and Sutcliffe, 1972).

23. In this theory a crucial question is whether $\dot{p}$ is accommodated in the money stock, M. As no (mass) political pressures operate directly on M, we have chosen to concentrate the discussion on the other variables; but much of the discussion could be formulated in money stock terms. The main point, in both formulations, is that if all kinds of pressures force a government to keep u below u_p, then surely a nonaccommodating monetary policy is out of the question.

24. There are a number of closely related terms for this phenomenon. Kalecki speaks of "discipline"; others talk of "labor class militancy" or "workers' aggressivity." We prefer the neutral term "labor market climate."

25. The two classical results explaining c_n in the literature on the macroeconomic strike model (since Ashenfelter and Johnson 1969) are: (1) a negative coefficient of u; and (2) a negative coefficient of the lagged sum of real wage rises, $\dot{w}$. Both results hold up nicely for U.S. data, but fail to generalize. The most significant general result is the strong positive correlation with nominal wage rises, as shown in Figure 5b.

26. Because this result is contrary to most of the literature, it should be explained. Several explanations appear possible, but most evidence points to the crucial importance of the wage structure: Wage inflation, as well as real wage rises, must inevitably change some wages more than others in the short run. Hence some groups lose compared to others, and this is likely to generate conflicts.

27. The operationalization of the model is based on the discussions and empirical analysis in Paldam (1980, 1983). There the reader will find experiments with reformulations of the model, stability tests for changing time periods, reestimations with different estimation techniques, and the like—all done for 15-17 countries, using data for 1948 to 1975. The order of magnitude for the coefficients is, respectively, 1.7, -0.7, 0.2, and 0.4 for the four β's, and 3.0, -0.5, 0.6, and 0.5 for the four β's. The R^2 scores are 0.70–0.85, and DW falls nicely around 1.8–2.0.

28. A neomonetarist explanation would be that the Phillips curve has been "rationalized" away by all relevant actors, and hence $\dot{w}$ is explained exclusively by the money stock, M. Because of the fairly open capital markets, M in the different countries takes on a large international element. What is not explained by the neomonetarists is the role of the c_n series and, ultimately, the smoothness of the acceleration of the wage and price levels. Also, it proves that the M's of the different countries have relatively small international elements.

29. See Paldam (1979b) for a brief summary of the constant-wage-share hypothesis, as well as a discussion of the data mentioned above.

30. A fourth topic which could have been discussed is the large expansion in the public sector throughout the OECD area. It was omitted for reasons of space.

REFERENCES

Ashenfelter, O., and G. E. Johnson (1969). "Bargaining Theory, Trade Unions, and Industrial Strike Activity." *American Economic Review* 59:35–49.

Boddy, R., and J. Crotty (1975). "Class Conflict and Macro-Policy: The Political Business Cycle." *Review of Radical Political Economy* 7:1–19.

Breuss, F. (1980). "The Political Business Cycle: An Extension of Nordhaus's Model." *Empirica* 2:223–259.

Brown, B. W., and S. Maital (1981). "What Do Economists Know? An Empirical Study of Experts' Expectations." *Econometrica* 49:491–504.

Brunner, K. (ed.) (1978). "Keynesian Policies, the Drift into Permanent Deficits and the Growth of Government: A Symposium." Articles by R. J. Barro, D. F. Gordon, W. A. Niskanen, P. C. Roberts, J. Tobin, J. M. Buchanan, and R. E. Wagner. *Journal of Monetary Economics* 4:566–636.

Chan-Lee, J. H. (1980). "A Review of Recent Work in the Area of Inflationary Expectations." *Weltwirtschaftliches Archiv* 116:45–86.

Chrystal, K. A., and J. Alt (1979). "Public Sector Behavior: The Status of the Political Business Cycle." Discussion Paper No. 128, Department of Economics, University of Essex.

Feiwel, G. R. (1974). "Reflections on Kalecki's Theory of Political Business Cycles." *Kyklos* 27:21–48.

Figlewski, S., and P. Wachtel (1981). "The Formation of Inflationary Expectations." *Review of Economics and Statistics* 63:1–10.

Frey, B. S. (1976). "Theorie und Empirie Politischer Konjunkturzyklen." *Zeitschrift fur Nationallokonomie* 36:95–125.

Frey, B. S. (1978). *Modern Political Economy*. New York: John Wiley & Sons.

Frey, B. S., and Ramser, H. J. (1976). "The Political Business Cycle: A Comment." *Review of Economic Studies* 43:553–555.

Friedman, M. (1968). "The Role of Monetary Policy." Presidential address to the American Economic Association, December 1967. *The American Economic Review* 58:1–17.

Ginsburgh, V., and P. Michel (1983). "Random Timing of Elections and the Political Business Cycle."*Public Choice* 40:155–164.

Glyn, A., and B. Sutcliffe (1972). *British Capitalism, Workers and the Profit Squeeze*. London: Penguin.

Goldman, D. G., and J. M. Poterba (1980). "The Price of Popularity: The

Politica Business Cycle Reexamined." *American Journal of Political Science* 24:696–714.

Grossman, H. I. (1974). "The Cyclical Pattern of Unemployment and Wage Inflation." *Economica* 41:403–413.

Hibbs, D. A. (1980). "On the Demand for Economic Outcomes: Macroeconomic Performance and Mass Political Support in the United States, Great Britain and Germany." *Journal of Politics* 44:426–462.

Jonung, Lars (1981). "Perceived and Expected Rates of Inflation in Sweden." *American Economic Review* 71:961–968.

Kalecki, M. (1943). "Political Aspects of Full Employment." *The Political Quarterly* 14:322–331.

Kirchgässner, G. (1981). "On the Politico-Economic Theory of Optimal Government: Some Remarks on the Nordhaus and MacRae Models" (rev.). Zurich: Economic Institute, Zurich Polytechnic. (Mimeographed).

Kowalik, T. (1964). *Problems of Economic Dynamics and Planning: Essays in Honour of Michal Kalecki*. Warsaw: PWN.

Lecaillon, Jacques (1981). "Cycle electoral et repartition de revenu national." *Revue Economique* 32:213–236.

Lipsey, R. G. (1960). "The Relation between Unemployment and the Rate of Changes of Money Wage Rates in the UK, 1862–1957: A Further Analysis." *Economica* 27:1–31.

MacRae, C. D. (1977). "A Political Model of the Business Cycle." *Journal of Political Economy* 85:239–263.

Monroe, K. R., and M. D. Levi (1983). "Economic Expectations and Presidential Popularity: A Model of the Short-Term Politico-Economic Interaction," In K. R. Monroe (ed.), *The Political Process and Economic Change*. New York: Agathon Press, pp. 214–231 (this volume).

Monroe, K. R. (1979). "Econometric Analyses of Electoral Behavior: A Critical Review." *Political Behavior* 1:137–173.

Nordhaus, W. D. (1975). "The Political Business Cycle." *The Review of Economic Studies* 42:169–190.

Paldam, M. (1979a). "Is There an Electional Cycle? A Comparative Study of National Accounts." *Scandinavian Journal of Economics* 81:323–342.

Paldam, M. (1979b). "Towards the Wage-Earner State: A Comparative Study of Wage Shares, 1948–75." *International Journal of Social Economics* 6:45–62.

Paldam, M. (1983). "Industrial conflicts and economic conditions: a comparative empirical investigation." *European Economic Review* 20:231–256.

Paldam, M. (1980). "The International Element in the Phillips-Curve." *Scandinavian Journal of Economics* 82:216–239.

Paldam, M. (1981a). "An Essay on the Rationality of Economic Policy: The Test Case of the Electional Cycle." *Public Choice* 36:43–60.

Paldam, M. (1981b). "A Preliminary Survey of the Theories and Findings on Vote and Popularity Functions." *European Journal of Political Research* 9:181–199.

Paldam, M., and P. J. Pedersen (1982). "The Macroeconomic Strike Model: A Study of 17 Countries, 1948–75." *Industrial and Labor Relations Review*, 35:504–521.

Parsley, C. J. (1980). "Labor Union Effects on Wage Gains: A Survey of Recent Literature." *Journal of Economic Literature* 18:1–31.

Phelps, E. S. (1967). "Phillips-Curves, Expectations of Inflation and Optimal Unemployment over Time." *Economica* 34:254–281.

Phillips, A. W. (1958). "The Relation between Unemployment and the Rate of Change of Money Wage Rates in the United Kingdom, 1861–1957." *Economica* 25:283–299.

Robinson, J. (1943). "Planning Full Employment." *The London Times* (1966) January 22 and 23, 1943. In *Collected Economic Papers*, Vol. I, Oxford: Basil Blackwell.

Schneider, F. (1978). *Politisch-ökonomische Modelle*. Konigstein/Ts. Anton Hain Verlag.

Sherman, H. (1979). "A Marxist Theory of the Business Cycle." *Review of Radical Political Economics* 11(1):1–23.

Shiller, R. J. (1978). "Rational Expectations and the Dynamic Structure of Macroeconomic Models." *Journal of Monetary Economics* 4:1–44.

Solow, R. M. (1969). *Price Expectations and the Behavior of the Price Level*. Manchester: The University Press.

4: Inflation, Unemployment, and Electoral Terms: When Can Reform of Political Institutions Improve Macroeconomic Policy?

William R. Keech and Carl P. Simon

Is there a systematic relationship between the structure of democratic political institutions and the quality of public policy? Can institutions be designed to assure the best possible policy choices? This chapter will address these questions in the institutional context of electoral term length, and in the policy context of inflation and unemployment.

Democratic political institutions are characteristically evaluated on the grounds of fairness and decisiveness. Such analyses typically assume that whatever policies result from fair procedures are desirable in themselves. That is, institutions that aggregate people's preferences fairly and decisively into a collective decision are seen as producing the best policy. This perspective is most appropriate when there are no grounds for evaluating policy other than the distribution of people opposed to or in favor of the policy.

Despite this traditional view, however, there are other grounds for evaluating public policy—in particular, the quality of policy resulting from alternative institutional settings. But to use policy quality as the basis for evaluating institutions, one needs a theory that would help define and measure it independently of procedural considerations.

Analyses that systematically measure the desirability of outcomes are rare. Among the few available there are two that use cost-benefit analysis and prisoners' dilemma games to define and measure the quality of outcomes.[1] However, both these analyses are grounded in basically static and time-independent considerations of policy quality.

This chapter presents an explicitly intertemporal standard. The crucial analytical feature here is the difference between present and future welfare. The maximization of feasible welfare in the present may be at the expense of maximum feasible welfare over a longer period. If voters or politicians who appeal for their votes fail to understand these intertemporal trade-offs, or take a shortsighted view of them, society may be worse off over the long run than it would be otherwise.

Our question is whether institutional alternatives have some impact on the quality of outcomes in these terms. The particular alternative we will analyze is the length of electoral terms. The argument can readily be extended, however, into issues of term renewability, and the possibility in parliamentary systems of elections being called before the end of a fixed term. We hope this analysis will provide guidance and stimulus for more general thinking about the relationship between institutional alternatives and the quality of actual public policies.

The tool and substantive example of this analysis is a currently prominent theory of the relationship between inflation and unemployment: adaptive expectations. In this model, the government can reduce unemployment to points where it causes not only contemporaneous inflation but also delayed inflation. The delayed inflation persists even after unemployment returns to a point previously associated with lower rates of price increase. This model is also capable of generating "stagflation", the phenomenon in which inflation and unemployment increase simultaneously.

This model will be analyzed here in its own terms, making social welfare a function of inflation and unemployment. However, the illustration is also meant to be viewed as an application of a more general problem of "intertemporal choice." The essential characteristic of the problem is that the essential values of something chosen at one time affect the values of desired things available at other times. Examples include public policy on the use of renewable and nonrenewable resources, on investment and its effects on possibilities for consumption over time, on public pension systems, and on the maintenance of public roads and bridges.

The next section of this chapter reviews the discussion of optimal term length from *The Federalist Papers* to contemporary political science and economics. The following sections describe the vehicle for our analysis, William Nordhaus's model of the "political business cycle," and how we will use it. Next we present our main results, which show that the optimal term length is dependent on the parameters of the model, and how the choice of term length is more critical under some conditions than others. Finally, we draw implications for other aspects of electoral terms, such as their renewability.

ELECTORAL TERMS AND PUBLIC CHOICE

The length and renewability of electoral office is a recurring issue in American political life, as indicated by the ratification 30 years ago of the Twenty-Second Amendment to the U.S. Constitution (limiting presidents to two terms) and by more recent proposals for a nonrenewable 6-year presidential term by many observers, including former Presidents Johnson, Nixon, and Carter.[2] The relevance of term length to public choice problems with a time dimension is acknowledged in *The Federalist Papers*, where several different and not wholly compatible considerations are raised. The solution offered is a different term length for each elective office.

For example, in his discussion of the Senate, Madison observes that while some policies have immediately visible consequences, others depend on "a succession of well-chosen and well-connected measures which have a gradual and perhaps unobserved operation." Therefore, he argues, longer terms bring the period of accountability into line with the period in which policymaking has its consequences. Furthermore, some types of effective policymaking demand sustained activity, and longer terms provide an opportunity for such activity free of the pressure to produce immediate but short-lived results (No. 63).

In his discussion of the presidency, Hamilton identifies another reason why longer terms of office may be desirable. He argues that they lead to more personal firmness, where short and secure terms produce "feebleness and irresolution." He observes that while the people commonly intend the public good, they sometimes err, and suggests that brief terms do not give officeholders the security they need to resist transient impulses the people may receive from those who "flatter their prejudices to betray their interests" (No. 71). Hamilton is also a firm advocate of reeligibility, which gives the incumbent an opportunity to "act his part well" and an opportunity for the people to continue him in office when they approve his conduct (No. 72).

In contrast to Hamilton, who intimates that people can misperceive their interests, Madison argues that the people are dependable judges of their own best interests, and that shorter terms are accordingly preferable:

As it is essential to liberty that the government in general should have a common interest with the people, so it is particularly essential that (The House of Representatives) should have an immediate dependence on, and an intimate sympathy with, the people. Frequent elections are unquestionably the only policy by which this dependency and sympathy can be effectually secured (No. 52).

Thus *The Federalist Papers* contain arguments for both shorter terms and longer terms. The differences between the arguments hinge on assumptions about the time it takes to carry out a successful policy, about whether voters know what is in their best interest, and about what elected officials will do in the absence of electoral constraints. Each of these assumptions can be represented in the model we will use, and the arguments concerning electoral terms can be assessed accordingly.

Recent empirical work has also addressed these questions. James Kuklinski (1978) has found that the voting records of California assemblymen exhibit a continually high level of representation of their constituents' preferences. He attributes this to the fact that assemblymen are elected every 2 years, and thus face a "continuing electoral process." California senators, however, vote most congruently with their constituents' preferences at 4-year intervals, when their cohort is up for election, and much less so in the remaining 3 years of their terms. The longer terms seem to provide the senators the freedom to deviate from their constituency's preferences as long as they return to those preferences when the voters are paying the most attention.

Amacher and Boyes (1978) argue similarly that the classes of the U.S. senators facing election several years hence behave more independently of the wishes of their constituents than those facing election soon.[3] While Kuklinski does not directly address the question of optimal term length, Amacher and Boyes do, and they implicitly assume that voters' preferences are equivalent to their interests. They suggest that deviation of public policy from voter preferences (which they define as "external costs") is minimized when electoral terms are as short as possible, that is, approaching zero:

... an elected official may behave in a manner not representative of his polity and... as the length of time he has between the time he is "rehired" increases, the probability he may behave in an unrepresentative fashion increases. (p. 9)

Amacher and Boyes argue that the only valid reason for not making electoral terms as short as possible is that the decision costs for such terms would be prohibitive. They see optimal term length as one which minimizes the sum of external and decision costs (1978, pp. 8–10).

This argument does not acknowledge that voters might misperceive their interests, and it does not include the element of intertemporally interdependent choices. One modern work that does include these features is C. Duncan MacRae's paper on "A Political Model of the Business Cycle" (1977). Using a model very much like the one used here, MacRae concludes that the optimal (welfare-maximizing) term length is infinite—that is, no elections at all after a first one. His rationale is that with long terms, the economy displays "turnpike behavior," moving after an election toward the long-run optimal levels of inflation and unemployment. With an infinite electoral term, then, the economy will continue to move at the long-run optimum. Otherwise, whenever an election approaches, the economy moves away from an optimum because "the planning horizon of the party in power shortens with the approaching election year" (1977, pp. 250–252).

One of the purposes of this chapter is to sort out these issues. We focus on issues of intertemporal choice because they are of substantive importance in their own right, and also because they allow a demonstration of the crucial possibility that voters may misperceive their interests. This possibility will be the basis for our analysis of term length.

THE VEHICLE: NORDHAUS'S MODEL
OF THE POLITICAL BUSINESS CYCLE

In order to address these questions with precision and clarity, we need an indicator of the desirability of public policies, which we will call a welfare function; a model of political decision making with explicit institutional features; and a model of policy dynamics. These ingredients will enable us to identify the behavior to be anticipated under alternative institutions and to relate this behavior to the desirability of public policy. The model of policy dynamics is an extra necessity in this particular problem, where delayed consequences and the possibility of inappropriate time perspectives play major roles in the normative evaluation.

William Nordhaus's seminal article on "The Political Business Cycle" (1975) provides these ingredients in the form of a mathematical model of a dynamic policymaking process. The general elements of such a model are goal-oriented, utility-maximizing policymakers who try to win popular votes in order to retain public office. These policymakers control such instruments as fiscal and monetary policy, which enables them to manipulate policy outcomes such as the unemployment and inflation rates. These outcomes, in turn, are part of voters' utility functions, and therefore define the results of subsequent elections. The model of policy dynamics makes outcomes at any time dependent on choices made previously. Thus voters may be induced to support incumbents because policy outcomes at election time look good, even though this situation may be the result of less desirable outcomes early in the term, or may cause less desirable outcomes after the election.

Following Nordhaus's model, we will use inflation and unemployment as the policy outcomes affecting voter's choices. Not only do these economic variables play an important role in voters' decisions, but they are also modeled so as to display in a straightforward manner the delayed policy effects that are important to this model.

For purposes of this study, the measure of the quality of policy is a social welfare function, $g(U, \dot{P})$, where U is the rate of unemployment and $\dot{P}$ is the rate of inflation. (The symbol $\dot{P}$ is based on P for prices, with $\dot{P}$ the rate of change of the price level, i.e., inflation.) We assume that welfare is negatively related to the rates of inflation and unemployment in that a decrease in either will improve the welfare of society.

The welfare function just noted measures social welfare at any instant in time. Since we are interested in the value of welfare over time, this function must be integrated or "summed" so that we will have a measure of aggregate welfare over this period of concern. In Nordhaus's formulation, this is

$$W = \int_0^\infty g(U, \dot{P}) e^{-\rho t} \, dt \tag{1}$$

or the integral over infinite time of welfare as a function of inflation and unemployment, discounted at rate ρ so that values close to the present count for more than values in the distant future.

The model of political decision making assumes that politicians maximize votes over each single finite electoral period. Votes are dependent on unemployment and inflation in basically the same functional form that welfare is, with two crucial differences. The first is that votes are a function of unemployment and inflation integrated over the electoral period, rather than over infinite time. The second is that different times are weighted in a way opposite to that used in the welfare function. That is, times near the election count for more than times early in the electoral term. The vote function is

$$V = \int_0^\theta g(U, \dot{P}) e^{\mu t} \, dt \tag{2}$$

where θ is the electoral period, and μ is a factor that represents the voters' discounting or forgetfulness of values early in the term. The model assumes that a single incumbent elected official (whom we will call the president) maximizes votes in each electoral period by manipulating the unemployment rate.

Thus what maximizes votes and what maximizes welfare *at any given time* are exactly the same thing. The fundamental difference between the two formulations is the amount of time considered, and the way different times are weighted. Votes are defined over a finite electoral period, with the weight on outcomes increasing the closer one comes to the election. Welfare is defined over infinite time, with the weight on outcomes declining the further into the future one goes. This formulation implies that voters' preferences may be at odds with their welfare only in a very restricted sense. Voters are seen as accurately perceiving their interests at a given time, but as possibly unable to see these interests accurately for longer time periods and unable to communicate their longer-term interests effectively to policymakers.[4]

The model of policy dynamics is an adaptive expectations model of inflation:

$$\dot{P} = f(U) + \lambda \dot{P}_e \qquad f' < 0, 0 \le \lambda \le 1 \qquad (3)$$

$$d/dt \, \dot{P}_e = \gamma (\dot{P} - \dot{P}_e) \qquad (4)$$

where $\dot{P}_e$ is expected inflation. The model generates a short-run "naive" Phillips curve, wherein inflation is a negative function of unemployment at any given time, $\partial \dot{P} / \partial U = f' < 0$. The model also generates a long-run Phillips curve, which represents the trade-off between inflation and unemployment when inflation equals expected inflation, $\partial \dot{P} / \partial U |_{\dot{P} = \dot{P}_e} = f'/1 - \lambda$. This long-run trade-off is steeper than the short-run trade-off when λ is greater than zero; and when $\lambda = 1$, the long-run Phillips curve has an infinite slope. That is, the long-run curve becomes a vertical line at the "natural rate" of unemployment, representing no trade-off at all between inflation and unemployment.[5]

The dynamics of the model are as follows: When $\dot{P} = \dot{P}_e$, the existing combination of unemployment and inflation is on the long-run curve (LL in Figure 1), and the system is in equilibrium at a noninflationary rate of unemployment. However, when unemployment moves to a point off the long-run curve, inflation will no longer equal expected inflation, and the latter will change at a rate defined by γ in Eq. (4). This means that when unemployment moves to the left of the long-run curve, the immediate inflationary consequence is represented by movement on the short-run curve, but the delayed inflationary consequence is represented by the full Eq. (3), in which $\dot{P}_e$ will have increased to equal $\dot{P}$.

For example, in Figure 1, a drop in the unemployment rate from U_0 to U_1 implies an immediate change in the inflation rate from $\dot{P}_0$ to $\dot{P}_1$, as implied by the short-run move from point A to point B on short-run

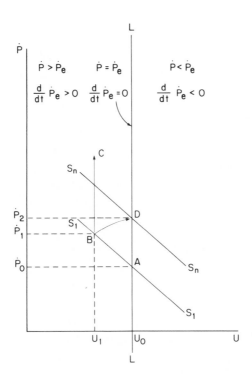

FIG. 1.   Long-run and short-run Phillips curves.

curve S_1S_1. Since B lies to the left of LL, the long-run curve, inflation at B will be greater than the expected inflation rate, and will drive the expected inflation rate higher, by Eq. (4). If unemployment is kept at U_1, the long-run inflationary result will be an inflationary path, represented by the arrow C. Even temporary reductions of unemployment below equilibrium will have lasting inflationary consequences, unless they are later compensated for by increases of unemployment above equilibrium. This is shown by the return of the unemployment rate from U_1 to U_0. By the time this is achieved, expected inflation will have increased, by Eq. (4), which implies that the movement of unemployment is along a series of higher short-run curves, one for each new expected rate of inflation. When unemployment returns to U_0, the natural rate, it is accompanied by a higher rate of inflation, $\dot{P}_2$, because of the rise in expected inflation.

The only way to bring inflation back down is to move unemployment to the right of U_0, which will create a decline in *expected* inflation.

Although the short-run Phillips curves point to the once-familiar movements of inflation and unemployment in opposite directions, the dynamic just described represents the more modern phenomenon of stagflation, wherein inflation and unemployment increase at the same time.[6]

The elements described above create the basis for a conflict between political incentives and maximum feasible welfare. If politicians decide to maximize voter support rather than public welfare, they may choose values of unemployment that are excessively high at the beginning of their terms, or whose full inflationary consequences will be delayed until after the next election, or some combination of both. These possibilities are the basis of Nordhaus's conclusion that

under conditions where voting is an appropriate mechanism for social choice, democratic systems will choose a policy on the long-run trade-off that has a lower unemployment and a higher inflation than is optimal. (1975, p. 178)

Our question is whether institutional arrangements such as term length can be changed so as to reduce the divergence between welfare-maximizing and vote-maximizing policy.

THE METHOD OF ANALYSIS

We begin by giving specific functional form to the model. Following Nordhaus, we let $g(U, \dot{P}) = -U^2 - \beta\dot{P}$, and $f(U) = \alpha_0 - \alpha_1 U$. Consequently, the welfare function (1) becomes

$$W = \int_0^\infty \left(-U^2 - \beta\dot{P} \right) e^{-\rho t} \, dt \qquad (5)$$

the vote function (2) becomes

$$V = \int_0^\theta \left(-U^2 - \beta\dot{P} \right) e^{\mu t} \, dt \qquad (6)$$

the inflation function (3) becomes

$$\dot{P} = \alpha_0 - \alpha_1 U + \lambda \dot{P}_e \qquad (7)$$

and the expected inflation equation (4) becomes

$$d/dt \, \dot{P}_e = \gamma \left(\alpha_0 - \alpha_1 U - (1 - \lambda) \dot{P}_e \right) \qquad (8)$$

The officeholder will choose a policy of unemployment rates $U(t)$ during his term from 0 to θ, with the goal of maximizing the vote function Eq. (6). This problem is one of dynamic constrained optimization or "optimal control theory" Eq. (7). Using the Maximum Principle just as Nordhaus did, one can solve for the optimal unemployment rate strategy:

$$U^*(t) = \left(\tfrac{1}{2}\alpha_1 \beta + B/A \right) e^{A(t-\theta)} - B/A \qquad (9)$$

where

$$A \equiv \gamma(1 - \lambda) - \mu \quad \text{and} \quad B \equiv -\tfrac{1}{2}\alpha_1 \beta(\gamma - \mu)$$

This solution, $U^*(t)$, is a function of the electoral period θ and of the various economic and political parameters in Eqs. (6), (7), and (8). One of Nordhaus's major conclusions is that the optimal unemployment policy has the unemployment rate *decreasing* throughout the term from

$$U^*(0) = \left(\tfrac{1}{2}\alpha_1 \beta + B/A \right) e^{-A\theta} - B/A \qquad (10)$$

to

$$U^*(\theta) = \tfrac{1}{2}\alpha_1 \beta \qquad (11)$$

Our next task is to use our social welfare function (5) to assess the welfare consequences of the length of the electoral period, θ. Let $U^*(t; \theta)$ be the optimal unemployment strategy of Eq. (9), where we explicitly keep track of the dependence on θ. The welfare function in Eq. (5) might be evaluated over an infinite time horizon and discounted appropriately. For our purposes, we need to normalize the welfare function in terms of electoral periods. First, longer terms will usually mean larger accumulations of welfare, so we need to work with average social welfare by integrating from 0 to θ and then dividing by θ. Furthermore, we choose to drop the social discount rate, ρ, not only because we are now using a finite time horizon, but also because we think it is reasonable for society to take a long view and value all time points between elections equally. Thus our criterion is

$$\frac{W^*(\theta)}{\theta} = \frac{1}{\theta} \int_0^\theta \left[-U^*(t; \theta)^2 - \beta \dot{P}^*(t; \theta) \right] dt \qquad (12)$$

Here $\dot{P}^*(t; \theta)$ is the rate of inflation that corresponds to $U^*(t; \theta)$, and is obtained by substituting the formula (9) for U^* into Eqs. (7) and (8). The average welfare function is a rather complicated function of θ and all the parameters. We write it out explicitly, along with $\dot{P}^*$, in Appendix 1.

Our problem now is to compute for each choice of the parameters α_0, α_1, β, γ, λ, μ, and $\dot{P}_{e_0}$ that θ^* that maximizes $W^*(\theta)/\theta$. (To aid the reader's interpretation of our results, we have summarized the economic and political meaning of these parameters in Appendix 2.) The resulting θ^* should, of course, be a function of the parameters

$$\theta^*\left(\alpha_0, \alpha_1, \beta, \gamma, \lambda, \mu, \dot{P}_{e_0}\right) \tag{13}$$

computed by setting

$$\frac{d}{d\theta}\left(\frac{W^*(\theta)}{\theta}\right) = 0 \tag{14}$$

and solving for θ. Unfortunately, the formulas for $W^*(\theta)/\theta$ as listed in Appendix 1 are far too complex to carry out this process and arrive at a closed form solution, as in Eq. (13). This problem is complicated by the fact that, for many values of the parameters, $W^*(\theta)/\theta$ is not a concave function of θ (unless $\lambda = 1$). It can have several local maxima and minima or no interior maxima. We used a computer to solve for the optimal θ^* for many reasonable values of the parameters. Some of the results are summarized in Appendix 3. In the next section, we use comparative statistics to study the behavior of θ^*.

THE OPTIMAL ELECTORAL PERIOD

The most general results of our analysis is that the optimal period depends on the parameters of the model. Thus there is no single optimal period for all social and political conditions. Our conclusion, therefore, differs from that of Amacher and Boyes (1978), who suggested that the optimal period for minimizing divergence between public policy and popular interests was the shortest possible term (subject to the need to minimize decision costs as well as external costs). However, Amacher and Boyes dealt with a conceptualization of policy that did not incorporate our problem of intertemporal choice, so the results are not strictly comparable.

Our conclusion also diverges from that of MacRae (1977), who suggested that the welfare-maximizing electoral period was infinite. MacRae did deal with problems of public intertemporal choice in very much the same form as ours. While our conclusion is more ambiguous, it is not so distressing as MacRae's from the point of view of democratic values. Our results show that within the assumption of our model, the optimal or welfare-maximizing electoral period varies between zero and very large numbers. Its exact value depends on such things as society's relative valuation of inflation and unemployment, how expectations of inflation affect inflation, and the degree to which voters remember values of unemployment and inflation from the beginning of a term.

Dependence of the Optimal Term Length on Parameters

Although one cannot generally expect an explicit formula for θ^* as a function of the parameters, as in Eq. (13), one can nonetheless ask how θ^* changes as any of the considered parameters changes.[8] For example, if we want to know how θ^* changes when parameter μ increases, we are interested in differentiating Eq. (13) with respect to μ and in calculating the sign of $\partial\theta^*/\partial\mu$.

We present and interpret here the results of these calculations for the case where coefficient λ of expected inflation in the inflation Eq. (7) is fixed at $\lambda = 1$. We choose this value for three reasons. First, many macroeconomists of various theoretical persuasions suggest that λ is very close to 1, if not identical to 1, in contemporary inflation models.[9] This is equivalent to arguing that the long-run Phillips curve is vertical. Second, by standard continuity arguments, our results for $\lambda = 1$ also hold for λ close to 1. Finally, as noted in Appendix 1, the formula for $W^*(\theta)/\theta$ is much simpler for $\lambda = 1$ than it is for $\lambda < 1$. We describe the calculations in Appendix 5.

1. $\partial\theta^*/\partial\mu < 0$. As μ increases, the optimal length decreases. When $\mu = 0$, voters weigh all days of the incumbent's entire term equally in making their reelection decision. When μ becomes large, voters consider only the actions of the incumbent just before the election. We show in Appendix 6 that $\theta^* = \infty$ when $\mu = 0$. In this case, the voting function

has exactly the same form as the undiscounted social welfare function. Therefore, a politician motivated solely by the desire to gain votes will in this case maximize social welfare and votes at the same time. In such an ideal situation, there would be no loss in social welfare from leaving the politician in office for a long time.

In the second case (μ large), the goals of vote maximization and of welfare maximization diverge. A vote-maximizing politician will choose excessively high unemployment rates early in his term in order to "invest" in low rates of expected inflation. This low $\dot{P}_e$ will permit unsustainably low rates of both inflation and unemployment at the end of the term. A large μ implies that the voters will forget the high unemployment early in the politician's term and remember only the unrealistically low inflation and unemployment at the end of that term. In this case, therefore, the term of office should be made short enough to be remembered in its entirety by the voters.

The fact that $\partial\theta^*/\partial\mu < 0$ analytically demonstrates what happens to the optimal θ^* for intermediate values of μ. If the voters' span of consideration were to increase a little ($\Delta\mu < 0$), it would be safe to increase the term of office ($\Delta\theta^* > 0$) correspondingly.

At this point, it is easy to see that there are economic and political circumstances (e.g., μ very small) under which MacRae's (1977) suggestion of a long-as-possible term length is optimal, and others (e.g., μ very large) under which Amacher and Boyes's (1978) suggested short-as-possible term length solution holds (see Appendix 6).

2. $\partial\theta^*/\partial\beta > 0$. As β increases, so does the optimal term length. An increase in β implies an increased concern for inflation relative to unemployment in the priorities of the electorate. More precisely, the higher β is, the more unemployment society is willing to tolerate in order to decrease inflation by 1%.[10] As β increases, so will society's tolerance (as defined by the welfare function) of higher unemployment at the beginning of electoral terms. By Eq. (15), the longer the period between elections, the higher the unemployment at the beginning of the electoral term. As β increases, so will the society's tolerance, for the higher unemployment that characterizes longer terms:

$$\partial U^*/\partial\theta|_{t=0} = \tfrac{1}{2}\alpha_1\beta\gamma\lambda e^{-A\theta} > 0 \qquad (15)$$

3. $\partial\theta^*/\partial\alpha_1 > 0$. As α_1 increases, so does the optimal term length. An increase in α_1 means an increase in the steepness of the short-run Phillips curve. As a result, a unit increase in unemployment will now lead to a much sharper drop in inflation. Thus, the deflationary gains from the higher unemployment rates that accompany longer electoral terms will increase, and unemployment will not have to be raised so high in order to make possible low inflation and unemployment at the end of the term. Accordingly, electoral terms will not have to be shortened so much in order to avoid high unemployment in the beginning.

4. $\partial\theta^*/\partial\alpha_0 < 0$. If α_0 increases, each short-run Phillips curve moves up, so that any given amount of unemployment will lead to a higher rate of inflation. The higher unemployment rates that accompany longer electoral periods will be associated with higher levels of inflation than they were previously—to the detriment of society's welfare. In such an instance, a shorter term will reduce the period of high unemployment.

5. The sign of $\partial\theta^*/\partial\gamma$ is indeterminate; it is the same as the sign of

$$\alpha_0/\alpha_1 - \tfrac{1}{2}\alpha_1\beta$$

The first term is the "natural rate of unemployment," that is, the location of the long-run Phillips curve, and the rate of unemployment that corresponds to constant (nonaccelerating) inflation at any level, including zero. The second term is $U^*(\theta)$, the vote-maximizing unemployment rate at the end of the term. The sign of this derivative is the same as the sign of $\dot{P}(\theta) - \dot{P}_e(\theta)$, which determines whether expected inflation is increasing or decreasing at the end of the term [see Eq. (4)].

If these signs are positive, the final unemployment rate is below the natural rate, and therefore inflationary. In this case, a longer term is appropriate because it will compensate for this inflation with a longer deflationary period early in the term. If the signs are negative, the final unemployment rate is above the natural rate, which is deflationary. In this case, a shorter term is appropriate because it is not necessary to compensate for an inflationary final stage with more early deflation.

6. In general, the very existence of the problem of public intertemporal choice depends on the parameters in a straightforward way. If any one of the parameters α_1, β, γ, or λ is zero, the problem ceases to be one of intertemporal choice and becomes one of static optimization. Since the

time framework then is no longer relevant to the solution, all term lengths are equally desirable in this model, and we may return to the static optimization defined by Amacher and Boyes (1978).

For example, if $\alpha_1 = 0$, $\partial \dot{P}/\partial U = 0$, and there is no relationship between inflation and unemployment, the optimal policy for the officeholder would be to set U as low as possible, since he cannot affect $\dot{P}$ even indirectly. Similarly, if $\beta = 0$, inflation has no weight in the voting function. The optimal policy, again, would be to set U as low as possible, since the resulting high inflation will have no cost in terms of votes or welfare.

If $\gamma = 0$, $\dot{P}_e$ will also be zero and expected inflation will be a constant, independent of U and $\dot{P}$. If $\lambda = 0$, expected inflation will have no effect on inflation, and policies will have no lagged consequences. In either case, inflation will vary only with unemployment, and the inflation-unemployment relationship will be entirely contemporaneous and without lags. The optimal rate would be $U^* = \frac{1}{2}\alpha_1\beta$, where the short-run Phillips curve is tangent to an iso-vote curve.

Mathematically, in all these extreme cases, $W(\theta)/\theta$ is independent of θ, and there is no best term length. Empirically, however, there is no reason to believe that any of these parameters is zero.[11]

How Much Difference Does the Choice of Term Length Make?

Since the optimal term length depends so heavily on a spectrum of economic and political variables, a governmental body considering a change in the length of any electoral term would need some sort of "red flag" or indicator of the risks and returns involved in the proposed change. Fortunately, there is one important combination of the variables that plays exactly that role, differentiating conditions under which a change in term length would lead to small variations in social welfare from conditions under which such a change could lead to disastrous decrease in social welfare. This parameter,

$$A = \gamma(1 - \lambda) - \mu$$

is an index of lagged consequences and the voters' awareness of them.

When A is negative (e.g., $\lambda = 1$ and μ is positive), then $W^*(\theta)/\theta$ drops off to minus infinity as the term length, θ, increases, so that small changes in term length can lead to large drops in social welfare. On the other hand, when A is positive, then $W^*(\theta)/\theta$ moves within some bounded range, no matter how large or small θ is. Appendix 7 sketches an analytic proof of the statements in this paragraph and describes the conditions under which $W^*(\theta)/\theta$ moves in a small range as θ varies from zero to infinity. When these latter conditions prevail, the economic and political variables we consider play a small role in determining the optimal term length.

The reasons for the divergent behavior for $A > 0$ and $A < 0$ can be seen in formula (9) for the vote-maximizing pattern of unemployment rates. Recall that the optimal strategy for the politician is to raise U to $U^*(0)$, as in Eq. (10), at the beginning of his term, and to let U decrease, as in Eq. (9), to the $U^*(\theta)$ in Eq. (11). Since $\partial U^*/\partial\theta|_{t=0} > 0$ by Eq. (15), the longer θ is, the higher the officeholder will want to raise U^* at the beginning of his term. When $A > 0$, there is a bound,[12] *independent of θ*, on the height to which the officeholder will want to raise the unemployment rate. On the other hand, if A is negative, the officeholder will want to raise unemployment to a higher and higher rate the longer his term in office is, with the rate becoming arbitrarily large as θ increases. This large increase in U can have a strong negative impact on the social welfare function.

What is the economic and political interpretation of this important parameter A? The parameters γ, λ, and μ have already been described. In particular, μ is the rate at which voters discount past information. The larger μ is, the more voters disregard past events in making present decisions. The parameter $\gamma(1 - \lambda)$ is the intrinsic rate of decay of expected inflation. This follows from the fact that rearrangement of Eq. (8) leads to

$$d/dt\, \dot{P}_e = -\gamma(1 - \lambda)\dot{P}_e + \gamma(\alpha_0 - \alpha_1 U)$$

If $\gamma(1 - \lambda)$ is large, $\dot{P}_e$ changes quickly and $\dot{P}_e$ and $\dot{P}$ equilibrate rapidly. The macroeconomic situation is a more or less contemporaneous one without lags. Similarly, if $(1 - \lambda)$ is large (i.e., close to 1), then the slope of the short-run Phillips curve $(f'(U))$ is close to the slope of the long-run Phillips curve, $f'(U)/(1 - \lambda)$, so that lag effects are very small.

Returning to $A = \gamma(1 - \lambda) - \mu$, we note that if A is negative, then $\gamma(1 - \lambda)$ is small relative to μ. The smallness of $\gamma(1 - \lambda)$ points to large lag effects, meaning that past events have a large effect on the present situation. The relative largeness of μ implies that voters discount the past in their decision making. To summarize: If $A < 0$, past events play a major (possibly welfare-diminishing) role, yet voters ignore them; if $A > 0$, the voters' frame of reference extends to those past periods that are still influencing the present economic situation. The important parameter A, then, is truly the index of lagged consequences and the voters' awareness of them.

In general, the condition that has the simplest and probably the most powerful effect on whether long terms can bring disastrous consequences because of vote maximizing is the voters' memory. As the voters' memory gets longer, μ approaches zero. A cannot be negative when μ is zero, and vote maximizing cannot lead to precipitous welfare losses relative to feasible possibilities.

IMPLICATIONS AND CONCLUSIONS

Under the assumptions of our model, then, the choice between a 4-year and a 6-year term depends on the values of the political and economic parameters. Accordingly, we have no general recommendation on term length. We can, however, infer the direction of change in term length implied by changes in the parameters, and we have pointed out the importance of the complex parameter A as a measure of the seriousness of the term length issue. We have also shown that neither the longest nor the shortest possible term lengths will minimize the welfare loss of politicians' vote-maximizing behavior under all conditions.

Our model has some implications for whether electoral terms should be renewable, but these should not be taken too seriously because these emerge from our assumptions rather than from the analysis. Specifically, since there are only two objective functions in the model—votes and welfare—we could infer that by ruling out the possibility of reelection, we would ensure that incumbents will act to maximize welfare instead of votes.

In fact, we acknowledge that politicians eligible for reelection do not necessarily maximize votes, and that those who are ineligible do not necessarily maximize welfare. Our model helps us to see how outcomes might be less than optimal if politicians did maximize votes according to a simple deterministic model. But the assumptions we have made for purposes of analysis should not be permitted to undermine awareness of the many other dimensions of behavior of elected officials. Renewable terms allow the public to evaluate a politician's competence, integrity, and performance on issues not involving intertemporal choice. Renewable terms allow the voters to keep favored officials in office longer than those found wanting (see above).

Our model also has some implications for parliamentary-style variable terms. Within the model, the incumbent has no incentive to call an election before his maximum term has elapsed because to do so would constrain his ability to create a desirable final period within the voters' memory. Thus, if the government has a majority, there is no reason to expect that an opportunity to call early elections will make any difference in the deterministic world we have created.

However, if governments typically do not have a majority, as in Canada, the incentives are quite different. When the government commands only a minority of seats, the *opposition* can call an early election by choosing to defeat the government. The ability of the opposition to force an election would lead the government to avoid the high levels of unemployment (and low levels of welfare) it might otherwise choose early in its term. When the opposition can call an election at any time, the government has a strong incentive to keep inflation and unemployment at optimal sustainable levels. It will avoid creating low welfare levels early in the term for the purpose of engineering unsustainably high welfare levels near the election.

We have analyzed a model that uses certain simplifying assumptions about voters, politicians, and the economy to relate political institutions to the quality of policy. In the real world, neither votes nor the economy are as controllable as both are in this model. The less controllable they are, the less likely it is that politicians will try to manipulate the economy for electoral gain at the expense of society's well-being. This makes choosing the optimal term length somewhat less urgent than it might be under the worst-case assumptions of our model.

Surely the most general and significant finding of this analysis is that there is no one single best term length for all conditions. This conclusion is congruent with several others on related matters. Ian Lustick (1980) argues that the relative desirability of incrementalist and synoptic decision-making strategies depends on four characteristics of the task environment. Dennis Mueller (1979) finds that the relative desirability of unanimity and majority rule depends on whether the issue is allocation or redistribution. Finally, Orbell and Wilson (1978) show that the choice of the best constitutional mechanisms depends on configurations of the opportunity costs of cooperation and the magnitude of the social fine in prisoners' dilemma games:

> Without solid knowledge about the empirical character of such configurations, advocacy of particular constitutional mechanisms is likely to be based on simple ideological assertion at best, and to be cynically self-serving at worst. (p. 419)

Thus there seems to be ample reason for caution in considering institutional reform. The "best" institutions are situation-specific.

Acknowledgments. The research reported here has been supported by National Science Foundation grants SES 80-06562 and MCS 79-00993. We are grateful for the comments of many colleagues, especially Claudio Cioffi-Revilla, Michael Cohen, Philip Cook, James Kuklinski, Donald Liner, and Robert Strauss.

NOTES

1. Weingast (1979) uses cost-benefit analysis to argue that universalist decision-making rules (or norms) are socially preferable to minimum winning coalition norms in distributive legislative policymaking. Orbell and Wilson (1978) show that the superiority of majoritarian democracy over uncoordinated individualism and selfish dictatorship in n-person prisoners' dilemma games depends on the relationship between the opportunity costs of cooperation and the size of the social fine.

2. See Cronin (1980, pp. 353–361) for examples of rationales and for a general discussion.

3. Rather than independently measuring the congruence between the votes of members of both houses and the preferences of their respective constituencies, as Kuklinski (1978) did, Amacher and Boyes (1978) use voting scores of members of the House as a yardstick for assessing how close senators from the same state are to the views of their constituents at different stages of their terms. That is, they

assume what Kuklinski measured: that representatives' votes are closer to constituency preferences than are senators' votes. With this assumption, they found some evidence that the closer a senator is to the next election, the more congruent that senator's votes are with the preferences of his constituency (as measured by House votes).

4. One could begin, as Nordhaus (1975) did, with a voting function instead of a welfare function. In this perspective, $g(U, \dot{P})$ would be an aggregate voting function that reflects the percentage of the electorate that would support the president when the inflation rate is $\dot{P}$ and the unemployment rate is U. One then constructs a social welfare function from the aggregate voting function as in Eq. (1), allowing a policy to be evaluated by the fraction of the electorate voting for it, discounted over time at rate ρ. For purposes of this model, we assume that $g(U, \dot{P})$ is a well-behaved function, differentiable in both variables and quasiconcave.

5. See Ackley (1978; Chap. 14) for further explication.

6. The following simplified scenario demonstrates how inflation and unemployment can rise simultaneously: Let $\dot{P} = 6 - U + \dot{P}_e$, where $\dot{P}_e = \dot{P}_{-1}$, the previous period's inflation, and the natural rate of unemployment is 6.

Year	$\dot{P} = 6 - U + \dot{P}_{-1}$	*Comment*
0	$0 = 6 - 6 + 0$	Neither inflation nor expected inflation, with U at natural rate.
1	$1 = 6 - 5 + 0$	A drop in U below natural rate brings immediate inflation.
2	$2 = 6 - 5 + 1$	Leaving U below natural rate brings both immediate and expected inflation.
3	$4 = 6 - 4 + 2$	A further drop in U brings accelerating inflation.
4	$6 = 6 - 4 + 4$	Leaving U below natural rate continues acceleration.
5	$7 = 6 - 5 + 6$	*Rising U may be accompanied by rising inflation,* i.e., *stagflation.*
6	$7 = 6 - 6 + 7$	Return of U to natural rate will continue expected
7	$7 = 6 - 6 + 7$	inflation... indefinitely.
8	$6 = 6 - 7 + 7$	U may have to be raised *above* the natural rate to lower inflation...
9	$4 = 6 - 8 + 6$	And it may take a lot of sustained unemployment to wipe out expected inflation.

7. See Intriligator (1971: Chap. 14) or Clark (1976) for an introduction.

8. This is the process called *comparative statics* in economic theory. Appendix 4 outlines the mathematical principles behind such an analysis.

9. See, for example, Ackley (1978, p. 478), Dornbusch and Fischer (1978, p. 404), and Turnovsky (1977, p. 76).

10. In economic terms, $-\beta/2u$ is society's marginal rate of substitution of unemployment for inflation.

11. See Gramlich (1979) for some relevant estimates.

12. If $A = \gamma(1 - \lambda) - \mu > 0$, then $\gamma > \mu$ and $B = -\frac{1}{2}\alpha_1\beta(\gamma - \mu)$ is negative. By Eq. (10)

$$U^*(0; \theta) = \left(\frac{1}{2}\alpha_1\beta + \frac{B}{A}\right)e^{-A\theta} - \frac{B}{A}$$

$$= -\frac{\alpha_1\beta\gamma\lambda}{2A}e^{-A\theta} + \left|\frac{B}{A}\right|$$

$$\leq \left|\frac{B}{A}\right|$$

When $A < 0$, it is obvious from the above equation that $U^*(0, \theta) \to +\infty$ as $\theta \to +\infty$.

REFERENCES

Ackley, G. (1978). *Macroeconomics: Theory and Policy*. New York: Macmillan.

Amacher, R. C., and W. J. Boyes (1978). "Cycles in Senatorial Voting Behavior: Implications for the Optimal Frequency of Elections." *Public Choice* 33:5–13.

Clark, C. W. (1976). *Mathematical Bioeconomics*. New York: Wiley-Interscience.

Courant, R. (1937). *Differential and Integral Calculus*. New York: Interscience.

Cronin, T. E. (1980). *The State of the Presidency* (2nd ed.). Boston: Little, Brown.

Dornbusch, R., and S. Fischer (1978). *Macroeconomics*. New York: McGraw-Hill.

Gramlich, E. M. (1979). "Macro Policy Responses to Price Shocks." *Brookings Papers on Economic Activity* 1:125–166.

Hibbs, D. A., Jr. (1977). "Political Parties and Macroeconomic Policy." *American Political Science Review* 71:1467–1487.

Intriligator, M. D. (1971). *Mathematical Optimization and Economic Theory*. Englewood Cliffs, NJ: Prentice-Hall.

Kuklinski, J. H. (1978). "Representativeness and Elections: A Policy Analysis." *American Political Science Review* 72:165–177.

Lustick, I. (1980). "Explaining the Variable Utility of Disjointed Incrementalism: Four Propositions." *American Political Science Review* 74:342–353.

MacRae, C. D. (1977). "A Political Model of the Political Business Cycle." *Journal of Political Economy* 85:239–263.

Mueller, D. C. (1979). *Public Choice*. New York: Cambridge University Press.

Nordhaus, W. D. (1975). "The Political Business Cycle." *Review of Economic Studies* 42:169–190.

Orbell, J. M., and L. A. Wilson II. (1978). "Institutional Solutions to the *N*-Prisoners' Dilemma." *American Political Science Review* 72:411–421.

Tufte, E. R. (1978). *Political Control of the Economy*. Princeton: Princeton University Press.

Turnovsky, S. (1977). *Macroeconomic Analysis and Stabilization Policies*. Cambridge: Cambridge University Press.

Weingast, B. R. (1979). "A Rational Choice Perspective on Congressional Norms." *American Journal of Political Science* 23:245–262.

APPENDIX 1

Optimal inflation policy $\dot{P}^*(t)$ and the average welfare $W^*(\theta)/\theta$ for each term length θ.

(a) $0 < \lambda < 1$:

$$\dot{P}^*(t) = \alpha_0 - \alpha_1 E e^{A(t-\theta)} + \alpha_1 \frac{B}{A}$$

$$+ C\lambda e^{-\lambda(1-\lambda)t} + \frac{\lambda}{1-\lambda}\left(\alpha_0 + \alpha_1 \frac{B}{A}\right)$$

$$- \frac{\alpha_1 \gamma \lambda E}{A + \gamma(1-\lambda)} e^{A(t-\theta)}$$

where

$$A \equiv \gamma(1-\lambda) - \mu,$$

$$B \equiv -\frac{1}{2}\alpha_1\beta(\gamma - \mu),$$

$$E \equiv \frac{1}{2}\alpha_1\beta - \frac{B}{A} = -\frac{\alpha_1\beta\gamma\lambda}{2A}$$

and

$$C \equiv \dot{P}_{e_0} - \frac{1}{1-\lambda}\left(\alpha_0 + \alpha_1 \frac{B}{A}\right) + \frac{\alpha_1 \gamma E}{A + \gamma(1-\lambda)} e^{-A\theta}$$

$$\frac{W^*(\theta)}{\theta} = C_0 + C_1\left(\frac{1-e^{-A\theta}}{A\theta}\right) + C_2\left(\frac{1-e^{-2A\theta}}{2A\theta}\right)$$

$$+ \left(C_3 + C_4 e^{-A\theta}\right)\left(\frac{1-e^{-\gamma(1-\lambda)\theta}}{\gamma(1-\lambda)\theta}\right)$$

where

$$C_0 \equiv - \left\{ \frac{\beta}{1-\lambda}\left(\alpha_0 + \alpha_1 \frac{B}{A}\right) + \frac{B^2}{A^2} \right\}$$

$$C_1 \equiv \frac{2E^2\gamma(1-\lambda)}{A + \gamma(1-\lambda)}$$

$$C_2 \equiv -E^2$$

$$C_3 \equiv \frac{\beta\lambda}{1-\lambda}\left(\alpha_0 + \alpha_1 \frac{B}{A}\right) - \beta\lambda \dot{P}_{e_0}$$

$$C_4 \equiv \frac{2AE^2}{A + \gamma(1-\lambda)}$$

(b) $\lambda = 1$:

$$\dot{P}^*(t) = \alpha_0 + \dot{P}_{e_0} - \frac{1}{2}\alpha_1^2\beta\left(1 - \frac{\gamma}{\mu}\right)$$

$$+ \gamma\alpha_0 t - \frac{1}{2}\alpha_1^2\beta\gamma\left(1 - \frac{\gamma}{\mu}\right)t$$

$$- \frac{\alpha_1^2\beta\gamma}{2\mu}\left(1 - \frac{\gamma}{\mu}\right)e^{\mu(\theta - t)} - \frac{\alpha_1^2\beta\gamma^2}{2\mu^2}e^{\mu\theta}$$

$$\frac{W^*(\theta)}{\theta} = - \frac{\alpha_1^2\beta^2}{4}\left(1 - \frac{\gamma}{\mu}\right)^2 - \beta\left[\alpha_0 + \dot{P}_{e_0} - \frac{1}{2}\alpha_1^2\beta\left(1 - \frac{\gamma}{\mu}\right)\right]$$

$$- \beta\gamma\left[\alpha_0 - \frac{\alpha_1^2\beta}{2}\left(1 - \frac{\gamma}{\mu}\right)\right]\frac{\theta}{2}$$

$$+ \frac{\alpha_1^2\beta^2\gamma^2}{4\mu^2}\frac{1 - e^{2\mu\theta}}{2\mu\theta} + \frac{\alpha_1^2\beta^2\gamma^2}{2\mu^2}e^{\mu\theta}$$

APPENDIX 2

Meaning of the Parameters

θ Length of the electoral period.

α_0 Constant term in unemployment-inflation function. ("Natural unemployment" rate occurs at α_0/α_1.)

α_1 Coefficient on unemployment in the unemployment-inflation function. (Slope of the short run Phillips curve is $-\alpha_1$.)

λ Coefficient of expected inflation in the unemployment-inflation function. (Slope of long-run Phillips curve is $-\alpha_1/(1-\lambda)$, or ∞ when $\lambda = 1$.)

β Weight on inflation in vote and welfare functions. (The larger β is, the more unemployment society is willing to suffer for a unit decrease in the inflation rate.)

γ Rate of adjustment of expected inflation to discrepancies between actual and expected inflation.

μ Rate at which voters discount past (welfare-related) information. The smaller μ is, the longer is the voters' frame of reference regarding past economic conditions.

$\dot{P}_{e_0}$ Expected inflation at the beginning of the term. This is the initial condition necessary for a full solution of the differential Eqs. (4) and (8).

APPENDIX 3

Tables of θ^* as Functions of the Parameters

(a) $\alpha_0 = 4.8, \alpha_1 = 1, \lambda = .5, \gamma = .5, \dot{P}_{e_0} = 1$

	μ			
β	.09	.1	.15	.3
6	0	0	0	0
6.5	22.9	16.5	7.6	0
7	33.4	19.8	8.8	0
7.5	∞	23.2	9.7	
8	∞	27.1		
10	∞	∞		

(b) $\alpha_0 = 4.8, \alpha_1 = 1, \beta = 6, \mu = .09, \dot{P}_{e_0} = 1$

	γ					
λ	.2	.3	.4	.5	.6	.7
.5	0	0	0	0	0	∞
.7	0		13.44	15.00	16.96	20.04
.8	0	11.98	13.02	13.90	14.79	15.80
.9	0	11.91	12.56	13.02	13.41	13.78

APPENDIX 4

Comparative Statics: Principles

In many social science models, one wants to solve for a variable x an equation $F(x; p) = 0$, which depends on a parameter p. If one changes p, one obtains a new equation and a new solution x. We will write $x^*(p)$ as the solution of $F(x, p) = 0$ when the parameter is fixed at p. Two natural questions are: (i) Is

$x^*(p)$ a well-behaved function of p? (ii) How does x^* change as p changes? The Implicit Function Theorem (Courant, 1937; p. 480) answers both of these questions.

By definition of $x^*(p)$, $F(x^*(p), p)$ is identically zero for all p. Differentiating this expression with respect to p yields

$$\frac{\partial F}{\partial x}\frac{dx^*}{dp} + \frac{\partial F}{\partial p} = 0$$

or

$$\frac{dx^*}{dp} = -\frac{\partial F}{\partial p}\Big/\frac{\partial F}{\partial x}, \quad \text{at } (x^*(p), p)$$

The Implicit Function Theorem tells us that if the denominator $\partial F/\partial x$ is not zero at $(x^*(p), p)$, then $x^*(p)$ is a continuously differentiable function of the parameter p, and its derivative is given by the above equation.

APPENDIX 5

Comparative Statics for Θ^*

We apply the theory of Appendix 4 to Eq. (14), the equation which determines the optimal Θ^* as a function of the other parameters in Appendix 2.

Let $h(x)$ denote the function

$$h(x) = \frac{1 - e^x}{x}$$

which occurs in the next to last term of the expression for $W^*(\Theta)/\Theta$ in part (b) of Appendix 1. Since the Taylor series of e^x is $\Sigma_0 x^n/n!$, the Taylor series for $h(x)$ is

$$h(x) = -\sum_0^\infty \frac{x^n}{(n + 1)!} = -1 - \frac{1}{2}x - \frac{1}{6}x^2 - \cdots$$

The function h is always negative. It tends to 0 from below as $x \to -\infty$, and it drops off monotonically toward $-\infty$ as x increases to $+\infty$.

The equation (14) which determines Θ^* is

$$\frac{\partial}{\partial\Theta}(W^*(\Theta)/\Theta) = -\frac{1}{2}\alpha_0\beta\gamma + \frac{1}{4}\alpha_1^2\beta^2\gamma - \frac{\alpha_1^2\beta^2\gamma^2}{4\mu}$$

$$+ \frac{\alpha_1^2\beta^2\gamma^2}{2\mu}h'(2\mu\Theta) + \frac{\alpha_1^2\beta^2\gamma^2}{2\mu}e^{\mu\Theta}$$

In line with our discussion in the previous appendix, we will call this function

$F(\Theta; p)$, where p is any one of the parameters $\alpha_0, \alpha_1, \beta, \gamma, \mu$. Furthermore, if $\Theta^*(p)$ is the solution of

$$F(\Theta; p) = 0$$

for fixed p, then

$$\frac{\partial \Theta^*}{\partial p} = -\frac{\partial F}{\partial p} \Big/ \frac{\partial F}{\partial \Theta}$$

Since we are interested in interior maxima of $W^*(\Theta)/\Theta$, the denominator $\partial F/\partial \Theta$, which is the second derivative of $W^*(\Theta)/\Theta$ with respect to Θ, will be nonpositive at $\Theta^*(p)$. Consequently, $\partial \Theta^*/\partial p$ has the same sign as $\partial F/\partial p$, i.e., as

$$\frac{\partial^2}{\partial p\, \partial \Theta}\left(\frac{W^*(\Theta)}{\Theta} \right)$$

We now compute this sign.

(i) α_0:

$$\frac{\partial F}{\partial \alpha_0} = -\frac{1}{2}\beta\gamma < 0$$

(ii) α_1: We first divide F (or $W^*(\Theta)/\Theta$) by α_1^2, an operation which will not change the optimal $\Theta^*(\alpha_1)$. We then compute

$$\frac{\partial}{\partial \alpha_1}\left(\frac{1}{\alpha_1^2} F(\Theta; \alpha_1) \right) = \frac{\partial}{\partial \alpha_1}\left(-\frac{\alpha_0\beta\gamma}{2\alpha_1^2} \right)$$

$$= \frac{\alpha_0\beta\gamma}{4\alpha_1^3} > 0$$

(iii) β: First, divide $F(\Theta; \beta) = 0$ by β^2, and then take the derivative with respect to β:

$$\frac{\partial}{\partial \beta}\left(\frac{1}{\beta^2} F(\Theta; \beta) \right) = \frac{\partial}{\partial \beta}\left(-\frac{\alpha_0\gamma}{2\beta} \right)$$

$$= \frac{\alpha_0\gamma}{2\beta^2} > 0$$

(iv) γ: First, divide $F(\Theta; \gamma) = 0$ by γ^2, and then take the derivative with respect to γ:

$$\frac{\partial}{\partial \gamma}\left(\frac{1}{\gamma^2} F(\Theta; \gamma) \right) = \frac{\partial}{\partial \gamma}\left(-\frac{\alpha_0\beta}{2\gamma} + \frac{\alpha_1^2\beta^2}{4\gamma} \right)$$

$$= \frac{\beta}{2\gamma^2}\left(\alpha_0 - \frac{\alpha_1^2\beta}{2} \right) = \frac{\alpha_1\beta}{2\gamma^2}\left(\frac{\alpha_0}{\alpha_1} - \frac{1}{2}\alpha_1\beta \right)$$

(v) μ:

$$\frac{\partial F}{\partial \mu} = \frac{\alpha_1^2 \beta^2 \gamma^2}{4\mu^2}\{1 + 4\mu\Theta h''(2\mu\Theta) - 2h'(2\mu\Theta) - 2e^{\mu\Theta} + 2\mu\Theta e^{\mu\Theta}\}$$

The term in brackets is zero when $\Theta = 0$. We will show that its derivative with respect to Θ is negative for $\Theta > 0$. This implies that it (and therefore $\partial F/\partial \mu$) is negative for $\Theta > 0$.

Let $x = \mu\Theta$ in the bracketed formula above. The formula becomes

$$b_1(x) = 1 + 4xh''(2x) - 2h'(2x) - 2e^x + 2xe^x$$

Its derivative is

$$b_1'(x) = 2x(4h'''(2x) + e^x)$$

The term in parentheses is the third derivative of

$$b_2(x) = \tfrac{1}{2}h(2x) + e^x$$

Since h is analytic, $b_1'(x)$ will be negative for $x > 0$ if all the coefficients in the Taylor series (about 0) for $b_2(x)$ are negative from the x^3 term on. The Taylor series for $b_2(x)$ can easily be derived from the above series for h:

$$b_2(x) = -\sum_0^\infty \frac{2^{n-1}x^n}{(n+1)!} + \sum_0^\infty \frac{x^n}{n!}$$

$$= \sum_0^\infty \frac{(-2^{n-1} + (n+1))}{(n+1)!}x^n$$

One checks readily that the coefficients of x^n are nonpositive for $n \geq 3$. When one computes the third derivative of $b_2(x)$, the first three terms drop out, and consequently all the terms of $b_2'''(x)$ have nonpositive coefficients. This implies that

$$b_1'(x) = 2xb_2'''(x)$$

is less than or equal to zero for $x \geq 0$ and, since $b_1(0) = 0$, that $b_1(x) \leq 0$ for $x \geq 0$.

APPENDIX 6

Cases Where $\Theta^* = \infty$ and $\Theta^* = 0$

(a) We first consider the case where $\lambda = 1$ and $\mu = 0$. In this case, we want to maximize

$$V = \int_0^\Theta (-u^2 - \beta(\alpha_0 - \alpha_1 U + \dot{P}_e)) \, dt$$

subject to $\dot{P}_e = \gamma(\alpha_0 - \alpha_1 U)$. By the usual optimal control theory techniques, it follows that

$$U^*(t) = \tfrac{1}{2}\alpha_1\beta(1 - \gamma(t - \Theta))$$

and

$$\frac{W^*(\Theta)}{\Theta} = \frac{V(u^*)}{\Theta}$$

$$= -\beta\left(\alpha_0 - \frac{1}{2}\alpha_1^2\beta + \dot{P}_{e_0}\right)$$

$$- \frac{1}{2}\left(\alpha_0\beta\gamma + \frac{1}{2}\alpha_1^2\beta\gamma\right)\Theta$$

$$+ \frac{1}{12}\alpha_1^2\beta^2\gamma^2\Theta^2$$

Since this is a quadratic function of Θ with a positive Θ^2 term,

$$\frac{W^*(\Theta)}{\Theta} \to \infty \quad \text{as} \quad \Theta \to \infty$$

i.e., optimal term length is as large as possible.

(b) We return now to the more general case described in Appendix 5, where $\lambda = 1$ and $\mu > 0$. Recall that

$$\frac{\partial}{\partial\Theta}(W^*(\Theta)/\Theta) = -\frac{1}{2}\beta\gamma\left(\alpha_0 - \frac{1}{2}\alpha_1^2\beta\right)$$

$$+ \frac{\alpha_1^2\beta^2\gamma^2}{4\mu}\{-1 + 2h'(2\mu\Theta) + 2e^{\mu\Theta}\}$$

When $\Theta = 0$, the expression in brackets is zero. Furthermore, a Taylor series analysis, as we used in Appendix 6, shows that this expression is negative for all $\Theta > 0$. Consequently, if

$$\left(\alpha_0 - \frac{1}{2}\alpha_1^2\beta\right) > 0$$

then $(\partial/\partial\Theta)(W^*(\Theta)/\Theta)$ is negative for all Θ and $W^*(\Theta)/\Theta$ is a decreasing function of Θ. Under these circumstances, the optimal term length is $\Theta^* = 0$.

APPENDIX 7

The Influence of the Sign of $A \equiv \gamma(1 - \lambda) - \mu$

(a) Behavior of $k(x) \equiv (1 - e^{-x})/x$. By L'Hopital's rule, $k(0) = 1$. One can easily show that:

(i) k is always positive
(ii) As $x \to -\infty$, $k(x) \to +\infty$

(iii) As $x \to +\infty$, $k(x) \to 0$

(iv) k' is always negative; so k is a monotonically decreasing function.

(b) If $A < 0$, $W^*(\theta)/\theta \to -\infty$ as $\theta \to +\infty$. Recall the formula for $W^*(\theta)/\theta$ from Appendix 1(a):

$$\frac{W^*(\theta)}{\theta} = C_0 + C_1 k(A\theta) + C_2 k(2A\theta)$$

$$+ \left(C_3 + C_4 e^{-A\theta}\right) k(\gamma(1 - \lambda)\theta)$$

When A is negative, $k(A\theta)$, $k(2A\theta)$, and $e^{-A\theta}$ all tend to (positive) infinity as $\theta \to \infty$. However, their coefficients have different signs, so a more sensitive estimate must be made. Since $k(\gamma(1 - \lambda)\theta)$ tends to zero, we can ignore the C_0 and C_3 terms in our analysis. The remaining constants C_1, C_2, and C_4 are each divisible by E^2. To simplify our notation, we divide these constants through by E^2 but use the same letters for them.

We will need two algebraic facts which the reader can verify directly:

$$k(2A\theta) \equiv \left(\frac{1 - e^{-2A\theta}}{2A\theta}\right) = \left(\frac{1 + e^{-A\theta}}{2}\right)\left(\frac{1 - e^{-A\theta}}{A\theta}\right) \tag{16}$$

and

$$C_4 e^{-A\theta} k(\gamma(1 - \lambda)\theta) = -AC_4 \left(\frac{1 - e^{-\gamma(1-\lambda)\theta}}{(1 - \lambda)}\right)\left(\frac{1 - e^{-A\theta}}{A\theta}\right)$$

$$+ C_4 k(\gamma(1 - \lambda)\theta) \tag{17}$$

Putting this all together,

$$C_1 k(A\theta) + C_2 k(2A\theta) + C_4 e^{-A\theta} k(\gamma(1 - \lambda)\theta)$$

$$= C_1 k(A\theta) - \frac{1}{2}(1 + e^{-A\theta}) k(A\theta) - AC_4 \left(\frac{1 - e^{-\gamma(1-\lambda)\theta}}{\gamma(1 - \lambda)}\right) k(A\theta)$$

$$+ C_4 k(\gamma(1 - \lambda)\theta)$$

by (16) and (17)

$$= \left\{C_1 - AC_4 \left(\frac{1 - e^{-\gamma(1-\lambda)\theta}}{\gamma(1 - \lambda)}\right) - \frac{1}{2}(1 + e^{-A\theta})\right\} k(A\theta)$$

$$+ C_4 k(\gamma(1 - \lambda)\theta) \tag{18}$$

As $\theta \to \infty$, $k(\gamma(1 - \lambda)\theta) \to 0$,

$$\left(\frac{1 - e^{-\gamma(1-\lambda)\theta}}{\gamma(1 - \lambda)}\right) \to \frac{1}{\gamma(1 - \lambda)}$$

$$-\frac{1}{2}(1 + e^{-A\theta}) \to -\infty \qquad \text{since } A < 0$$

and

$$k(A\theta) \to +\infty$$

Consequently, the entire expression in (18) tends to $-\infty$ as θ becomes large; and so does $W^*(\theta)/\theta$.

(c) If $A > 0$, $W^*(\theta)/\theta$ is bounded away from $+\infty$ and from $-\infty$. This fact follows from the description of k in part (a) for $x \geq 0$, i.e., k falls slowly from 1 to 0 as θ goes from 0 to ∞. In fact,

$$\left.\frac{W^*(\theta)}{\theta}\right|_{\theta=0} = \frac{1}{4}\alpha_1^2\beta^2 - \alpha_0\beta - \beta\lambda\dot{P}_{e_0}$$

and

$$\left.\frac{W^*(\theta)}{\theta}\right|_{\theta\to\infty} = C_0$$

If the constants C_1, C_2, C_3, and C_4 are all small and $A > 0$, then $W^*(\theta)/\theta$ will move over a small range of numbers as θ varies between 0 and ∞. This will occur, for example, when $\mu = 0$, γ is arbitrary, and α_0, α_1, β, λ, and $\dot{P}_{e_0}$ are small.

5: Can Income Policies Work?

R. Robert Russell

Incomes policy is the generic term for centralized efforts to control prices
and wages (and sometimes other forms of income). Virtually every
Western industrialized country has experimented with such policies. The
programs have varied considerably. In most cases, the primary objective
is to reduce inflation; frequently, however, there are other goals—most
notably, income redistribution. In some, coverage is comprehensive; in
others, coverage is limited to a few highly concentrated sectors of the
economy. Most are administered by the government, but in some countries—especially those with economy-wide bargaining between national
labor and business organizations—the incomes policies are privately
administered, presumably because the bargaining parties consider
voluntary restraint to be in their enlightened self-interest. Some pro-
rams require a large bureaucracy; others are much less ambitious.
Some are essentially voluntary, with the role of the central authorities limited primarily to exhortation and admonition; others entail
detailed regulations backed by the force of law, with civil penalties for
violations.

The persistent popularity of incomes policies has perplexed many economists.[1] Their repeated adoption despite widespread verdicts of past failures is in part attributable to their simple appeal: they constitute the most direct, and most easily understood, assault on inflation. In addition, they are attractive to elected officials, who are eager to avoid the political costs of alternative antiinflation policies. Many economists, especially in the United States, view these popular perceptions as naive and the decisions to adopt incomes policies as political opportunism.

There is, nevertheless, an economic case to be made for such policies, which is presented in the following section. Next, I examine the case against incomes policies. It will be apparent that may basic predisposition is mildly favorable to such policies; while I attempt to be fair, I make no attempt to disguise my belief that income policies can be useful complements to fiscal and monetary restraint. Whether they have been effective is an arguable empirical question. Thus I present some econometric evidence on the effectiveness of three incomes policies adopted in the United States: the Kennedy/Johnson guideposts, the Nixon administration's Economic Stabilization Program (ESP), and the Carter administration's Pay and Price Standards Program.[2] This evidence is reasonably representative of the econometric results obtained in the analysis of these programs by other investigators. Finally, I present some concluding remarks.

THE RATIONALE FOR INCOMES POLICIES

Support for incomes policies among economists, such as it is, reflects disillusionment with the efficacy of fiscal and monetary policies as antiinflation instruments. Since these policies dampen inflationary pressures by lowering aggregate demand,[3] an inevitable concomitant is greater excess capacity, resulting in lower capital utilization rates and higher unemployment rates. The attendant social costs—principally lower aggregate output[4]—are large.

A consensus estimate is that an engineered decline in the growth of nominal GNP on average is split nine to one between output and prices in the short run (see Okun, 1978).[5] Lowering the inflation rate by one percentage point through restraint of aggregate demand, according to these estimates, costs about 10% of 1 year's GNP, or $300 billion at today's output level.

The theoretical foundation for this phenomenon—the perverse short-run trade-off between inflation and unemployment—has been the subject of considerable investigation in recent years. The simple explanation is market imperfections, that is, discretionary pricing power, especially in highly concentrated markets. Such imperfections are the original micro-economic foundation of the cost-push theory of inflation. However, while the traditional microeconomic theory of imperfect competition can explain relatively high prices in imperfectly competitive markets, it does not adequately explain price rigidity. Two prominent lines of research in recent years help to elucidate the sluggish adjustment of prices and wages (and the concomitant fluctuations of output and employment).

The first is an information-based theory of market disequilibrium, developed by, among others, Alchian (1969), Phelps (1968, 1969, 1979), Holt (1970), Mortenson (1970), and Lucas (1972). The basic idea is that economic agents confuse absolute price changes with relative price changes. For example, a disinflation policy designed to lower the absolute level of wages would be resisted by individual workers—and perhaps by employers as well—because they misperceive the decline in individual wage rates as changes in their wages relative to those of others, when in reality there is an equiproportional decline in all wage rates. The result is increased unemployment in those sectors of the economy where such resistance occurs. Eventually, as workers become unemployed and as information about the average wage level becomes widely disseminated, the resistance to wage cuts diminishes. This phenomenon generates a downward-sloping short-run Phillips curve. Of course, the same type of mechanism can work in product markets.

An alternative explanation of wage and price rigidity, which has grown in part out of skepticism that informational disequilibrium can persist long enough to explain sustained periods of recession, is based on the theory of implicit contracts, developed primarily by Azariadis (1975), Baily (1974), D. Gordon (1976), and Okun (1975, 1981). The basic idea, as applied to labor markets, is that when hiring a worker, a firm enters into an implicit agreement [the "invisible handshake," Okun (1981) calls it] restraining what the employer can do to the worker's wages and other terms of employment in the future. These implicit contracts are to be distinguished from explicit contracts; the former are informal, nonbinding, and long-term, whereas the latter are binding and short-term (typically 1–3 years).

Implicit contracting is most likely to occur in the "career labor market" (see Okun, 1981) and in cases where a worker incurs substantial mobility costs or other transaction costs in taking a new job. The implicit contract induces employee loyalty. The polar case of this model is the Japanese system of guaranteed lifetime jobs. While the United States labor market is a long way from this system, it is also, according to this theory, a long way from the classical model of instantaneous adjustment of wages to changes in labor market equilibrium. The primary response, at least initially, to a policy of disinflation in an economy characterized by implicit labor contracts is likely to be reduced hiring of new workers, and hence higher unemployment rates, rather than lower wage rates (or lower rates of wage increases.)[6] The same phenomenon occurs in product markets, Okun (1981) argues, where sellers implicitly pledge to keep their prices reliable and competitive. Therefore, the buyer avoids the heavy transaction costs of shopping around for the lowest prices, and the seller develops customer loyalty.

In theory, each of these models can explain substantial sluggishness in the adjustment of prices and wages to changes in the equilibrium price level. Empirical verification of these theories is difficult, however, and no one has yet devised a practical test that can discriminate between the two. In any event, there may well be a substantial amount of truth in both theories since, after all, they are not mutually exclusive.

Either theory can provide the intellectual foundation for an incomes policy. Thus, in the context of the information-theoretic model, pay and price guidelines can provide information about the average wage and price levels, thus lowering the resistance to wage and price reductions. A slightly different statement of this effect is that incomes policies can alter inflation expectations, thus shifting the Phillips curve downward. Alternatively, an incomes policy can be interpreted as a social compact which supersedes the implicit contracts of individual economic agents.[7]

THE CASE AGAINST INCOMES POLICIES

The many arguments against incomes policies can be organized under four different assertions:

Assertion 1: Incomes policies can't work—ever.

Assertion 2: Incomes policies might lower the inflation rate temporarily, but they can have no lasting effect.

Assertion 3: Incomes policies may have a lasting effect, but the costs generated by induced inefficiencies and market distortions exceed the benefits.

Assertion 4: Whether or not incomes policies work, they shouldn't be tried because they are anathema to the American way of life.

I consider in turn the arguments underlying each of these assertions.

Incomes Policies Can't Work—Ever

This point of view is associated primarily with the monetarist school of thought, though by no means do all monetarists subscribe to it. In its extreme form, the argument is that the inflation rate is determined exclusively by the growth rate of the money supply. This proposition is grounded in the classical economic dichotomy, which states that relative prices are determined by fundamental microeconomic phenomena, and the absolute price level is determined by the amount of money in circulation. The formal expression is the quantity theory equation, $MV = PQ$, where M is the money supply, V is the velocity of money (roughly speaking, the number of times per period that a dollar is used in transactions), P is the price level, and Q is real output (hence, PQ is nominal output, say, nominal GNP).[8] Thus percentage rates of change are related by $\dot{M}/M + \dot{V}/V = \dot{P}/P + \dot{Q}/Q$. If the velocity of money is institutionally determined (independent of economic conditions) and the rate of growth of output is determined by the microeconomic fundamentals, the inflation rate is determined exclusively by the growth of the money supply. Thus, the argument goes, an incomes policy is at best useless, and more likely, deleterious, because of induced distortions of relative prices.

As an arithmetic tautology, this argument is indisputable. As a theory and as a policy, it is deficient. The problem is that the predicates are demonstrably false: Velocity is not independent of economic conditions (it is procyclical) and, most important, output is not independent of the money supply. Econometric evidence supports the notion of a close relationship between the money supply and nominal GNP (see, e.g., Mayer, 1978), but the effect is split between output and prices. In the short run, most of the effect of change in the rate of growth of the money supply is on output growth, and most of the long-run effect is on prices. In other words, in the long run, the Milton Friedman (1961, p. 18) dictum that inflation "is always and everywhere a monetary phenomenon" is fundamentally true. However, between long-run (steady-state) equilibriums, monetary restraint can result in huge output losses.

Let us put the matter a little differently. Suppose that OPEC doubles the price of oil. Without doubt, the Federal Reserve can prevent the price increases of imported oil from getting built into the overall domestic inflation rate by a sufficiently restrictive monetary policy. That is, the Federal Reserve can simply refuse to monetize the higher oil prices, instead forcing the economy to a new relative-price equilibrium with higher prices of energy-intensive commodities, lower prices of non-energy-intensive commodities, and an absolute price level that is unaffected by the oil price increase. This restrictive monetary policy, however, while designed to lower non-energy-intensive prices, will have output effects as well as price effects. The result will be a slower rate of growth and higher unemployment rates. Alternatively, the monetary authorities can completely monetize the oil price increase, increasing the money supply by enough to accommodate the higher prices of energy-intensive commodities with no downward adjustment required on the part of non-energy-intensive commodities. In this case, there would be no output effects, but the inflation rate would accelerate.

Given any reasonable social welfare function guiding the decisions of the monetary authorities, however, the policy response to the oil price increase is likely to be one of partial monetarization. The result, then, is some acceleration of inflation and some retardation of real growth.[9] An extreme monetarist might argue that this acceleration of the inflation rate is a monetary phenomenon; after all, it would not have happened had the Federal Reserve system simply refused to monetize the oil price increases. This statement is true but uninteresting. While the increase in the money supply is the proximate cause of the additional inflation, the fundamental cause is the international oil price increase. It is therefore unenlightening to argue that this acceleration in the inflation rate was caused by the acceleration in the growth of the money supply.

Consider now an example that is more relevant to this paper. Suppose that the government institutes an incomes policy that, through its effect on expectations and/or the operation of implicit contracts (and some such phenomena are required to explain the real-output effects of monetary policy), causes a downward shift in the Phillips curve. This shock would allow the monetary authorities to lower the rate of growth of the money supply painlessly. That is, because a lower inflation rate is now consistent with any given unemployment rate, the monetary authorities can retard the rate of growth of the money supply without affecting the unemployment rate. Of course, in this example, we would observe, *ex post facto*, commensurate declines in the rate of growth of the money supply and the inflation rate. A monetarist might say that the retardation of the inflation rate was caused by the decline in the growth of money. Again, however, the lowering of the rate of growth of the money supply is only the proximate cause (the disinflation would not have occurred without the cooperation of the monetary authorities); the fundamental cause is the success of the incomes policy.

To summarize, the extreme monetarist view that incomes policies cannot affect the inflation rate, while based on a premise that is not only true but indeed tautological, is surely as simplistic as the popular view that the most effective method of arresting inflation is the direct control of prices and wages.

Incomes Policies Might Lower the Inflation Rate Temporarily, but They Can Have No Lasting Effect

This assertion stems from several points of view, some naive and some sophisticated. The first line of argument is only a slightly less strident version of the monetarist notion that an incomes policy can never have a salutary effect. As the argument goes, an incomes policy might put a cap on inflationary pressures while the monetary authorities continue to inflate the money supply, but once the controls are lifted—as inevitably they will be when the induced distortions become intolerable—the pent-up demand will cause the inflation to burst forth with renewed vigor. This statement makes sense if the incomes policy is used as a substitute for fiscal and monetary restraint, but there is certainly no reason to presuppose that it must be. To the extent that an incomes policy is designed to complement restrictive fiscal and monetary policies, this argument is invalid.

Unfortunately, there was a tendency to such substitution in all three of the incomes policies adopted in the United States over the last two decades. The Kennedy administration implemented expansionary policies, but initially, because there was substantial excess capacity, such policies were not deemed to be inflationary. Eventually, however, when the Johnson administration injected some $20 billion per year of Vietnam War expenditures into an already overheated economy, the Kennedy-Johnson guideposts came to be seen as a substitute for fiscal and monetary restraint (Johnson repeatedly resisted the entreaties of his economic advisers to raise taxes). It is also well known that the Nixon administration used its mandatory controls program to keep the lid on prices while it pumped up the economy in preparation for the 1972 election. Finally, although the Carter administration stressed the complementary roles of the Pay and Price Standards Program and restrictive fiscal and monetary policies, the latter were clearly inadequate to the task (only the credit controls of early 1980 had a significant effect). The standards came to seen as "the only game in town" and ultimately as the scapegoat for the apparent failure of the administration's antiinflation policies.

Thus the more sophisticated version of the assertion that incomes policies are unlikely to have a salutary long-term effect is based on a political consideration, namely, that the policy provides vote-sensitive politicians with an excuse for failing to bite the bullet and adopt the socially painful fiscal and monetary policies required to control inflation. It is contended that, despite the best of intentions when a program is promulgated, the temptation to substitute it for traditional antiinflation policies becomes irresistible. At the least, it is argued, incomes policies

divert attention from the other (more important) antiinflation instruments. History indicates that this is a valid point. However, blaming
incomes policies for the failure to adopt proper fiscal and monetary
policies is hardly a dispositive argument. Rather, this characteristic of
past antiinflation policies underscores the need to combine restrictive
fiscal and monetary policies with incomes policies. In other words, this
argument points to the need for a political solution to the problem of
misuse of incomes policies; as an economic argument, it is not compelling.

There is, however, an economic argument that supports the view that
incomes policies can, at best, only temporarily lower inflation rates. This
notion, proposed by Gordon (1973) and Blinder and Newton (1981), is
that the postcontrol corrections of relative-price distortions induced by
the program result in price levels equal to or greater than what would
have prevailed in the absence of the program. That is, when the controls
are lifted, the new equilibrium is achieved not because prices and wages
that are too high come down, but rather because prices and wages that
are too low come up. The downward rigidity of prices and wages results
in a postcontrols surge in the overall price level.

The Blinder-Newton econometric analysis of the Nixon administration's mandatory controls program provides support for this hypothesis.
They find that the program suppressed the rate of price inflation by
about a percentage point while it was in effect, but that the postcontrols
surge in inflation offset the earlier gain. It is important to note that this
calculation takes fiscal and monetary policies as given. Thus the inflationary effects of the political decision to inflate the economy while using
controls to keep the lid on prices must be added to the postcontrols
catch-up to arrive at the full effect of the Nixon program in exacerbating
inflation.

The strength of this argument is, of course, directly related to the
extent to which a program distorts relative prices. But the seriousness of
the distortions caused by a program depends significantly on its design
characteristics. The Gordon-Blinder-Newton thesis about the Nixon program is corroborated by a myriad of horror stories about market disruptions, distortions, and shortages (see, e.g., Eads, 1976, and Schultze,
1980). Perhaps most important is the fact that the early phases of the
Nixon program checked price inflation without having any effect on

labor costs, thus squeezing profit margins (see Gordon, 1973, and discussion below in this chapter). These margins bounced back after the controls were lifted.

There is much less evidence of induced distortions in either the Kennedy/Johnson guideposts or the Carter Pay and Price Standards Program. To a certain extent, this reflects differences in design features (these programs were more flexible than the Nixon program), but the principal reason is probably that the Nixon program was mandatory whereas the guideposts and the standards program were essentially voluntary (the former more so than the latter). The Nixon program entailed two mandatory price freezes and, during its critical Phase II, required prenotification of price increases by larger (Tier I) companies; they were not allowed to implement the increases until they obtained approval.[10] The Kennedy/Johnson program established guidelines for voluntary restraint (in fact, according to some of its promulgators, for "educational purposes"), although there were some notorious cases of presidential jawboning, especially during the Johnson years. The Carter program embodied a procurement sanction (a threat to debar noncompliers from bidding on large government contracts), but it became less and less credible as the program proceeded. It was essentially a voluntary program, relying primarily on the willingness, if not eagerness, of employers to use the pay standard to hold down wage increases.

Typically, when a market becomes very tight, companies in that industry have the opportunity to make large profits. Because compliance with the Carter administration's standards was voluntary, companies could choose, without fear of penalty of law, not to adhere to the standards if adherence meant substantial losses in profit. For example, six producers of cement and other building materials were listed as noncompliers because they refused to adhere to the program when the market was tight. Had the program not been voluntary, there might well have been a shortage of cement.

No significant distortions caused by the Kennedy/Johnson guidelines have been documented. Although there is no convincing evidence that the Carter administration's price standards created perceptible distortions in the overall economy, or that the program distorted the labor cost/price ratio, there is ample evidence that the pay standards distorted the structure of wage rates. In particular, complying employee groups

covered by multiyear contracts that included formal cost-of-living adjustments clauses (COLAs) received much larger pay increases than did
complying workers without such protection. This occurred because the
inflation assumptions under the standard were 6% in the first year and
7.5% in the second year, while the actual inflation rates were much
higher. As the consumer price index (CPI) accelerated above the assumed
inflation rate, workers with COLAs received wage increases that were not
charged against the pay standard, while non-COLA workers were held to
the maximum increase allowed under the standard. Despite this distortion, there is little evidence of a postcontrols catch-up of suppressed wage
rates. Thus the Gordon-Blinder-Newton phenomenon appears to be
applicable to only one of the three incomes policies adopted in the
United States in the last two decades. (It should be noted that these
authors did not attribute this phenomenon to either of the voluntary
programs.)[11]

Incomes Policies May Have a Lasting Effect, but the Costs Exceed the Benefits

Some who reach this conclusion stress the social costs of induced
inefficiencies (through the distortion of relative prices). Others emphasize
the direct administration costs—the administrative burden placed on
companies and/or the social costs of the "bureaucratic army" required
to enforce the guidelines. There are no reliable estimates of these costs
for any program. As the Council on Wage and Price Stability was going
out of business, it surveyed the companies it had been monitoring to
ascertain their administrative costs of complying with the program. The
resulting estimate, which is subject to the usual response-error biases, was
on the order of $300 million for the 2-year program. The government
administrative costs were comparatively small—less than $10 million.
Darby (1976) roughly estimates the total cost of the ESP at no more than
$2 billion—$1 billion for administrative costs and $1 billion for induced
inefficiencies.

The social benefits of a reduction in the inflation rate cannot be
measured directly. If, however, we are willing to take as given the social
commitment to lower the inflation rate, then we can measure the benefits

of the program by referring to the social costs of reducing the inflation rate by alternative methods—namely, fiscal and monetary restraint. As noted below, our best estimate of the effect of the Carter program was that it reduced the inflation rate by something like one percentage point. Recall from the discussion above that the consensus estimate of the output costs of lowering the inflation rate by one percentage point through fiscal and monetary restraint is on the order of $300 billion. Both estimates are, of course, inferential and subject to statistical error. Moreover, the estimates of the administrative costs in the paragraph above are crude and the social costs of any induced inefficiencies are unquantifiable. However, even if the estimates of both benefits and costs are off by several orders of magnitude, the Carter administration's program was clearly cost-effective.

Whether or Not Income Policies Work, They Shouldn't Be Tried Because They Are Anathema to the American Way of Life

According to this point of view, even if such programs are cost-effective, they should not be used because they assault fundamental freedoms that Americans cherish. Perhaps the most forceful proponent of this position among trained economists is Herbert Stein (1980), who argues that such programs " violate the rules of the economic and political game we play here." The political game we play, according to Stein, is the game of "free enterprise."

The critical question, of course, is this: What are the rules of the game? If the rule is laissez faire, it has surely been honored more in the breach than in the observance. The U.S. government has repeatedly intervened in the economy—sometimes rationally, sometimes irrationally.

The conventional wisdom among economists is that government should intervene in the marketplace only when an externality or a public good is at issue. The classic example of an externality is the consumption of clean air and water. The social costs of pollution are not taken into account by individual decision makers. The reason is that no one has property rights over the waste-disposal capacity of the environment; hence, the environment is consumed up to the point where the private value of another unit of consumption vanishes, even though the marginal cost to society is far from zero. As a result, in the absence of government intervention to internalize those externalities (using pollution taxes or an artificial market for pollution rights), there is an excessive amount of pollution. A classic example of a public good is national defense. The security provided by a defense system can be enjoyed by one person without any diminution in the amount of security enjoyed by others. A laissez-faire economy would produce too little national defense.

The critical question, then, is whether inflation can be seen as a negative externality (or a public "bad"). Indeed, it is the popular viewpoint, as well as the view of most economists, that inflation does impose costs on society that are not taken into account by agents with discretionary pricing power. It is argued that everybody would be better off if the rates of growth of all wages and prices were simultaneously lowered without any effect on relative prices.

Several explanations of the social costs of inflation have been put forward by economists (see Ackley, 1978). One stresses the uncertainty caused by high inflation rates. An attractive feature of the perfectly competitive model of economic behavior is its informational efficiency. Economic decision makers in a competitive environment need only know prices of items that they buy and sell in order to make economically rational (i.e., profit-maximizing or utility-maximizing) decisions. Inflation, however, can reduce the informational content of prices because it forces decision makers to distinguish price changes that are real (i.e., that constitute relative changes in the prices of commodities they buy and sell) from those that are nominal (i.e., equiproportionate changes in all prices). The former, of course, affect consumer and business decisions whereas the latter do not. Moreover, the informational inefficiencies caused by inflation worsen as the inflation rate grows because there is evidence that higher inflation rates are associated with greater variability of relative prices (see Okun, 1979; Logue and Willett, 1976; and Klein, 1976).

A second explanation of the social costs of inflation argues that high inflation rates cause a shift of investment funds away from productivity-enhancing capital investment projects towards goods that are primarily hedges against inflation (such as houses and works of art).

A third explanation says that inflation exacerbates the distortions caused by taxation. In part, this is simply because the share of GNP taken by the government tends to increase with inflation as a result of the progressivity of the tax structure. This is offset to some degree by periodic discretionary tax cuts, but there is a lag between the inflation and the legislative action. Moreover, the discretionary tax cuts have typically been slanted more toward individual taxes than business taxes, thus tending to increase the corporate income tax. This, in turn, tends to depress the real after-tax rate of return on capital. The problem is compounded by the treatment of depreciation allowances for firms: because these allowances are based on historical rather than replacement costs, true depreciation is understated during periods of rapid inflation. Both of these phenomena tend to depress the rate of capital formation.

The characterization of inflation as an externality has inspired proposed solutions to inflation that are incomes-policy analogues of pollution taxes and artificial markets in pollution rights. They are known, respectively, as tax-incentive policies (TIPs) and market antiinflation plans (MAPs).

Tax-based incomes policies were first proposed by Wallich and Weintraub (1971) and have been the subject of considerable analysis since then (see, e.g., Seidman, 1978; Dildine and Sunley 1978; and Okun 1978). The idea is to use the tax system to penalize companies for "inflationary" price or wage increases (and alternatively, to reward companies with tax subsidies for compliance with a wage or price guideline). These selective taxes would be designed to internalize an inflation externality just as a pollution tax is designed to internalize a pollution externality. TIPs have been criticized primarily on the ground of administrative infeasibility (see especially Dildine and Sunley, 1978).

The market anti-inflation plan was first proposed by Lerner (1977); see also Lerner (1978) and Lerner and Colander (1979). Firms would be given marketable rights for average wage and/or price increases.[12] Since companies would be able to buy and sell these marketable rights, relative wages and prices would be allowed to adjust in response to changing market conditions, while the overall inflation level would be held to some prescribed rate. This approach to the inflation problem is the incomes-policy analogue of artificial markets for pollutions rights, and its objective is to internalize the inflation externalities precisely as the artificial markets internalize pollution externalities. The administrative complexity of such a plan—amounting to the establishment of a second currency—can hardly be overestimated.

ECONOMETRIC EVALUATION OF U.S. INCOMES POLICIES

The foregoing discussion should have made it clear that definitive judgments about the effectiveness of incomes policies cannot be made on *a priori* grounds. Effectiveness is ultimately an empirical question. Unfortunately, the historical record is inconclusive.

There are essentially two types of evaluations of particular incomes policies: case studies (which may include before-and-after comparisons of inflation rates) and econometric analyses. Case studies of incomes policies in seven Western European countries in the 1960s can be found in Ulman and Flanagan (1971). Rockoff (1981) evaluates four wartime control programs in the U.S. (the two World Wars, the Korean War, and the Vietnam War). The most thorough examination of the Kennedy/Johnson guideposts is by Sheehan (1967). The Nixon administration's Economic Stabilization Program generated a spate of postmortems, including those of Bosworth (1972), Dunlop and Fedor (1977), Lanzillotti et al. (1975), Weber (1973), and Weber and Mitchell (1978). The last publication of the now-defunct Council on Wage and Price Stability (1981) qualifies as a case study (as well as an econometric evaluation). These studies provide useful insights into both the economics and the politics of incomes policies, but they do not add up to a consensus about the efficacy or propriety of these programs.

A truly rigorous evaluation of the quantitative effects of an incomes policy requires an estimate of what would have happened to prices and wages in the absence of the program. Such estimates can be obtained by traditional econometric techniques. An econometric model of the wage-price process can be used to assess the effects of these programs on pay and price trends, assuming that incomes policies were the principal cause of any changes in key relationships in the wage-price process during the respective periods of operation. Econometric analyses of incomes policies in this country can be found in Blinder and Newton (1981), Council on Wage and Price Stability (1981), Darby (1976), Eckstein and Brinner (1972), Feige and Pearce (1976), Frye and Gordon (1981), Gordon (1973, 1975), McGuire (1976), Pencavel (1980), and Perry (1970, 1980). Lipsey and Parkin (1970) have conducted an econometric analysis of incomes policies in Great Britain. A thoughtful critique of the techniques used in these studies can be found in Oi (1976).

The remainder of this paper describes the econometric evaluation of three recent U.S. incomes policies (the Kennedy/Johnson guideposts, the Nixon administration's Economic Stabilization Program, and the Carter administration's Pay and Price Standards Program) by the Council on Wage and Price Stability (1981).[12a] These results are reasonably consistent with those obtained by others; differences, where they occur, will be pointed out.

The analysis entails the estimation of two equations: one models the process of nominal pay rate determination, the other the process of price determination. Below, I describe the specifications of these equations and then report the empirical results. Finally, I evaluate these econometric results.

Specification of the Pay and Price Equation

PAY EQUATION The specification of the pay equation is conventional (see, e.g., Perry, 1980): the dependent variable is a measure of the percentage change in hourly compensation, and the explanatory variables reflect the influences of price inflation, labor market disequilibrium, changes in social insurance taxes, changes in the minimum wage, and incomes policies.

The dependent variable (CHPAY) is calculated by multiplying the Bureau of Labor Statistics Average Hourly Earnings Index by the ratio of total compensation to the value of wages and salaries, both from the National Income Accounts. Thus the pay variable includes fringe-benefit costs and employer contributions for social insurance as well as hourly wages and salaries. (This variable is used rather than the Total Hourly Compensation series from the National Income Accounts because the latter, unlike the Hourly Earnings Index, does not correct for overtime or for changes in the industrial mix of employment.)

The first of the explanatory variables is past rates of price inflation, which affect workers' expectations of future inflation and thus the expected real value of any nominal wage increase. The price inflation variable is specified as a distributed lag on the percentage increases in the Consumer Price Index (CHCPI). The sum of the distributed lag coefficients is expected to be positive; a sum equal to 1 means that there is no money illusion in the labor market (i.e., in the long run, real wages are independent of the inflation rate).

Labor market disequilibrium is reflected through the unemployment rate for civilian workers adjusted by a measure of the natural, or full-employment, unemployment rate (UR). The coefficient should be negative because an increase in labor market slackness normally results in a slowdown of nominal wage growth.

The Social Security tax variable (SSTAX) is included in a traditional format: the percentage change in the inverse of 1 minus the employer's effective tax rate. A coefficient of 1 would indicate that in the short run no portion of any change in the tax is shifted back to employees in the form of changed compensation.

Statutory changes in the minimum wage rate substantially affect compensation to those working in low-wage occupations. The overall effect of such changes is estimated by including the percentage change in the hourly minimum wage as a variable (CHMINWAGE).

The effects of the Kennedy/Johnson incomes policy of the 1960s (GUIDEPOSTS), Nixon's Economic Stabilization Program of the early 1970s (ESP1 for Phases I and II, and ESP2 for Phases III and IV), and the Carter administration's pay and price standards program (STANDARDS) are represented by dummy variables.

The Kennedy/Johnson GUIDEPOSTS dummy variable is phased in in equal increments starting in 1962:I (.25 for 1962:I, .5 for 1962:II, .75 for 1962:III), is equal to 1 from 1962:IV to 1966:IV, and is phased down to zero in four equal increments beginning in 1967:I to represent the gradual phase-out of the program in 1967. (See Perry, 1970, for a discussion of the construction of this variable.)

The ESPI and ESP2 variables are phased in and out to reflect the fact that they were in effect for parts of quarters when they were instituted and discontinued. To reflect a possible wage rebound after ESP, a dummy variable for the year following the controls (POSTCONTROL) has been added.

The STANDARDS variable is equal to zero before 1978:IV and to 1 thereafter.

PRICE EQUATION   The price equation is also conventional: the dependent variable is the percentage change in the Consumer Price Index for all urban consumers (CHCPI), and the explanatory variables reflect the effects of changing unit labor costs, changes in energy prices and home-purchase and financing costs (which typically are not closely related to labor cost trends), and income policies. Measures of product market disequilibrium, such as the GNP gap or the ratio of unfilled orders to production capacity, were found to be insignificant in the price equation.

The labor cost variable is the percentage change in trend unit labor costs (TRENDULC); it is entered both currently and lagged one and two quarters. The pay component of the unit-labor-cost variable is CHPAY, and the trend-productivity-growth component is constructed by regressing the percentage change in nonfarm output per man-hour on time and cylical variables. The coefficient should be positive and about equal to labor's share of production costs.

Because pricing decisions may be affected by current as well as by trend growth of unit labor costs, the deviation of current from trend productivity growth (PRODEV) is included as an explanatory variable. When PRODEV is positive, current unit labor costs are rising more slowly than trend unit labor costs, placing downward pressure on prices; hence, this coefficient should be negative.

The effect of energy price increases on inflation is estimated by including a free-form three-quarter distributed lag on the weighted percentage change in the energy price component of the Consumer Price Index (ENERGY), where the weight is the relative importance of energy in the CPI. The current weighted percentage change in the price index for home purchase and financing costs (HOMEPUR & INT) is also included; again, the weight is the relative importance of this component in the CPI. The coefficients of these variables are expected to be positive. The incomes policy variables are the same as in the pay equation.[13]

The Glossary at the end of the chapter defines the variables with greater precision and describes their construction where appropriate.

Empirical Results

Tables 1 and 2 display the ordinary least-squares estimates of the pay and price equations.

PAY EQUATION   The coefficients of the principal explanatory variables of the pay equation in Table 1—lagged price inflation, the adjusted unemployment rate, and the employment tax and minimum wage variables—all

TABLE 1. Pay Equation[a]

CONSTANT	3.479
	(18.507)
CHCPI[b]	.705
	(17.130)
UR	−.550
	(−6.307)
SSTAX	1.087
	(8.689)
CHMINWAGE	.010
	(3.580)
DATADUM[c]	−1.731
	(−1.984)
GUIDEPOSTS	−.857
	(−3.450)
ESP1	.321
	(.789)
ESP2	−1.127
	(−2.350)
POSTCONTROL	.513
	(.842)
STANDARDS	−.978
	(−2.020)
RBSQ	.880
DW	1.935
SE	.843

[a] The dependent variable is CHPAY. The numbers in parentheses are t statistics. The sample period is 1954:II to 1980:III.
[b] Entered as a third-degree polynomial distributed lag, with the far endpoint constrained to equal zero. The lag length is 12 quarters, starting with the variable lagged 1 quarter.
[c] A dummy equal to 1 in 1964:I and zero elsewhere to reflect the joining of two Average Hourly Earnings Index series in the construction of CHPAY.

have the expected signs, are of reasonable magnitudes, and are highly statistically significant. The sum of the coefficients on the price variables, .7, however, is statistically significant below 1, indicating the presence of some money illusion.[14]

The estimates indicate that the Kennedy/Johnson guidelines depressed the rate of wage inflation by almost a full percentage point; moreover,

TABLE 2. Price Equation[a]

CONSTANT	.107
	(.476)
TRENDULC	.289
	(3.921)
TRENDULC$_{-1}$	.269
	(3.626)
TRENDULC$_{-2}$	.127
	(1.695)
PRODDEV	−.107
	(−3.048)
ENERGY	.687
	(4.807)
ENERGY$_{-1}$	−.015
	(−.101)
ENERGY$_{-2}$	.358
	(2.540)
HOMEPUR & INT	.860
	(6.373)
GUIDEPOSTS	.496
	(1.657)
ESP1	−1.198
	(−2.427)
ESP2	2.215
	(4.008)
POSTCONTROL	.158
	(.250)
STANDARDS	−.315
	−(.481)
RBSQ	0.929
DW	1.867
SE	1.029

[a]The dependent variable is CHCPI. The same period is 1954:II to 1980:III.

the estimated coefficient is decidedly statistically significant.[15] The ESP1 and ESP2 coefficients suggest that Phases I and II were probably ineffective in restraining pay and that the acceleration in prices during Phases III and IV was not passed through in the usual manner to wages.[16]

Finally, the coefficient on the STANDARDS variable is negative and significantly different from zero at the 95% confidence level. Thus there is a high probability that this program slowed the rate of growth of pay. Most likely, the annual percentage growth would have been about a percentage point greater without the program, as indicated by the estimated coefficient on STANDARDS.

PRICE EQUATION   The principal structural coefficients of the price equation in Table 2—changes in trend unit labor costs, deviations of productivity growth from trend, energy price changes, and changes in home purchase prices and mortgage interest costs—for the most part have the expected signs, are statistically significant, and are of reasonable magnitudes. The trend-unit-labor-cost coefficients sum to about .7, which is roughly equal to the share of total costs accounted for by labor. The estimated coefficients of PRODEV indicate that about 10% of short-run productivity variations are reflected in price changes (the remainder presumably are absorbed in profit changes). Finally, the sum of the coefficients of the energy price variable and the coefficient of the home-purchase-and-mortgage-interest-cost variables are close to 1, indicating that the feedback effects of shocks in these sectors are adequately picked up by the unit-labor-cost variables.

The coefficients of the dummy variables for the 1960s guideposts and the early 1970s ESP are somewhat surprising. The positive coefficient of the GUIDEPOSTS variable, while not highly statistically significant, suggests that the labor cost savings attributable to that program were not fully passed through in the form of commensurately lower price inflation (a coefficient of +.6—obtained by multiplying .86 by .7, the sum of the coefficients on trend unit labor costs—would completely nullify the negative .86 percentage point effect of the program on pay). While this result is consistent with the design and administration of the guideposts program—which focused primarily on the fairly rigid 3.2% wage guidepost—it is not consistent with the conventional wisdom that product markets are sufficiently competitive to assure a pass-through of labor cost savings generated by a wage-side incomes policy. The coefficients on ESP1, ESP2, and POSTCONTROL suggest that a large (and statistically significant) catch-up, which more than offset the salutary effects of Phases I and II, took place during the period of gradual decontrol (Phases III and IV) rather than after the program ended.[17]

Finally, the STANDARDS coefficient suggests that the Carter program directly reduced the rate of increase of the CPI by 0.3 percentage points. This effect, however, is not statistically different from zero.

EVALUATION OF THE RESULTS   A reasonable interpretation of these results is that the Nixon controls program was probably ineffective but that
both the Kennedy/Johnson guideposts program and the Carter standards program lowered the rate of wage inflation by about one percentage point and that, at least in the latter program, this lower rate of
labor cost inflation was passed through in the form of commensurately
lower price inflation. Because the unit-labor-cost coefficients in the price
equation sum to 0.7, a one-percentage point decline in wage inflation
lowers price inflation by about 0.7 percentage point. This calculation,
however, reflects only the direct effect of the lowering of labor cost
inflation. Because the change in the price level is an explanatory variable
in the pay equation, there is a feedback effect that must be taken into
account in assessing the full impact of these two programs. Using the
method of postsample simulation,[18] the Council on Wage and Price
Stability estimated the total effect of the standards program on price
inflation, taking into account the interaction between prices and wages,
at about one full percentage point.[19]

Econometric wage and price equations tend to be nonrobust, i.e., the
estimated coefficients and hypothesis tests are often quite sensitive to the
specification of the model. In order to test for the robustness of its
results, the Council carried out an extensive sensitivity analysis. In
particular, in the pay equations, it experimented with alternative forms of
the lag on the CPI, alternative measures of labor market slack (e.g., the
gap between actual and potential GNP and the unemployment rate of
prime-age males), different forms of dummies for the Nixon controls
program, and different measures or prices. In the price equation, it
examined the effect of eliminating the energy and home-purchase and
interest variables, of including measures of market slackness, and of
using different dummies for the Nixon controls program.

The estimates of the effects of the incomes policies on wage inflation
were found to be insensitive to all changes in the specifications save one:
use of the Fixed Weight Consumption Expenditure deflator from the
GNP accounts instead of the CPI as a measure of changes in the cost of
living. This substitution had no effect on the estimated effects of the
guideposts program and the ESP, but it did cut the effect of the standards
program in half and lowered the t statistic to 1.0. The principal difference
between these two measures of price inflation is inclusion of mortgage

interest rates and home purchase prices in the CPI but not in the PCE index. The two indexes behaved almost identically during the guidepost and ESP periods, but diverged markedly during the standards program, when soaring interest rates and home purchase costs drove the CPI up by 1.7 percentage points per year more than the PCE index.

The specification using the PCE index assumes that none of the extra housing-cost inflation in the CPI feeds through to wage changes. The Council concluded, however, that the specification using the CPI results in the more reliable estimate of the effects of the standards program on wage inflation. The equation using the CPI fits the data better, suggesting that the CPI is the better measure of price inflation for the purpose of explaining pay rates, i.e., that pay rates are responsive to changes in home purchase prices and mortgage interest costs. Moreover, when the Council tested this hypothesis directly by including the percentage change in the home-purchase-and-mortgage-interest-cost component of the CPI in the equation using the PCE index, the coefficient was statistically significant at the 95% confidence level. This indicates that the equation using the PCE index is misspecified.

The only finding in the sensitivity analysis of the price equation that needs explanation is the result that, when the energy and housing cost variables are excluded from the price equation, the goodness of fit deteriorates considerably and the price standard is estimated to have *increased* price inflation by four percentage points.

This result is understandable if one considers what happened to these variables during the time the standards program was in place. Over the entire estimation period, the energy price variable (ENERGY) averaged 0.5% and the housing cost variable (HOMEPUR & INT) averaged 1.0%. There were two periods, however, when energy prices exploded: 1973:IV–1974:II, when the (weighted) percentage change averaged 3.4; and 1979:I–1980:II, when it averaged 3.9. Similarly, the weighted percentage change in housing costs exploded to an average of 2.4 over the period 1973:III–1975:II and to 4.2 over the 1978:II–1980:II period. When energy prices and housing costs are dropped from the equation, the coefficients on TRENDULC, ESP2, POSTCONTROL, and STANDARDS change markedly, because each of these variables is highly correlated with energy and housing: ESP2 and POSTCONTROL came into effect during the first period, STANDARDS was on during most of the second price explosion, and TRENDULC was relatively high in both periods.

The decision on whether to include or exclude energy prices from the price equation turns on the degree of their exogeneity. The Council's treatment assumes that energy prices are exogenous. To the extent that they are, excluding them from the equation results in upward biases in the coefficients of other variables. This can explain the excessively large coefficients on trend unit labor costs in the equation, which sum to .95 (indicating a more-than-proportional passthrough of labor cost increases). The equation with these variables omitted also ascribes to the ESP, as well as to the associated postcontrols catch-up, a large positive effect on the inflation rate, presumably because of the upward bias caused by the failure to take account of the effects of the 1973–74 energy crisis. Similarly, to the extent that energy prices are endogenous, the Council's basic equation, which includes these variables, attributes too much of the inflation increases of the 1970s to energy (an upward bias on its coeffi cients) and too little to the rise in unit labor costs, ESP2, POSTCON-TROL, and STANDARDS (a downward bias).

Similarly, housing costs are included as an explanatory variable because home prices and interest rates are not directly determined by the other explanatory variables in the price equation—most notably, unit labor costs. Again, however, to the extent that increases in such costs simply reflect increases in the overall inflation rate, the coefficient on housing costs is biased upward, while the STANDARDS coefficients is biased downward.

On balance, however, the Council's basic conclusion, which is that the price standard had no net effect on price inflation, is the more believable. It fits the data better, and the coefficients on unit labor costs are more plausible.

SUMMARY REMARKS AND AFTERTHOUGHTS

The debate about incomes policy tends to turn on strongly held ideological and theoretical preconceptions. Partly this is because there are respectable theories and ideologies to support both sides of this policy debate, and partly it is because the empirical evidence about the efficacy of incomes policies is inconclusive. Judged against the unrealistic expectations held by many—especially in European countries (see Ulman and Flanagan, 1971)—incomes policies would have to be deemed dismal failures. They cannot be used as an alternative to macroeconomic restraints, and they are not the answer to stagflation.

The econometric evidence about the efficacy of incomes policies is mixed. In standard econometric models of the wage-price process, the coefficients of dummy variables representing various incomes policies are sometimes statistically significant and sometimes not. Moreover, since these hypothesis tests lack robustness, reasonable changes in the specification of the wage and price equations often result in opposite conclusions about the effectiveness of incomes policies. Therefore search can typically uncover plausible models of wage and price determination that support either point of view.

The econometric analysis in this paper of the effectiveness of three incomes policies adopted in the United States in the last two decades is unlikely to convert either avid proponents or staunch opponents of such policies. It marshals strong evidence that the Kennedy/Johnson guideposts restrained the rate of inflation, and it provides an arguable case for a modest effect of the Carter standards program. The much more ambitious mandatory controls program of the early 1970s, however, appears to have done more harm than good. Thus both proponents and opponents can justifiably point to the success or failure of previous experiments with direct government attempts to restrain wage and price increases.

As I read the record of income policies, I believe they can be effective instruments of antiinflation policies for very short periods of time. If intelligently designed and prudently administered, they can generate a small one-time downward shift in the Phillips curve, thus facilitating the implementation of restrictive macroeconomic policies. It is, however, a mistake to perceive them as long-term antiinflation policies. The longer such policies are in effect, the more complicated and legalistic they become. Distortions and market disruptions, which may initially be of minimal proportions, gradually accumulate until the induced inefficiency costs of the program become onerous. In addition, the program inevitably becomes entangled in controversy over issues of equity. There are an untold number of design issues whose resolution will inevitably work to the benefit of some and the disadvantage of others. Important and powerful political-economic groups will have selfishly different views of what constitutes equity in the design and implementation of the incomes policies. Moreover, incomes policies are vulnerable to extraneous shocks (such as the world oil price explosion). Finally, the political temptation to relax fiscal and monetary policies, under the delusion that incomes policy alone can keep the lid on inflation, can generate inflationary pressures that torpedo the incomes policy. Perhaps Arthur Okun said it best:

In attempting to offer an overall appraisal of informal programs of wage restraint, I am remined of P. T. Barnum's statement that a lamb can be kept in a lion's cage if one has an adequate supply of lambs. I believe these programs can make a noticeable contribution for a substantial period of time, but they are ultimately doomed by various types of lions—excess demand, people determined to be noncooperative, or unrelated cost disturbances. (1981, p. 345)

GLOSSARY*

CHPAY	percentage change in PAY.
PAY	$J \times WSS/WS$.
J	Average Hourly Earnings Index of production workers in the total private nonfarm sector. This series is adjusted for overtime (in manufacturing) and for interindustry shifts in employment. Bureau of Labor Statistics (BLS).
WSS	compensation of employees. National Income Accounts (NIA).
WS	wages and salaries (NIA).
CHCPI	percentage change in the Consumer Price Index for urban consumers (all items) (BLS).
UR	unemployment rate for civilian workers less the natural unemployment rate calculated by Gordon (1978) (BLS).
SSTAX	percentage change in $1/(1 - TWER/WS)$.
TWER	employer contributions for social insurance (NIA).
CHMINWAGE	percentage change in the minimum hourly wage for all covered and nonexempt workers (not seasonally adjusted) (Office of Fair Labor Statistics, Department of Labor).

*Unless otherwise noted, all variables are seasonally adjusted. All percentage changes are at annual rates.

GUIDEPOSTS	.25 for 1962:I, .5 for 1962:II, .75 for 1962:III, 1 for 1964:II–1966:IV, .75 for 1967:I, .5 for 1967:II, .25 for 1967:III, zero otherwise.
ESP1	.5 for 1971:III, 1 for 1971:IV–1972:IV, .167 for 1973:I, zero otherwise.
ESP2	.833 for 1973:I, 1 for 1973:II–1974:I, .333 for 1974:II, zero otherwise.
POSTCONTROL	1 for 1974:III–1975:II, zero otherwise.
STANDARDS	1 for 1978:IV–1980:III, zero otherwise.
TRENDULC	CHPAY less TRENDPROD.
TRENDPROD	estimated trend rate of productivity growth, obtained by regressing CHPROD on CHGAP, $CHGAP_{-1}$, TIME, and DEOE, the period of estimation being 1953:I–1980:III, and using the fitted values setting CHGAP, $CHGAP_{-1}$, and DEOE equal to zero.
CHPROD	percentage change in output per man-hour in the non-farm business sector (BLS).
CHGAP	percentage change in (GNP72/POTGNP72)
TIME	1 for 1953:I, 2 for 1953:II, and so on.
DEOE	end-of-expansion dummy constructed by Gordon (1979).
ENERGY	weighted percentage change in the energy component of the Consumer Price Index, the weight being its relative importance in the CPI (not seasonally adjusted). Constructed using BLS data.
HOMEPUR & INT	weighted percentage change in the home-purchase and mortgage-interest-cost component for the Consumer Price Index, the weight being its relative importance in the CPI (not seasonally adjusted). Constructed using BLS data.
PRODEV	CHPROD less TRENDPROD.
ESPG1	1 for 1971:III–1972:IV, zero elsewhere.
ESPG2	1 for 1974:II–1975:I, zero elsewhere.

NOTES

1. In this country, polls typically reveal a substantial popular (nearly two-to-one) preference for wage and price controls (see *The Gallup Opinion Index*, June 1979, Report No. 167, p. 20). Professional economists, on the other hand, typically express skepticism, if not adamant opposition (see Kearl et al., 1979).

2. It is only fair to warn the reader that I helped design and administer the last-mentioned program.

3. Lowering aggregate demand, that is, below what it would be in the absence of the restraint. This may only mean lower growth; it need not mean recession.

4. Recession (lower growth), like inflation, has significant income-redistribution effects, but whether they are deemed social costs depends on one's values.

5. The short run here is a year. The conventional wisdom has adopted the "accelerationist" theory of Friedman (1961) and Phelps (1968) that in the long run there is no trade-off between unemployment and inflation; that is, the long-run Phillips curve is vertical (see Frisch, 1981). The short-run Phillips curve, however, is very flat; during the long disequilibrium period of disinflation, the short-run trade-off can impose huge costs on society.

6. The theory of implicit contracts is a close cousin to the explanation of unemployment and downward wage rigidity recently proposed by Solow (1980). The genesis of Solow's notion can be found in the classical treatise of Pigou (1933, p. 225): " ... public opinion in a modern civilized State builds up for itself a rough estimate of what constitutes a reasonable living wage." Pigou was referring specifically to minimum wage laws, but Solow (1980, p. 5) suggests that such feelings "also come into play as a deterrent to wage cutting in a slack labor market. Unemployed workers rarely try to displace their employed counterparts by offering to work for less."

7. An alternative explanation of downward wage-price rigidity was articulated recently by Cagan (1981). Briefly, the output-loss response to a reduction in the money supply is characterized as a second-best solution to a prisoner's dilemma game. The best outcome of a reduction in the money supply would be for all agents to reduce their prices immediately to the new equilibrium level, thus obviating the output losses. If, however, only some agents react instantaneously by reducing their prices to the new equilibrium levels, the result will be some output loss and some redistribution of wealth from those who cut prices immediately to those who do not. Consequently, agents rationally postpone cutting their prices until they are convinced that others are doing the same. I believe that this conception is closer to the mark than either of the theories discussed in this chapter—it certainly corresponds closely to the rhetoric of organized labor and the business community in discussions of wage and price restraint—but it has not yet been developed into a rigorous theory of the wage-price process. In this perception, incomes policies provide the first-best solution to the prisoner's dilemma game by convincing price setters that all will simultaneously adjust to the new equilibrium.

8. The original formulation is $MV = PT$, where T is the number of transactions per period (hence, PT is the value of transactions). In practice, however, the equation simply defines the velocity of money. Thus, $V = PQ/M$ is the output-based (e.g., GNP-based) velocity, and $V = PT/M$ is the transactions-based velocity. Indeed, velocity is also sensitive to the definition of the money supply and the price level.

9. See Gramlich (1979) for a thorough analysis of macroeconomic policy responses to inflation shocks.

10. In fact, it may be that the short-term effectiveness of the program was primarily attributable to the resultant *delays* in price increases. Note that this could also be a factor in the postcontrols price surge.

11. Pencavel (1980) suggests that the Kennedy/Johnson wage guidelines primarily affected collective bargaining settlements, resulting in a narrowing of the union-nonunion wage differential, and that this in turn led to a spate of large settlements in the late 1960s that restored the differential.

12. The most recent version (Lerner and Colander, 1979) entails marketable rights for increases in value added (essentially labor and capital costs). The total amount of "antiinflation credit" would be determined by the economy-wide productivity growth rate, and the initial allocation to firms would be based on their initial levels of net sales.

12a. The analysis was carried out under my direction by the staff of the Council—especially John Hagens.

13. The dummy variables model the effects of incomes policies as shifts in the intercepts of the wage and price equations. This can be interpreted as vertical displacements of the (short-run) Phillips curve, without changing its slope. An objective of such policies, however, may be to change the slope of the Phillips curve—i.e., to improve the trade-off between unemployment and wage inflation, thus lowering the cost of restrictive monetary and fiscal policies. This effect can be modeled by an interactive dummy, in which the incomes policies change the coefficient of UR in the wage equation. Unfortunately, attempts to estimate this effect were unsuccessful, presumably because of the fierce multicollinearity between UR and, say, STANDARDS*UR (the interactive variable). Similar attempts to model the effect of incomes policies on price expectations (on the coefficients of CHCPI in the wage equation) met the same fate.

14. More likely is a statistical confounding of the coefficients of the price variables and the constant term, which can be interpreted as trend productivity growth (the growth rate of hourly labor compensation in a stable price environment). A larger coefficient sum on prices and a lower constant term would be more reasonable (since annual productivity growth averaged much less than 3.5% over the estimation period).

15. This result is consistent with results obtained by others (see, e.g., Eckstein and Brinner 1972; and Perry, 1970, 1980).

16. Other econometric analyses of the ESP focus exclusively on prices, either because of the supposition that the program had no direct effect on wages (see, e.g., Blinder and Newton, 1981) or because such effects are taken into account

indirectly through the effect of unit labor costs on prices (see, e.g., Frye and Gordon, 1981).

17. Blinder and Newton (1981) and Frye and Gordon (1981) both conclude that the catch-up occurred after the controls ended. Of course, their model specifications differ from those of the Council's (as they do from each other) in several respects. In any event, whether the catch-up took place during the period of decontrol or after the program was abolished is not a matter of great importance.

18. The postsample simulation approach uses preprogram data to estimate econometric models which are then used to predict endogenous variables during periods when the program is in effect. The estimated effect of the program during each period is the discrepancy between the predicted and the actual values of the endogenous variables.

19. Frye and Gordon (1981) obtain a similar point estimate, but their coefficient is statistically insignificant (their t statistic is -1.08).

REFERENCES

Ackley, G. (1978). "The Costs of Inflation." *American Economic Review* 68:144–154.

Alchian, A. A. (1969). "Information Costs, Pricing and Resource Unemployment." *Western Economic Journal* 7:109–128.

Azariadis, C. (1975). "Implicit Contracts and Unemployment Equilibria." *Journal of Political Economy* 83:1183–1202.

Baily, M. N. (1974). "Wages and Employment under Uncertain Demand." *Review of Economic Studies* 41:37–50.

Blinder, A. S., and W. J. Newton (1981). "The 1971–1974 Controls Program and the Price Level: An Econometric Post-Mortem." *Journal of Monetary Economics* 8:1–23.

Bosworth, B. (1972). "Phase II: The U.S. Experiment with an Incomes Policy." *Brookings Papers on Economic Activity* 2:343–384.

Cagan, P. (1981). "Comment." Presented at the Conference on Expectations Formation and Economic Disequilibrium, C. V. Starr Center for Applied Economics, New York University.

Council on Wage and Price Stability (1981). *Evaluation of the Pay and Price Standards Program*.

Darby, Michael R. (1976). "Price and Wage Controls: The First Two Years." In K. Brunner and A. Meltzer (eds.), *The Economics of Price and Wage Controls*. Carnegie-Rochester Conference Series, Vol. 2. University of California at Los Angeles, Los Angeles, Calif.

Dildine, L. L., and E. M. Sunley (1978). "Administrative Problems of Tax-Based Incomes Policies." In A. M. Okun and G. L. Perry (eds.), *Curing Chronic Inflation*. Washington, D.C.: Brookings Institution.

Dunlop, J. T., and K. J. Fedor (1977). *The Lessons of Wage and Price Controls—the Food Sector*. Boston: Division of Research, Graduate School of Business Administration, Harvard University.

Eads, G. (1976). *The Commodity Shortages of 1973–1974: Case Studies*. National Commission on Supplies and Shortages.

Eckstein, O., and R. Brinner (1972). "The Inflation Process in the United States." Joint Economic Committee report.

Feige, E. L., and D. Pearce (1976). "Inflation and Incomes Policy: An Application of Time Series Models." In K. Brunner and A. Meltzer (eds.), *The Economics of Price and Wage Controls*. Carnegie-Rochester Conference Series, Vol. 2. Eau Claire, Wisc.: University of Wisconsin, Dept. of Economics.

Friedman, Milton (1961). "The Lag in the Effect of Monetary Policy." *Journal of Political Economy* 69:447–466.

Frisch, H. (1981). "Inflation Theory 1963–1975: A 'Second Generation' Survey." *Journal of Economic Literature* 19:1289–1317.

Frye, J. F., and R. J. Gordon (1981). "Government Intervention in the Inflation Process: The Econometrics of 'Self-Inflicted Wounds.'" *American Economic Review* 71:288–244.

Gordon, D. F. (1976). "A Neo-Classical Theory of Keynesian Unemployment." In K. Brunner and A. Meltzer (eds.), *The Phillips Curve and Labor Markets*. Amsterdam: North-Holland.

Gordon, R. J. (1973). "The Response of Wages and Prices to the First Two Years of Controls." *Brookings Papers on Economic Activity* 3:765–778.

_____ (1975). "The Impact of Aggregate Demand on Prices." *Brookings Papers on Economic Activity* 3:613–662.

_____ (1978). *Macroeconomics*. Boston: Little, Brown.

_____ (1979). "The End-of-Expansion Phenomenon in Short-Run Productivity Behavior." *Brookings Papers on Economic Behavior*, pp. 447–461.

Gramlich, E. M. (1979). "Macro Policy Responses to Price Shocks." *Brookings Papers on Economic Activity* 1:125–166.

Holt, C. C. (1970). "Job Search, Phillips' Wage Relation, and Union Influence: Theory and Evidence." In E. S. Phelps (ed.), *Microeconomic Foundations of Employment and Inflation Theory*. New York: W. W. Norton.

Kearl, J. R., C. L. Pope, G. C. Whiting, and L. T. Simmer (1979). "What Economists Think.' A Confusion of Economists?" *American Economic Review* 69:28–37.

Klein, B. (1976). "The Social Costs of the Recent Inflation: The Mirage of Steady 'Anticipated' Inflation." *Journal of Monetary Economics* 3:185–212.

Lanzillotti, R. F., M. T. Hamilton, and B. R. Roberts (1975). *Phase II in Review: The Price Commission Experience*. Washington, D.C.: Brookings Institution.

Lerner, Abba P. (1977). "Stagflation—Its Cause and Cure." *Challenge* 20:14–19.

———— (1978). "A Wage-Increase Permit Plan to Stop Inflation." In A. M. Okun and G. L. Perry (eds):, *Curing Chronic Inflation*. Washington: Brookings Institution.

————, and D. C. Colander (1979). "MAP: A Cure for Inflation." In D. C. Colander (ed), *Solutions to Inflation*. New York: Harcourt Brace Jovanovich.

Lipsey, R. G., and J. M. Parkin (1970). "Incomes Policy: A Reappraisal." *Economica* 37:1–31.

Logue, D. E., and T. D. Willett (1976). "A Note on the Relation Between the Rate and Variability of Inflation." *Economica* 46:151–158.

Lucas, R. E., Jr. (1972). "Expectations and the Neutrality of Money." *Journal of Economic Theory* 4:103–124.

Mayer, T. (1978). *The Structure of Monetarism*. New York: W. W. Norton.

McGuire, T. W. (1976). "On Estimating the Effects of Controls." In K. Brunner and A. Meltzer (eds.), *The Economics of Price and Wage Controls*. Carnegie-Rochester Conference Series, Vol. 2. Pittsburgh: Carnegie-Mellon University.

Mortensen, Dale T. (1970). "A Theory of Wage and Employment Dynamics." In *Microeconomic Foundations of Employment and Inflation Theory*, New York: W. W. Norton.

Oi, W. Y. (1976). "On Measuring the Impact of Wage-Price Controls: A Critical Appraisal." In K. Brunner and A. Meltzer (eds.), *The Economics of Price and Wage Controls*. Carnegie-Rochester Conference Series, Vol. 2. Rochester, N.Y.: University of Rochester.

Okun, A. M. (1971). "The Mirage of Steady Inflation." *Brookings Papers on Economic Activity* 2:485–498.

———— (1975). "Inflation: Its Mechanics and Welfare Costs." *Brookings Papers on Economic Activity* 2:366–373.

———— (1978). "Efficient Disinflationary Policies." *American Economic Review* 68:348–352.

———— (1979). "A Reward TIP." In D. C. Colander (ed.), *Solutions to Inflation*. New York: Harcourt Brace Jovanovich.

———— (1981). *Prices and Quantities: A Macroeconomic Analysis*. Washington, D. C.: Brookings Institution.

Pencavel, J. H. (1980). "The American Experience with Incomes Policies." Discussion Paper No. 26, Stanford University Workshop on the Microeconomics of Inflation.

Perry, G. L. (1970). "Changing Labor Markets and Inflation." *Brookings Papers on Economic Activity* 3:411–448.

———— (1980). "Inflation in Theory and Practice." *Brookings Papers on Economic Activity* 1:207–241.

Phelps, E. S. (1968). "Money-Wage Dynamics and Labor-Market Equilibrium." *Journal of Political Economy* 76: 687–711.

———— (1969). "The New Microeconomics of Inflation and Employment Theory." *American Economic Review* 59:147–167.

_____ (1979). "Introduction: Developments in Non-Walrasian Theory." In E. S. Phelps (ed.), *Studies in Macroeconomic Theory: Employment and Inflation*. Vol. 1. New York: Academic Press.

Pigou, A. C. (1945). *Lapses from Full Employment*. London: Macmillan.

Rockoff, H. (1981). "Price and Wage Controls in Four Wartime Periods." *The Journal of Economic History* 61:381–401.

Schultze, C. L. (1980). "Why Controls Don't Work." *Wall Street Journal*, February 27.

Seidman, L. S. (1978). "Tax-Based Incomes Policies." In A. M. Okun and G. L. Perry (eds.), *Curing Chronic Inflation*. Washington, D.C.: Brookings Institution.

Sheehan, J. (1967). *The Wage-Price Guideposts*. Washington, D.C.: Brookings Institution.

Solow, R. M. (1980). "On Theories of Unemployment." *American Economic Review* 70:1–11.

Stein, H. (1980). "Dear C.O.W.P.S." *Wall Street Journal*, July 19.

Ulman, L., and R. J. Flanagan (1971). *Wage Restraint: A Study of Incomes Policies in Western Europe*. Berkeley: University of California.

Wallich, H. C., and S. Weintraub (1971). "A Tax-Based Incomes Policy," *Journal of Economic Issues* 5:1–19.

Weber, A. R. (1973). *In Pursuit of Price Stability: The Wage Price Freeze of 1971*. Washington, D.C.: Brookings Institution.

_____ , and D. J. B. Mitchell (1978). *The Pay Board's Progress: Wage Controls in Phase II*. Washington, D.C.: Brookings Institution.

6: Politics and Economics
in Everyday Life

Donald R. Kinder and Walter R. Mebane, Jr.

Over the past dozen years, social scientists have ratified what American politicians have known in their bones since FDR: that prosperity enhances the electoral chances of incumbents, sustains a president's popularity, and strengthens the political hand of the sitting government (e.g., see Kramer, 1971; Tufte, 1975, 1978; Bloom and Price, 1975; Frey and Schneider, 1978; Hibbs, 1982; Kernell, 1978). Citizens' political preferences, everyone knows, are creatures of economic circumstance. But just how does this happen? Precisely how do people know whether incumbents have succeeded or failed? What kinds of economic evidence do they weigh? Preoccupied as we are with such questions, we develop in this chapter an argument about the political economy of *individuals*, not governments, about the intertwining of economics and politics in everyday life.

Central to our argument is the claim that people possess and can articulate beliefs about the causes of and responsibilities for economic circumstances—their own and the country's. Such beliefs constitute what we will call "ordinary economic theory." However unsophisticated or peculiar they may seem to economists, such theories should reveal a great deal about the connections people make, and fail to make, between their own economic circumstances, the economic circumstances of the nation, and the performance of government.

Our efforts here are motivated in part by the puzzles left by previous work. The effects of aggregate economic conditions on collective political outcomes are of course compatible with any number of theories about people. Attention has so far concentrated on just two. The first and more popular emphasizes the political significance of personal economic circumstances. Pocketbook voters, as we call them, support candidates and parties that advance their economic interests and oppose candidates and parties that seem to threaten them. Such a political calculus is attractive because it appears to promise drastic reductions in the costs that are otherwise incurred in learning about politics. "In order to ascertain whether the incumbents have performed poorly or well, citizens need only calculate the changes in their own welfare" (Fiorina, 1981, p. 5).

This pocketbook logic can be traced back at least to Hobbes. In one form or another, it is insinuated throughout contemporary political analysis. There's just one problem: while the economic circumstances of personal life do occasionally influence political choice, the effects are never very strong and usually they are utterly trivial. For example, declining financial condition, job loss, preoccupation with personal economic problems—none of these seems generally to motivate presidential voting (Fiorina, 1981; Kiewiet, 1981; Kinder and Abelson, 1981; Kinder and Kiewiet, 1981; Sigelman and Tsai, 1982).[1] Results are even less friendly to pocketbook assumptions in House elections (Fiorina, 1981; Kinder and Kiewiet, 1979, 1981).[2]

Nor do matters improve when we consider other kinds of political effects. Personal economic adversity has virtually no influence on Americans' allegiance to party (Fiorina, 1981; Kinder and Kiewiet, 1981). Similarly, job loss and diminishing financial position have little to do with the confidence Americans express in government (Denney et al., 1980; Kinder, 1981; Kinder et al., 1983). Finally, economic self-interest has modest, highly specific, and often negligible effects on which policies people endorse (e.g., see Hibbs, 1979; Kinder, et al., 1983; Schlozman and Verba, 1979; Sears et al., 1978, 1980).

So the reality of pocketbook politics in no way measures up to its mythology. To be sure, there are indications of economic self-interest at work in American mass politics, but the indications are more intermittent and uniformly weaker than originally imagined. One purpose of this chapter is to offer a general way of understanding why it is that pocketbook assumptions fail empirical tests so regularly—and why it is that they occasionally succeed.[3]

Whereas pocketbook voters might ask the political system and its officials, "What have you done for *me* lately?," voters of another mind would ask, "What have you done for the *country* lately?" We call such creatures "sociotropic" voters (Kinder and Kiewiet, 1979, 1981; Kinder, 1981; Kinder et al., 1983). Their political preferences are shaped by the country's economic condition, not their own. Sociotropic voters support candidates and parties that appear to further the nation's economic well-being and oppose candidates and parties that seem to threaten it. Although less popular than pocketbook assumptions, a sociotropic political calculus constitutes a second and competing general approach to individual political economy—and one which has met with rather more empirical success.

A first question for a sociotropic calculus is, of course, whether people distinguish between their own economic circumstances and the nation's. If they do not, then we have written a very short chapter. They do and we haven't. In assessing the nation's economic condition, people do not simply extrapolate from their own difficulties or achievements. Personal economic predicaments are largely autonomous from judgments Americans reach about economic problems in society (Kinder and Kiewiet, 1981; Mebane, 1982; the same holds true in Britain; Alt, 1978).[4] Moreover, assessments of the nation's economic condition do seem to affect political choice: in the votes Americans cast in presidential elections, presidential primaries, and House elections; in the identifications they develop with political parties; in the approval they confer upon the incumbent president; and more generally, in the confidence they express in their national government (Fiorina, 1981; Kiewiet, 1981; Kinder and Abelson, 1981; Kinder and Kiewiet, 1979, 1981; Kinder, 1981; Kinder et al., 1983). All this suggests the promise of the sociotropic view.[5]

The chief business of this chapter, taking into account the foregoing results, is to present and then test a general approach to understanding the intertwining of economics and politics in everyday life. In so doing, we will move beyond the starkest version of the pocketbook-sociotropic contrast, seeking to elucidate the possibly intricate details of how people understand the relation between economic and political realities. We approach this problem by taking seriously the ordinary person's theory of economics. Just what we mean by this is set out in the next part of the chapter. From there we move on to explore what form such theories take and then to test whether, as we claim, such theories matter. The chapter closes by drawing out the implications of what we have learned so far, and speculating about what we should try to learn next.

ORDINARY ECONOMIC THEORIES

Our particular construction of the way people understand relations between economics and politics draws on a general theory of understanding being developed in cognitive science (e.g., see Anderson and Bower, 1973; Schank and Abelson, 1977). This theory (more precisely, this family of theories) takes understanding to be a process whereby new events are interpreted in terms of old knowledge. Happenings are understood to the degree they are recognized as particular instances of familiar general types. Thus the news that the Reagan administration is stepping up military assistance to El Salvador may be understood by some as one more doomed, imperialist misadventure. Understanding the particular event comes through the eliciting of a general interpretive framework.

In psychological parlance, such frameworks are customarily referred to as "schemas" (Bartlett, 1932; Taylor and Crocker, 1982). Schemas are informal, tacit theories people hold about the world—about other people (called "prototypes": Rosch, 1977; Cantor and Mischel, 1979); about groups in society ("stereotypes": Hamilton, 1981); and about sequences of events ("scripts": Abelson, 1981; Schank and Abelson, 1977). Such theories provide the context within which new developments are understood.

Our special interest here is in the informal, tacit theories people hold about economics. Such theories serve the average person much as formal, explicit theories serve the economist. They provide explanations. They furnish predictions. They supply proposals for intervention and reform.

There is, of course, every reason to expect that the economic theories of ordinary men and women will be less complete and less internally consistent than the formal theories of professional economists. What passes for credible theory in everyday discourse may severely disappoint economists, to say nothing of philosophers of science. This is especially true for ordinary beliefs about the national economy. The agents and mechanisms underlying national events may seem abstract and mysterious. They may be remote from the tangible details of everyday life. And even if ordinary Americans were conversant with contemporary economic theory, recent events would probably confuse them. Consider Heilbroner's (1979) confession:

> After years of intensive study, we [economists] still do not know whether an increase in the supply of money is the cause of inflation or merely its passive accompaniment. We do not know whether wage increases lead inflation or follow it. We do not know if falling productivity is the source of rising prices or a quite unconnected factor. We do not know whether inflations are cumulative, pressing insidiously toward a runaway hyperinflation such as that of Weimar, Germany, or whether inflation may have self-limiting properties. We do not know whether inflation mainly penalizes the poor or the rich, or whether it tends to raise income groups in roughly unchanged order, as an incoming tide raises all ships, large and small. Or, to put the matter differently, we can adduce facts and theories to support both sides of all these questions, blaming the monetary authorities or exonerating them, excoriating or excusing labor unions. The blame can be fixed in turn on the Arabs, the farmers, the government, the consumer, big business, or, in some vague way, on "us." (pp. 132–133)

Given disarray in expert opinion, it would be unreasonable to expect confident, coherent economic theory from average folks. Yet however confused or unsophisticated or just plain wrong such theories might turn out to be, they should nevertheless constrain the patterning of the ordinary person's economic and political beliefs.

By itself, the assertion that economic understanding entails the elicitation of informal, tacit theory is no great achievement. As Schank and Abelson remark:

> There is a very long theoretical stride... from the idea that highly structured knowledge dominates the understanding process, to the specification of the details of the most appropriate structures. It does not take one very far to say that schemas are important: one must know the content of the schemas. (p. 10)

We agree. We think that two features of ordinary economic theory are especially consequential. First are *causal propositions*. Ordinary economic theory consists in part in the explanations people offer for economic problems: both the economic problems of everyday personal life, and, on a grander scale, the problems that plague the nation. That is, people make sense of economic events partly through the imposition of assumptions about their causes. Consider, for example, the puzzle confronting the American public in the first several months of 1980, as the consumer price index rose at an annual rate of nearly 18%. By itself, this fact is ambiguous. Did prices soar because of President Carter's inability to control runaway federal spending? Because of escalating oil prices demanded by OPEC? Or is the real enemy us—our unwillingness to curtail the purchase of products we don't genuinely need? Meaning is ascribed to rising prices, as to other social facts, partly through the assignment of causality. It is one thing to understand inflation in terms of moral collapse on the part of American consumers; quite another to locate the source of rising prices in policy failure in the White House. By their causal assumptions, people confer political significance on some facts and withhold it from others (Tversky and Kahneman, 1978).

Ordinary economic theory consists of more than the assumptions people make about the origins of problems. People are at least as much concerned to know how problems may be solved, and more particularly they are concerned to know *who* will act to solve the problems they see. In deciding this, people probably go beyond judgments of causal efficacy (or even set them aside), making judgments of *moral accountability*. While causal assumptions are primarily bound up in perceptions of problems, moral accountability attaches primarily to solutions. Agents and institutions are invested with moral accountability to the degree they are assigned responsibility to provide remedies.

Cause and accountability are companion concepts, but they are not identical (cf. Brickman et al., 1982). People may well hold public officials morally accountable to fix problems they clearly had no part in causing. For example, even if Americans in 1981 believed President Reagan's argument that the country's economic ills were due to decades of profligate government spending, still they might judge his performance in office by how quickly he fulfilled his responsibility, as they saw it, to bring the whole mess right. Beliefs about moral accountability, like those regarding cause, are also central to ordinary theories of *personal* economic life. If people assign responsibility for solving their own economic problems not to government but to themselves, they should seldom lay the blame for their own economic failures (or the credit for their own economic successes) on the White House steps.

What we mean here by ordinary economic theory, in short, is the collection of beliefs people hold both about the causes of personal and national economic problems and about the locus of responsibility for solving these problems.[6] In keeping with Schank and Abelson's injunction, we next explore the content of such beliefs.

ORDINARY ECONOMIC THEORIES: DESCRIPTIVE EVIDENCE

There is nothing like a depression to quicken interest in the human costs of unemployment. The many studies undertaken during the 1930s provide a rich source of evidence on ordinary people's economic theories—especially on the unemployed's understanding of their own predicaments. Although this work does not summarize neatly, one theme does show up repeatedly. It is shame. Radical politics and moral indignation belonged much more to the investigators of unemployment than to its victims. Again and again, journalists, novelists, and social scientists recorded their disappointment that the unemployed blamed neither capitalism nor government, but mainly themselves (Bakke, 1940; Eisenberg and Lazarsfeld, 1938; Jahoda et al., 1971; Komarovsky, 1940).

With slender evidence, Garraty (1978) suggests that over the past 40 years, the psychology of unemployment has been transformed, thanks in large measure to Lord Keynes:

If, in order to cool an overheated economy, a government may deliberately cause workers to lose their jobs—and all governments claim and occasionally exercise this right, which is an essential weapon in the Keynesian arsenal—then those who lose their jobs are unlikely to feel either personally inadequate or the hopeless victims of an inscrutable fate. And even when the state is not applying the brakes to the economy, being unemployed cannot logically seem the fault of the jobless because maintaining full employment is (again by official declaration) the responsibility of the state. The force of this logic has permeated the consciousness of thousands who have never read Keynes's *General Theory*. As a

result, the irrational tendency of so many of the unemployed of the thirties to
blame themselves for their unfortunate condition, the tendency that puzzled
social scientists... and vexed radicals... is fast disappearing among the unemployed of the seventies. (pp. 251–252)

Garraty's faith in logic is touching, and not wholly misplaced. The
unemployed of the 1970s indeed do not seem to locate the sources of
their difficulties deep within themselves. In a small set of follow-up
interviews appended to their larger study of unemployment, Schlozman
and Verba (1979) found little evidence that the unemployed held themselves morally accountable for their plight. Shame was quite foreign to
their explanations. Instead, the unemployed provided pragmatic, neutral
accounts: " 'the plant closed'; 'business was slow'; 'I didn't get along
with my boss'; 'I wanted to try something else'; 'we lost a government
contract' " (p. 193; cf. Maurer, 1979).

If the "new" unemployed do not blame themselves, neither do they
blame government. The jobless interviewed by Schlozman and Verba
"did not see themselves as victims of broad social forces or governmental
ineptitude but of specific events connected with their particular employment circumstances" (1979, p. 194). This preoccupation with the proximal and the particular is most significant. Failing to understand their
own predicament as tied to others, as produced by collective forces, the
unemployed are likely to treat their own experience as *irrelevant* to
societal economics or to government performance.

Government customarily escapes accountability also in the reasons
people give for their general personal economic achievements and failures.
With regularity since 1952, interviewers from the Survey Research Center
(SRC) have pestered Americans for assessments of their family's economic standing. Intermittently since 1960, interviewers have also asked
why the family's financial situation had improved or declined. This
evidence indicates that virtually no one sees government policy contribut-
ing to their family's economic achievements or setbacks. In any single
national survey, no more than 1% of those interviewed point directly to
government. Instead, like Schlozman and Verba's unemployed, most
evoke proximal causes: more work, better pay, higher income on the up
side; less work, lower pay, less income for those whose economic standing had declined. Inflation is in fact the only collective force named by

more than a handful of respondents. Thus personal economic problems are rarely ascribed to government incompetence or malfeasance; and except for inflation, they are seldom ascribed to collective causes of any kind.

What about *solutions* to personal economic problems—is government invisible there as well? Nearly so. The best evidence on the point comes from Brody and Sniderman's (1977) analysis of the 1972 National Election Study. Respondents were first asked to name their most pressing personal problem. Almost one-quarter mentioned some form of personal economic distress. Respondents were then asked whether their problem "is something you have to work out on your own, or is there someone who *ought* to be helping you with this?" Overall, one-half the sample declared that they should go it alone. Among these who cited personal economic problems as their most serious, about three-quarters chose the self-reliant course. In American society, moral accountability for solving personal economic problems rests mainly with individuals, not government.[7]

Nearly invisible in theories of personal economic predicaments, government becomes very prominent in the accounts people offer of the country's economic predicaments. The SRC's Survey of Consumers has typically asked respondents to forecast national economic conditions a year down the road. Upon occasion, respondents have also been asked to justify their forecast. As in the accounts they provide for their own achievements and failures, people are inclined to focus in the national case on proximal causes. Things will get better in the country because employment opportunities should improve; things will get worse because prices are going up. (These causes are so proximal that they bleed into their supposed effects.) But in sharp contrast to the personal case, where virtually no one implicated government economic policy, now government competes equally with other potential causes. In fact, since 1960, government is mentioned more often than any other cause (in roughly descending importance the others are: employment, prices, demand, and availability of credit). Thus many Americans believe that the economic fate of the country rests with decisions made by government.

We can look in somewhat greater depth at the assumed causal link between government and the course of the national economy by examining the explanations people offer for inflation in particular. Over the past several years, inflation has towered over other economic ills in the attention it has received from economists, in the pervasive concern expressed about it by the general public, and—not least—in the rhetoric and policies of presidents. So it was in the early spring of 1979, when we added a set of questions designed to reveal theories about inflation to the March Survey of Consumers.[8] Early in the interview, respondents were asked, "Why do you think prices have gone up as much as they have over the past couple of years?" Replies to this question, coded into general categories, are shown in Table 1. The most obvious point made there is the apparent diversity of causes singled out. Why, according to the American public, have prices risen? Because of big business profiteering, balance of trade deficits, wage increases, exorbitant union demands, wage-price spirals, soaring energy costs, consumer greed, government, and, undeniably, inflation. This diversity would seem to reflect faithfully the confusion of experts about the causes of inflation.

Although, as Table 1 shows, the public sees a variety of causes for rising prices, its favorite single source is government, mentioned by more than one person in six. And what did people mean by government? Extravagant federal spending. Government was spending too much—on defense, on foreign aid, on social welfare, or just in general. References to oppressive taxes, inflationary regulations, corruption in high places, or

TABLE 1. Causes of Inflation I

Why do you think prices have gone up as much as they have over the past couple of years?	
Government	17.5%
Energy costs	11.3
Wage increases	10.3
Consumer "greed"	9.7
Big business	9.5
Inflation	7.7
Unions	6.9
Balance of trade	5.2
Wage-price spirals	5.0

Source: Survey Research Center (SRC) Survey of Consumers, March, 1979. Sample $n = 769$. "Don't know" responses ($n = 98$) excluded.

even governmental inefficiency paled in comparison, cited by no more than a handful of people each.

Government as a major perpetrator of inflation comes through strongly in Table 2 as well. Later in the interview, respondents were confronted with the following request: "There may have been several causes of inflation during the past couple of years. For each of the following statements, please tell me whether you think this has increased inflation a great deal, somewhat, a little, or not at all." As indicated in Table 2, government was singled out for two sins in particular: for its deficit spending and, oddly, for "printing money with nothing to back it up." More than two-thirds of the public thought each had increased inflation "a great deal." Of the eight potential causes, only increases in oil prices was judged more potent.

The judgments summarized in Table 2 appear to reflect a coherent perception by people of government's overall role as a cause of inflation, at least within the bounds of the question they were asked here. A

TABLE 2. Causes of Inflation II

	Increased inflation			
Cause	*A great deal*	*Somewhat*	*A little*	*Not at all*
Cost of oil and other kinds of energy	75.2%	18.1%	5.7%	.9%
Washington spending more than it takes in	72.2	19.7	6.6	1.5
Washington printing money with nothing to back it up	67.1	19.9	9.0	4.0
Groups receiving unfairly large wage increases	51.7	29.8	14.8	3.8
Businesses raising prices to increase their profits	48.9	35.3	14.2	1.6
Increasing interest rates	37.7	41.4	17.3	3.6
Consumers buying products they don't really need	32.4	30.5	23.6	13.6
Government spending money to keep down unemployment	31.3	36.1	22.4	10.2

Source: SRC Survey of Consumers, March, 1979. $n = 769$. "Don't know" responses (average $n = 17$) excluded.

confirmatory factor analysis of these same items, reported in Table 3, shows that those items explicitly implicating government actions go together to indicate a single factor. People seem to think of these particular actions as aspects of a general inflationary role of the government, whether they think this role is of great importance currently or of less importance. Notice too that all but one of the remaining items from Table 2 load together on one factor. Evidently people have a coherent perception of the overall role of the private sector as a cause of inflation as well, this role being distinct from that of the government but not completely independent of it (note the fairly strong correlation between the two factors). All in all, the evidence in Tables 2 and 3 fortifies our earlier point that government looms large in the public's causal reasoning about inflation.

Remedies for inflation are also often political. We began a series of questions by asking respondents whether they thought *anything* could be done about rising prices. By March of 1979, slightly more than one-third

TABLE 3. Causes of Inflation Factor Analyzed

Cause	1	2
Government deficit spending	1.0^a	
Government printing money	1.69	
Government spending against unemployment	.87	
Business raising prices		1.0^a
Too-big wage increases		1.02
Rising interest rates		.96
Consumer greed		1.47
Energy costs	.81	0^b

Source: SRC Survey of Consumers, March 1979. Results taken from Confirmatory Maximum-Likelihood Factor Analysis (Jöreskog and Sörbom, 1978), using a matrix of polychoric correlations (Olsson, 1979) and the vector of standard deviations to generate the covariance matrix. $n = 769$. Overall chi-square (14 degrees of freedom) = 21.7. Coefficients are unstandardized factor loadings. Correlation between factors = .44. Overall model includes five correlated measurement errors not shown here. All free coefficients are significant past .001 level.
[a] Fixed by hypothesis.
[b] Found to be not significantly different from zero, and so fixed.

(35.3%) said no, that the country would just have to live with it. Those who said inflation could be controlled were then asked: "What do you think can be done about rising prices?" The public's proposals, sorted into general categories, are shown in Table 4. The most popular recommendation was simply to constrain prices. Of those who named this option, three-quarters explicitly mentioned price *controls*. Government in fact permeates Table 4, in explicit form, as in proposed reductions in federal spending, or implicitly, as in the recommendation to constrain wages.

Any hesitation about policy disappeared when respondents were asked, finally: "*Who* do you think is most responsible for doing something about rising prices?" Many named government. The relevant proportions, given in Table 5, indicate that responsibility was spread rather evenly among the president, Congress, and government generally. Although the consumer, along with business, must shoulder some of the responsibility for solving inflation, these results indicate that the job belongs primarily to government.

In summary, people account for their personal economic predicaments in terms that differ sharply from those they enlist to account for national economic problems. People seldom blame themselves for their own

TABLE 4. Solutions for Inflation

What do you think can be done about rising prices?[a]	
Constrain prices	28.4%
Consumerism	20.4
Constrain wages and prices	9.8
Constrain wages	9.3
Government (miscellaneous)	6.1
Cut government spending	5.6
Reduce energy costs	4.5
Electoral sanction	3.4
Cut money supply	1.9
Provoke recession	1.3

Source: SRC Survey of Consumers, March, 1979. $n = 769$. "Don't know" responses ($n = 75$) excluded.
[a]Asked only of the 64.7% of the sample who thought that something could be done about inflation.

TABLE 5. Responsibility for Solving Inflation

Who do you think is most responsible for doing something about rising prices?[a]	
Government (general)	23.8%
Congress	23.1
President	18.3
Consumers	17.6
Business	8.1
President and Congress	3.7

Source: SRC Survey of Consumers, March, 1979.
$n = 769$. "Don't know" responses ($n = 23$) excluded.
[a]Asked only of the 64.7% of the sample who thought that something could be done about inflation.

predicaments, but neither do they blame government. Nor do they look to government for assistance in solving their problems. They see their predicaments caused by proximal, particularistic forces (inflation being the salient exception), and they typically rely on their own resources in seeking solutions. In contrast, government is very prominent in popular accounts of national economic predicaments. Government is singled out as the most potent cause of economic conditions in general and inflation in particular; government is also widely understood to be responsible for solving inflation, though precisely how this is to be done is often hazy.

DO ORDINARY ECONOMIC THEORIES MATTER?

The preceding section of this chapter certainly suggests that they do. The prominence of government in everyday theories of national economic problems is of course consistent with muscular sociotropic effects, just as the invisibility of government in everyday theories of personal economic predicaments is consistent with frail pocketbook effects. Furthermore, our assumption that informal economic theory discloses much about the connections people draw, and fail to draw, between the domains of economics and politics, is consistent also with the patterning of pocketbook failures. For example, by several recent analyses, economic self-interest did modestly affect congressional voting in 1978, and in an intriguing way. Personal economic predicaments contributed to votes against incumbent senators more than to votes against incumbent representatives; and more to votes against representatives of the in-party (party of the president) than against representatives of the opposition (Hibbing and Alford, 1981; Kuklinski and West, 1981). These two results, both drawn from the 1978 election, and the generally stronger (though still modest) pocketbook effects found in presidential voting, may be of a single piece. In the public mind, who bears responsibility for economic caretaking? Presumably presidents do more than individual senators; senators more than representatives; and incumbent representatives of the president's party more than incumbent representatives of the opposition. The circumstances of personal economic life seem to find political expression *as if* voters were guided by tacit judgments of cause and accountability.[9]

A similar point can be made about the evidence marshalled earlier on behalf of the sociotropic citizen. Of the various ways sociotropic judgments have been represented, two have proven most successful in terms of predicting political choice: appraisals of government performance and assessments of party economic competence. Both, of course, reflect judgments about the nation's economic condition. Perhaps more important, both take for granted that the national condition is affected by government policy.

These patterns are encouraging for our general argument, but they fall far short of a convincing case. Moreover, what people say in a brief answer to a short question may not adequately reflect how (or whether) they put their economic theories to use (e.g., see Nisbett and Wilson, 1977). *If* the accounts people offer of problems and solutions faithfully represent their real understanding of economics, and *if* such accounts matter, then the pattern of relations among their various economic and political beliefs should vary predictably with the accounts they have given. Next we see, in various ways, whether this is so.

In the first test we make use of the March 1979 Survey of Consumers. In addition to the questions on inflation causes and solutions, alluded to earlier, the March survey included items tapping respondents' evaluations of President Carter's performance and their attachments to party. This enables us to trace out the political ramifications of economic experiences and judgments.

Also included in the survey was an extensive battery of questions designed to map personal economic distress. In March of 1979, there was a good bit of it. Most of those interviewed believed that their incomes would not keep pace with prices over the next several years; nearly one-third acknowledged that they had recently put off medical or dental treatment because of the cost; 4 in 10 said that they had used savings or had borrowed money to pay current bills; almost one-third reported that they were " very worried" about having savings for retirement; and so on (the exact questions and the corresponding sample frequencies are given in the Appendix).

The survey also included the normal SRC complement of questions about national economic conditions. If anything, Americans in the early spring of 1979 were gloomier about the country's condition than about their own. Almost one-half of the respondents believed business conditions had deteriorated over the past year. More than three-quarters declared the country to be in fair or in poor shape, and when asked to name particular problems, nearly 4 in 10 nominated the economy as the most pressing. Predictions about the nation's future were even bleaker. More than two-thirds predicted that the next 12 months would bring bad times; virtually everyone believed that prices would rise over the same period, with nearly one-quarter forecasting inflation to exceed 10%; most predicted that interest rates would also rise; and almost one-half thought that unemployment would increase as well (these questions are also given in the Appendix).

A first empirical point to make on the way to testing whether everyday economic theories matter is that, consistent with previous work, appraisals of personal and national economic conditions are distinct. Table 6 presents the results of factor analyzing the various pocketbook and sociotropic indicators. Following a principal factoring procedure, five factors were extracted and then rotated to an oblique solution. The resulting pattern is remarkably neat. Six of the eight sociotropic items fall together on a single dimension; *none* of the eight loads substantially on any of the four pocketbook factors. Conversely, the 14 pocketbook measures are distributed exclusively among four factors; none appears on the sociotropic dimension. In this respect, Table 6 provides further and

TABLE 6. Pattern of Economic Discontent

	Factors				
	1	*2*	*3*	*4*	*5*
Pocketbook					
Family progress	− .61				
Financial progress relative to expectations	− .37				
Family expectations	− .58				
Income rise more than prices?	− .42				
Fallen behind on rent or housing payments?		.56			
Used savings to pay bills?		.37			
Put off medical treatment?		.49			
Argue over money?		.41			
Worry about home heating costs?			− .44		
Worry about savings losing value?			− .68		
Worry about savings for retirement?			− .64		
Worry about losing a job?				.60	
Worry about paying bills?				.72	
Lost a job?				.26	
Sociotropic					
Predicting good times/bad times in country					.60
Business conditions					.52
Predicting business conditions					.56
Current shape of the country					.37
Predicting unemployment					.34
Life getting worse in U.S.?					.33
Predicting prices					
Predicting interest rates					

Source: SRC Survey of Consumers, March, 1979. Effective *n* for this analysis is 755. Only factor loadings greater than .25 are shown. Principal factoring, oblique rotation.

quite powerful evidence that people can and do distinguish their personal economic condition from the nation's.

Of more immediate importance is the determination of the effects of these pocketbook predicaments and sociotropic judgments on political preference, and particularly of how the pattern of such effects is shaped, if at all, by everyday economic theories. This requires first of all a model; ours is displayed in Figure 1. Among other things, it assumes that assessments of national economic conditions and evaluations of President Carter's performance affect one another. Just as believing the national

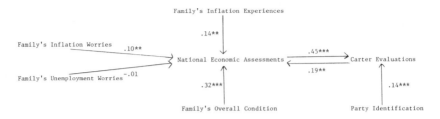

FIG. 1.   Economic-based evaluations of President Carter.

Source: SRC Survey of Consumers, March, 1979. *Notes*: $n = 742$. Estimates are based on two-stage least squares regression. Coefficients are unstandardized. Economic variables are factor scores, based on the analysis summarized in Table 6. Some variables have been reflected so that positive coefficients are expected in all instances.
$*p < .10; **p < .05; ***p < .01.$

economy is falling apart may influence evaluation of the incumbent president's performance, so, too, may evaluations of the president color judgments of national economic conditions. (This is especially plausible where, as here, assessments of national conditions include forecasts about future states.) The equation for national economic assessments implicit in Figure 1 is exactly identified: party identification is assumed to directly affect evaluations of Carter but not assessments of the national economy.[10] The equation for Carter performance evaluations is overidentified: Personal economic distress, in its multiple manifestations, is assumed to directly affect national economic assessments, but not evaluations of Carter's performance. Put another way, the model stipulates that pocketbook experiences and appraisals can influence evaluations of Carter only indirectly, by shaping assessments of national economic conditions. (This assumption is well supported by a test of overidentification, which tests the assumption, being assumed in the estimation of the Carter evaluation equation, that the coefficients of the excluded personal economic distress variables are zero; for this test, $F = .34, p = .79$.)

As represented in Figure 1, party identification takes three values: Republicans (1), Independents (3), and Democrats (5). Evaluations of President Carter's performance fall into four categories: "excellent" (2), "good" (1), "fair" (−1), and "poor" (−2). Finally, the four personal economic variables and the single national economic assessment variable are factor scores, based on the analysis summarized in Table 6.

Estimates of the various relations diagrammed in Figure 1 are provided by two-stage least squares regression (Johnston, 1972). These estimates indicate, first of all, that the indirect route by which personal economic distress affects evaluations of Carter has its origins overwhelmingly in overall assessments of the family's economic condition. Particular worries or specific experiences associated with unemployment or inflation had little to do with evaluations of national economic conditions. Job loss, postponing medical care, worrying about having sufficient savings for retirement—all of these and more no doubt are personally consequential, but they seem to bear little on the economic judgments people make about society. Global evaluations of the family's economic condition, however, do. People who believed that, materially speaking, things had gone well for their family and who expected more of the same in the future were also more upbeat and confident in their assessments of national economic conditions (as indicated by, in Figure 1, an unstandardized coefficient of .32). We will have reason to return to this relationship between global economic evaluations of family and nation later.

Figure 1 coefficients also support our starting assumption that assessments of the national economy both cause and are caused by presidential evaluations. Carter enthusiasts placed a rosier construction on the nation's economic health and prospects than did his critics ($b = .19$, standard error (SE) = 0.9; beta = .28, $p < .05$). At the same time—and this is crucial—assessments of the national economic scene shaped evaluations of Carter's performance ($b = .45$, SE = .11; beta = .30, $p < .01$). This is a substantial effect; according to the estimates provided in Figure 1, the impact of sociotropic assessments on Carter evaluations in fact surpassed that due to party identification. Democrats, of course, evaluated Carter more favorably than did Republicans—but this difference was smaller than the corresponding difference associated with a comparatively favorable versus a comparatively unfavorable reading of the national economy.[11] In short, the Figure 1 results sustain the sociotropic prediction: Presidential evaluations are, for the average American, very much creatures of national economic circumstances.[12]

We are, of course, especially interested in systematic variation about this imagined average American. We expect that the strength of the relationship between national economic assessments and presidential evaluations will vary in predictable ways, depending on the theories people adopt for economic events. We concentrate first on theories regarding *national* economic problems—who or what causes them; who or what is responsible for solving them. By what we call the "availability hypothesis" (Tversky and Kahneman, 1973), Americans who indict federal spending as a principal cause of inflation, or who assign to the president major responsibility for softening the consequences of inflation, should typically be sociotropic in their evaluation of the national government. That is, in appraising the president's performance, they should give special weight to the state of the economy (as they see it). Just the opposite should hold for those whose theories locate the causes of and responsibilities for national economic events outside government. By what we call the "discounting hypothesis" (Kelley, 1973), assessments of the health and vitality of the economy among such people should be less relevant to the president's standing.

Since the degree of relevance of economic affairs for evaluations of the president is a relative matter, testing these two general predictions—availability and discounting—involves making comparisons: setting those whose theories evidently suggest high relevance against those whose theories suggest low relevance. Ideally, we would like to design these comparisons to examine the two predictions independently. We would like to see, for example, as a test of availability, whether people who enlist government as a powerful cause of inflation weigh economic evidence more heavily when evaluating the president than do people who do not so enlist government, whatever the (common) degree to which they believe business profiteering also contributes to inflation. In practice, however, the two predictions have in varying degrees become confounded in our tests.

These tests of the availability and discounting predictions are reported in Table 7. Here we selected six paired subsamples out of the overall Survey of Consumers sample, based on evidence of divergent economic theories between pairs. Within each subsample, the model of presidential evaluation represented in Figure 1 was reestimated, again following a two-stage least squares (2SLS) procedure. The first pair of subsamples separates those who mention government, when asked to say why prices have gone up, from those who mention other conditions and agents, but not government. The second pair distinguishes those scoring high on the

TABLE 7. Direct Effect of National Economic Assessments on Evaluations of President Carter Within Subsamples Defined by Everyday Economic Theories

ENTIRE SAMPLE	
(n = 742); .45	
Predict stronger *effect*	*Predict* weaker *effect*
(*availability hypothesis*)	(*discounting hypothesis*)

CAUSES

Spontaneously mention government as cause of inflation (*n* = 164) .54**	Spontaneously mention energy costs, wage increases, etc., as cause of inflation (*n* = 473) .35**
High on government cause of inflation factor (*n* = 116) .41*	High on nongovernment cause of inflation factor (*n* = 178) .23

RESPONSIBILITIES

President should solve inflation (*n* = 133) .47**	Business, consumers, etc., should solve inflation (*n* = 333) .39**

Source: SRC Survey of Consumers, March, 1979. As in Figure 1, estimates are generated by two-stage least squares regression.
*$p < .10$; **$p < .05$; ***$p < .01$.

government factor underlying the inflation check-off list from those scoring high on the private sector factor (in view of the correlation between factors, these are not mutually exclusive groups). And in the third pair, those who said the president was responsible for doing something about rising prices are contrasted to those who did not name the president, but rather picked business, consumers, or some other nongovernmental agent. The overall effect of making these distinctions is clear. In each case, the coefficient representing the relationship between national economic assessments and presidential evaluations is greater for the group where high relevance is suggested than it is for the group where low relevance is suggested. The degree of contrast appears to be greater for the distinctions based on causes for national economic conditions than for those based on responsibilities for solving national economic predicaments.[13] Though it is hard to sort out the relative contributions of availability and discounting dynamics in these tests, still, here is the first compelling evidence that economic theories matter.

We next turn to the possibility that everyday theories about *personal* economic life might also matter. Naively considered, it seems reasonable to think that beliefs about personal economic events play a more consequential role than do those about national events. Surely people have more evidence, and more vivid and detailed evidence, about their own situation than about the nation's. No doubt they have thought more about themselves than they have about society. Their theories about personal economic life should be better established, and perhaps, therefore, more consequential. Let us see.

Making use again of the March 1979 SRC Survey of Consumers, we tested two possible paths by which everyday theories of personal economic life might matter, politically. As shown clearly in Figure 1, the effect of personal economic distress on evaluations of Carter's performance is wholly indirect; it derives primarily from the relationship between global evaluations of the family's economic condition and global evaluations of the nation's economic condition. So one way in which pocketbook predicaments could become politically more consequential would be through the strengthening of this relationship. And this in turn just might be a function of how people explain their family's economic condition. As we saw earlier, most explanations are privatistic, focusing on proximal, idiosyncratic causes. But explanations occasionally latch on to larger causes that touch many people and that therefore may properly fall within the province of government. People adopting explanations of the latter sort should be more apt to interpret the course of the national economy in personal terms. Because their own progress and prospects are profoundly affected by general forces (such as rising prices), their assessment of national economic conditions should closely reflect their assessment of their own condition.

This turns out to be true. Table 8 summarizes the results of reestimating (via 2SLS) the impact of overall assessments of the family's economic predicament on assessments of the nation's economic predicament within each of three subgroups: those whose explanations for why their family's finances had changed over the recent past, and in a separate question, why they expected their family's finances to change in the future, focused on privatistic causes (49%); those whose explanations emphasized both

TABLE 8. Direct Effect of Overall Assessment of Family's Economic Situation on Assessments of Nation's Economic Situation Within Subgroups Defined by Everyday Economic Theories

	Theory of family's economic predicament		
	Privatistic	*Mixed*	*Collective*
Family assessment	.26***	.52***	.67***
n	329	201	146

Source: SRC Survey of Consumers, March, 1979. Table entries are two-stage least squares (2SLS) regression coefficients (unstandardized).
*$p < .10$; **$p < .05$; ***$p < .01$.

privatistic and collective causes (30%); and those whose explanations focused on exclusively collective causes (22%).[14] As predicted, across the three groups the link between the family's and the nation's economic condition tightens substantially. Those who enlist privatistic causes to account for their own position—and they are many—see little connection between the economic course of their own life and that of the nation. The comparatively few who explain their own economic ups and downs as due to collective causes, in contrast, interpret the national economic scene very much in terms of their own achievements and failures. In this way, everyday theories of personal economic life can be said to matter.

A second possible pathway follows the same logic but is more direct. People who adopt collective interpretations of their family's economic predicament are prone to appraise national economic conditions in personal terms, as we have just seen. For identical reasons, they may also make political use of their own experiences, evaluating the president according to their own economic trials and tribulations. In short, they may be the pocketbook citizens so much of the literature yearns for.

It's not so, except in a curious way. As in the previous analysis, we first partitioned the sample into three groups, defined by the explanations they provided for their family's economic progress and prospects. We then explored whether, moving from the privatistic to the collective theory group, the direct effects of personal economic distress on evaluations of Carter's performance would begin to show up at statistically reliable levels. Generally they did not. The one exception, shown in Table 9, was unemployment. Whereas unemployment experiences and worries

TABLE 9. Direct Effects of Family Unemployment and National Economic
Assessments on Evaluations of President Carter Within
Subgroups Defined by Everyday Economic Theories

	Theory of family's economic predicament		
	Privatistic	*Mixed*	*Collective*
Family unemployment	− .01	− .05	.25**
National assessment	.33*	.30*	.88**
n	329	201	146

Source: SRC Survey of Consumers, March, 1979. Table entries are unstandardized
coefficients, generated by two-stage least squares regression.
*$p < .10$; **$p < .05$; ***$p < .01$.

were unrelated to evaluations of Carter's performance among those who
explained their positions in privatistic (unstandardized regression coefficient = − .01) or mixed (− .05) terms, such experiences and worries were
reliably related to evaluations of Carter among those whose explanations
emphasized collective causes (.25, $p < .05$). This is a peculiar confirma-
tion of pocketbook politics, however, since, among the collective rea-
soners, it is those who feel *most* threatened by unemployment who give
Carter the *highest* marks! This result suggests that the experiences of
unemployment may work to the general advantage of the Democrats (cf.
Kiewiet, 1981).

Explanations for personal economic predicaments seem also to
influence the political importance granted to national economic assessments. This is the final point made in Table 9. The coefficients arrayed
along the second row there indicate that, among those who explain their
family's economic predicament in collective terms, national economic
assessments play a dominant role in presidential evaluations ($b = .88$).

This result of course contributes to the general case that everyday
theories matter. At a more detailed level, it provides further evidence that
those who explain their family's economic predicament in collective
terms are very different creatures. They grant enormous political importance to national economic assessments. They interpret the course of
national economic events in terms of their own family's progress and
prospects. And their evaluation of the president reflects directly the
economic experiences of personal life. For those who enlist collective

causes in explaining personal predicaments, economic and political realities seem to be deeply intertwined.

Determining whether or not this intriguing result can be sustained in other contexts is our next and final empirical task. Here we examine whether people who reach for collective causes in accounting for their economic experiences give more weight to such experiences when they vote for president. Table 10 displays *logit* coefficients, estimated by a maximum-likelihood procedure, for an equation that supposes presidential voting to be a function of just two variables: party identification and family economic situation. (For an excellent account of this procedure, consult Hanushek and Jackson, 1977.) The coefficients were estimated for each National Election Study that asked people why their family's economic condition had improved or declined—1956, 1960, 1964, 1972, and 1976.[15] In the left-hand column of Table 10 we present the results for those voters who explained movement in their family's economic position in collective terms, and in the right-hand column, the results for all other voters. Our expectation is strongly supported. In four of the five elec-

TABLE 10. Direct Effect of Family Economic Trend on
Presidential Voting 1956–1976

	Voters who explain their family economic trend in collective terms	*All other voters*
1956	.155	.096***
n	(51)	(1,198)
1960	.113	.076*
n	(17)	(745)
1964	−.038	.036
n	(51)	(1,048)
1972	.178	.063
n	(100)	(575)
1976	.291*	.049
n	(57)	(852)

Source: SRC/CPS National Election Studies. Entries are logit coefficients. Standard errors for the left-hand column range from .148 to .217; for the right-hand column, from .031 to .049. In each instance, the estimating equation also included party identification.
*$p < .10$; **$p < .05$; ***$p < .01$.

TABLE 11. Pocketbook Voting in 1972:
Estimated Vote for President Nixon

	Family economic condition		
	Better	*Same*	*Worse*
Voters who explain their family economic trend in collective terms (*n* = 100)			
Democrats	.56	.47	.38
Independents	.77	.70	.63
Republicans	.91	.86	.81
All other voters (*n* = 575)			
Democrats	.50	.47	.44
Independents	.67	.64	.61
Republicans	.80	.78	.76

Source: SRC/CPS 1972 National Election Study. Probability estimates are derived from the logit equation described in the text.

tions, the coefficient associated with the impact of the family's economic condition increased among voters who explained fluctuations in their own economic position by enlisting collective forces. The 1964 election is the single exception, and in 1964, the amount of pocketbook voting was utterly trivial to begin with.[16]

To appreciate the magnitude of these effects, Table 11 translates the appropriate logit coefficients for the 1972 case into estimates of the probability that voters would support incumbent President Nixon. Table 11 displays two sets of probabilities, one calculated for collective reasoning voters (top panel), the other based on all other voters (bottom panel). As indicated there, the impact of personal economic predicaments on presidential voting in 1972 more than doubled among voters who explained their predicaments in collective terms.

CONCLUSIONS

In American society, collective political choice is profoundly shaped by aggregate economic circumstance. Our purpose here has been to elucidate how this interdependence gets played out, not in society and government but in the lives of individuals. Fortunately for that purpose, the connections Americans draw between their own economic predicaments, the economic predicaments of society, and the performance of their government are neither hopelessly complex nor infinitely idiosyncratic. Such beliefs form patterns—patterns, moreover, which seem interpretable in terms of ordinary economic theory. How people explain economic problems and how they assign responsibility for solving them appears to disclose much about the intertwining of economics and politics.[17]

Many Americans explain their economic ups and downs by citing proximal, particularistic causes. To borrow Lane's felicitous phrase, they "morselize" their experiences. What we found to be a strong tendency in Americans' causal understanding of personal economic events, Lane found in *Political Ideology* (1962) to be true more generally:

this treatment of an instance in isolation happens time and time again and on matters close to home: a union demand is a single incident, not part of a more general labor-management conflict; a purchase on the installment plan is a specific debt, not part of a budgetary pattern—either one's own or society's. The items and fragments of life remain itemized and fragmented. . . . (p. 353)

In our evidence, such morselizing works to nullify the political meaning latent in the economic setbacks and achievements of everyday life.

Although typically morselized, the ordinary person's theory of everyday economic events occasionally is not. When this happens, the consequences seem to be very great. Americans who depart from the conventional theory look at politics and economics in ways that differ radically from their morselizing compatriots. In particular, Americans who explain their family's economic predicament by citing collective forces see politics and economics as deeply intertwined. They assess the course of national economic events in terms of their own family's improvements and possibilities. Their feelings for the president are greatly influenced by how they size up the national economy, and, secondarily, by their own economic experiences. This result suggests that shifts in theoretical perspective regarding personal economic life are accompanied by pervasive alterations in the inferential pathways that connect economic and political realities. They also hint that such shifts are not easy to bring about. Ordinary people may cling to their economic theories just as stubbornly as social scientists cling to theirs.

Compared to theories of personal economic life, beliefs about the causes and remedies for national economic conditions may be rather superficial. Such beliefs do seem to matter. Americans who explain inflation by pointing to rapacious unions, profiteering corporations, or gluttonous consumers give less importance to the state of the economy in their presidential evaluations; those who think government is the chief perpetrator give somewhat more—but these effects are comparatively modest. For most Americans (though, as we have seen, not for all), the national economic scene is far removed from private life. Perhaps, then, the ordinary person's theory of national economic life is not deeply entrenched. Perhaps such theories reflect more or less what people are momentarily told in their newspapers and on their television sets, by journalists, experts, government officials, presidents, and other well-placed popularizers of the dismal science.

This hunch is in fact well supported by a series of experiments on agenda-setting (Iyengar, Peters, and Kinder, 1982; Kinder et al., 1983). Perhaps unremarkably, problems that capture the attention of network news programs become the problems the public believes to be the nation's most important.[18] More to the point here is that the public is influenced also by how news programs frame problems. In particular, viewers exposed to news coverage that implies presidential responsibility for economic difficulties are more likely, when they evaluate the president's performance, to weigh heavily their judgment of how the nation is faring on economic matters, than are those exposed to coverage that is agnostic on economic responsibility. This effect is most pronounced among politically naive viewers, whose theories about national economic life may be least well-developed. In how they choose to frame problems, therefore, those responsible for news programs may make available to the viewing public certain ways of understanding, and in so doing, invite or discourage the intertwining of political and economic realities.

The part played by mass media in the long-term cultivation and short-term prominence of popular economic thinking is one puzzle for future work. There are others. How stable are the beliefs that make up ordinary economic theory? What sorts of circumstances, for what kinds of people, bring about conversion from one theoretical perspective to another? How far should an analogy between ordinary theory and scientific theory be pursued? Is the core notion of ordinary theory applicable to problems outside economics?

However or whenever these puzzles are eventually resolved, one general conclusion now seems safe. The notion of "the average person," which we ourselves have used in various guises in this chapter, while it may occasionally be a useful literary device, is in fact a dreadful oversimplification. Not everyone embraces just the same economic theory. People differ from one another in the causes they identify and the responsibilities they assign. As we have shown, such differences matter, both for the way people arrive at their evaluations of political incumbents and for the way people understand their own economic circumstances. Perhaps to speak of the average person is to speak approximately of everyone, but it is certainly to speak precisely about no one. "The public" is a caricature.

The fact of individual diversity, while nearly always acknowledged in principle, is just as frequently ignored in practice. Thus there is the contemporary debate about the "American voter," quarreling over the relative importance of party, policy, and candidates in electoral choice. *Whose* electoral choice is seldom pondered. Or, closer to home, there are the disagreements concerning the extent to which the political preferences of "Americans" are shaped by their own economic circumstances as opposed to their assessments of the circumstances of the nation. To *which* Americans the principals in this debate have been referring has not previously been a concern. Our final and most general point is that resolutions of such debates in perfectly general terms are not possible. Nor are they desirable. For the answers will vary radically from one "average American" to the next. And as we have tried to show here, there is at least one useful way to represent differences among people, and that is by attending to the informal, tacit theories they hold—the ordinary and occasionally extraordinary ways each person understands his or her world.

Acknowledgments. We thank Richard Curtin, Shanto Iyengar, Kristen Monroe, Mary Grace Moore, Douglas Rivers, Steven J. Rosenstone, and Janet A. Weiss for their helpful comments on an earlier version of this chapter.

NOTES

1. One anomalous result in this literature is Tufte's (1978) discovery of substantial associations between presidential voting and assessments of family economic condition, when both are measured as voters leave the polling booths. That the close correspondence indicates voters aligning their presidential preferences with their economic predicaments seems most dubious. Most likely, it is the other way around (Sears and Lau, 1983).

2. Of course, it might be that the circumstances of personal economic life affect whether potential voters make it to the polls in the first place. In *Political Man*, for example, Lipset (1960) argued that the economically deprived turn to the political system for reparations and, as a consequence, participate more (other things equal) than the economically secure. However, the evidence runs the other way. Anomalously for pocketbook assumptions, personal economic adversity in fact *suppresses* turnout (Rosenstone, 1982; Kinder et al., 1983).

3. Kramer (1983) offers a powerful *methodological* argument why it is that cross-sectional survey-based tests of pocketbook voting fail so regularly. His argument depends in part on assumptions regarding how voters see their own circumstance in relation to national economic activity. In an indirect way, the evidence we present later is roughly consistent with Kramer's assumptions.

4. We should not overdraw this point. People do generally distinguish between their personal economic well-being and the well-being of the nation as a whole. But people do not conceive of the difference in a way that makes the course of their personal lives entirely independent of the course of the nation. No doubt people generally believe that there are significant commonalities and relations between their personal lives and the state of the nation. Probably they believe that what happens to the nation affects what happens in their personal lives, immediately in some ways, eventually in others. Probably they rely on what they personally experience to help them decide what's going on in the country. So it would be wrong to maintain that people see the interests of the nation as utterly divorced from their own. They do not. But the domains are largely separate.

5. The pocketbook and sociotropic theories do not exhaust the possibilities, of course. One plausible hypothesis, for example, is that political choice reflects assessments of the *group's* situation—where "group" might refer to women, blacks, air traffic controllers, social scientists with deep ties to the National Science Foundation, and so on (Miller et al., 1978; Rhodebeck, 1982).

6. Of course, the rendering of ordinary economic theory could be more complete on a number of counts. The perfect alignment of causal belief with problems and of moral responsibility assignment with solutions is overly simple. Clearly people assign blame for problems that already exist (or give credit for

accomplishments), and clearly they speculate about *how* problems may be solved, regardless of who they think should do the solving. Recognizing these complications makes clear the difficulties of drawing a precise boundary between causal beliefs and responsibility beliefs. Indeed, it is far from clear that there is a precise boundary. The theoretical untangling of all this presents a host of knotty problems which we finesse here. Another limitation on our current treatment is the restriction of popular attention to only the personal and the national domains. There is more to the world than this, as most people certainly know, and we think that a more complete description of ordinary economic theory should additionally include at least the domains of the local community and of the community of nations. Another bound on what we say is due to our limiting the scope of people's theories to just economics and politics. People certainly see other sorts of affairs as pertinent for what they know even about these two areas. Energy and natural resources, requirements for national warmaking power, and the facts of sexual and racial discrimination are just a few of the areas of obvious relevance to at least some people that are ignored here.

7. Just how self-reliant people are depends heavily on exactly how they define their economic problems. Those who said that rising prices was their most pressing personal problem were much less self-reliant, and more expectant of government assistance, than were those who mentioned unemployment (Kiewiet, 1983).

8. The questions were developed by Donald Kinder, Michael Denney, and Stephen Hendricks, and the work was supported by a grant to Denney and Hendricks from the Center for Energy Studies at the University of Texas at Austin.

9. Essentially the same point is made by pocketbook patterns in presidential evaluations. Personal economic predicaments generally have no bearing on presidential evaluations—with a single exception. People who expect their family's economic condition to improve evaluate the incumbent president more favorably than do those whose family expectations are pessimistic. The causal direction of this mild relation is, of course, ambiguous. By hindsight, we suspect it indicates that people's expectations about their economic futures are conditioned by the confidence they feel in the incumbent president. If the political actor most responsible for economic well-being seems capable, then citizens look to their own futures with more confidence than if the president seems inept. From the public's point of view, this calculation only makes sense if the president is likely to continue to hold the office—a contingency which strengthens our speculation, since it fits the pattern of results perfectly. The relation between presidential evaluations and family expectations held in three of four cases: for Nixon in the fall of 1972 on the eve of his greatest political victory; for Ford in 1974 just after assuming the presidency; and for Carter in the fall of 1978. It failed but once: for

President Ford in the fall of 1976 as he was about to relinquish his office (Kinder, 1981).

10. This assumption would seem to run against other claims: Fiorina's (1981), that party identification responds to evaluations of government performance; or Kinder and Kiewiet's (1979, 1981), that judgments of national economic conditions are often colored by partisan loyalties. In both instances, the conflict is more apparent than real, for here sociotropic assessments are represented by judgments of national economic conditions purged of any partisan connotation whatsoever. As expected, Democrats differed not at all from Republicans in their assessment of national economic conditions (Pearson r = .039, not significant).

11. According to the estimates in Figure 2, Democrats (coded 5) approved of Carter's performance more than did Republicans (coded 1) by an average of .56 along a four-point scale [(5–1) × .14 = .56]. The corresponding difference associated with a comparatively favorable reading of the national economy (coded + 1) versus a comparatively unfavorable reading (coded − 1) was .90 [(1 − − 1) × .45].

12. The results displayed in Figure 1 are important in their own right. The pattern of weak pocketbook effects and strong sociotropic effects reported widely in the literature could both be due to measurement problems. Perhaps with more sensitive and comprehensive indicators, pocketbook politics would become muscular. Perhaps with sociotropic measures purged of any explicit partisan coloration, sociotropic politics would become weak. Figure 1 reports no support for either allegation.

13. These are essentially independent tests. Beliefs about causes of and solutions for inflation are only faintly correlated.

14. People who explained past movement in their family's economic position by citing collective causes also tended to cite collective causes in justifying expectations for the family's economic future (tau-beta = .42).

15. The 1968 study also included this question. However, because Wallace's strong third party showing clouds the interpretation of anti-incumbent voting, we excluded the 1968 election from our test. The 1976 study did not include the question, but because the 1976 study served, in part, as the final interview of a three-wave panel, we were able to include it. Here *panel* voters were classified as collective, mixed, or privatistic based on their replies to the question from the 1972 study. Thus the 1976 results constitute a roundabout test of the stability of ordinary economic theory.

16. These results corroborate the analysis of the 1972 election undertaken by Feldman (1982), motivated by concerns similar to our own.

17. Although the differences we have identified between people who give different accounts for economic problems are in many respects striking, there is reason to believe that our results in fact understate how extensive the differences really

are. Analysis in progress of the March 1979 Survey of Consumers data, using multiple-indicator simultaneous equations methods, suggests in particular that the assumption we used that the factor model reported in Table 6 is valid for everyone is not fully justified. Although in broad outlines invariant across the subgroups we defined to generate the results reported in Tables 7, 8, and 9, the factor pattern underlying people's responses to questions about economic affairs (and about political affairs, actually) differs as the accounts they have given differ. Furthermore, for some people the various aspects of the national condition, lumped together as one sociotropic assessment in the results of Table 6, can be disaggregated, with the various aspects having different patterns of relationships with both personal and political assessments. Finally, the degree to which economic assessments of all kinds crystallize into *partisan* judgments varies with the particular economic theory a person adopts. We will report these results in greater detail elsewhere.

18. What *is* remarkable, perhaps, is that large alterations in viewers' priorities can be brought about by rather subtle variations in the priorities of news programs.

REFERENCES

Abelson, R. P. (1981). "The psychological status of the script concept." *American Psychologist*, 36:715–729.

Alt, J. E. (1979). *The Politics of Economic Decline*. London: Cambridge University Press.

Anderson, J., and Bower, G. (1973). *Human Associative Memory*. Washington, D.C.: Winston-Wiley.

Bakke, E. W. (1940). *Citizens Without Work*. New Haven: Yale University Press.

Bartlett, F. C. (1932). *Remembering*. Cambridge, England: Cambridge University Press.

Bloom, H. S., and H. D. Price (1975). "Voter response to short-run economic conditions." *American Political Science Review* 69:1240–1254.

Brickman, P. E., et al. (1982). "Models of helping and coping." *American Psychologist* 37:368–384.

Brody, R. A., and Sniderman, P. M. (1977). "From life space to polling place: The relevance of personal concerns for voting behavior." *British Journal of Political Science* 7:337–360.

Cantor, N., and Mischel, W. (1979). "Categorization processes in the perception of people." In L. Berkowitz (ed.), *Advances in Experimental Social Psychology*, (Vol. 12). New York: Academic Press, pp. 3–52.

Denney, W. M., Hendricks, J. S., and Kinder, D. R. (1980). "Personal stakes versus symbolic politics." Paper delivered at the Annual Meeting of the

American Association for Public Opinion Research, Cincinnati, May 29–June 3, 1980.

Eisenberg, P., and Lazarsfeld, P. F. (1938). "The psychological effects of unemployment." *Psychological Bulletin* 35:358–390.

Feldman, S. (1982). "Economic self-interest and political behavior." *American Journal of Political Science* 26:446–466.

Fiorina, M. P. (1981). *Retrospective Voting in American Presidential Elections.* New Haven: Yale University Press.

Frey, B., and Schneider, F. (1978). "An empirical study of politico-economic interaction in the United States." *Review of Economics and Statistics* 60:174–183.

Garraty, J. A. (1978). *Unemployment in History.* New York: Harper & Row.

Hamilton, D. L. (ed.) (1981). *Cognitive Processes in Stereotyping and Intergroup Behavior.* Hillsdale, NJ: Lawrence Erlbaum.

Hanushek, E., and Jackson, J. (1977). *Statistical Methods for Social Scientists.* New York: Academic Press.

Heilbroner, R. L. (1979). "Inflationary capitalism." *New Yorker,* October 8.

Hibbing, J. R., and Alford, J. R. (1981). "The electoral impact of economic conditions: Who is held responsible?" *American Journal of Political Science* 25:423–439.

Hibbs, D. A., Jr. (1979). "The mass public and macroeconomic performance: The dynamics of public opinion toward unemployment and inflation." *American Journal of Political Science* 23:705–731.

Hibbs, D. A., Jr. (1982). "A dynamic analysis of economic influence on political support for British governments among occupational groups." *American Political Science Review* 76:259–279.

Iyengar, S., Kinder, D. R., and Peters, M. D. (1982). "Priming effects in politics: The evening news and presidential performance." Unpublished manuscript, Center for Political Studies, The University of Michigan.

Iyengar, S., Peters, M. D., and Kinder, D. R. (1982). "Experimental demonstrations of the not-so-minimal consequences of television news programs." *American Political Science Review* 76:848–858.

Jahoda, M., Lazarsfeld, P. F., and Zeisel, H. (1971). *Marianthal.* New York: Aldine-Atherton.

Johnston, J. (1972). *Econometric Methods* (2nd ed.). New York: McGraw-Hill.

Jöreskog, K. G., and D. Sörbom. (1978). *LISREL IV: Analysis of Linear Structural Relationships by the Method of Maximum Likelihood—User's Manual.* Chicago: International Education Services.

_____ (1981). *LISREL V: Analysis of Linear Structural Relationships by Maximum Likelihood and Least Squares Methods—User's Guide* (preliminary ed.), University of Uppsala.

Kelley, H. H. (1973). "The processes of causal attribution." *American Psychologist* 28:107–128.

Kernell, S. (1978). "Explaining presidential popularity." *American Political Science Review* 73:506–522.

Kiewiet, D. R. (1983). *Macroeconomics and Micropolitics: The Electoral Effects of Economic Issues*. Chicago: University of Chicago Press.

―――― (1981). "Policy-oriented voting in response to economic issues." *American Political Science Review* 75:448–459.

Kinder, D. R. (1981). "Presidents, prosperity, and public opinion." *Public Opinion Quarterly* 45:1–21.

―――― *Economic Predicaments and Political Choice*. (In preparation.)

Kinder, D. R., and Abelson, R. P. (1981). "Appraising presidential candidates: Personality and affect in the 1980 campaign." Paper delivered at the Annual Meeting of the American Political Science Association, New York.

Kinder, D. R., Iyengar, S., Krasnick, J. A., and Peters, M. D. (1983). "More than Meets the Eye: The Impact of Television News on Evaluations of Presidential Performance." Paper delivered at the Annual Meeting of the Midwest Political Science Association, Chicago.

Kinder, D. R., and Kiewiet, D. R. (1979). "Economic discontent and political behavior: The role of personal grievances and collective economic judgments in congressional voting." *American Journal of Political Science* 23:495–527.

―――― (1981). "Sociotropic politics." *British Journal of Political Science* 11:129–161.

Komarovsky, M. (1940). *The Unemployed Man and His Family*. New York: Dryden Press.

Kramer, G. (1971). "Short-term fluctuations in U.S. voting behavior, 1896–1964." *American Political Science Review* 65:131–143.

―――― (1983). "The ecological fallacy revisited: Aggregate versus individual-level findings on economics and elections, and sociotropic voting." *American Political Science Review* 77:92–111.

Kuklinski, J. H., and West, D. M. (1981). "Economic expectations and voting behavior in United States House and Senate elections." *American Political Science Review* 75:436–447.

Lane, R. E. (1962). *Political Ideology*. New York: The Free Press.

Lipset, S. M. (1960). *Political Man*. New York: Doubleday.

Maurer, A. (1979). *Not Working*. New York: Holt, Rinehart, and Winston.

Mebane, W. R. Jr. (1982). "The warp of sociotropic thinking." Paper prepared for the Annual Meeting of the Midwest Political Science Association, Milwaukee.

Miller, A., Gurin, P., and Gurin, G. (1978). "Electoral implications of group identification." Unpublished manuscript, Institute for Social Research. Ann Arbor, Mich.

Nisbett, R. E., and Wilson, T. D. (1977). "Telling more than we can know: Verbal reports on mental processes." *Psychological Review* 84:231–259.

Olsson, V. (1979). "Maximum likelihood estimation of the polychoric correlation coefficient." *Psychometrika* 44:443–460.

Rhodebeck, L. (1982). "Group-based politics." Ph.D. dissertation, Department of Political Science, Yale University.

Rosch, E. (1977). "Classification of real-world objects: Origins and representations in cognition." In P. N. Johnson-Laird and P. C. Wason (eds.), *Thinking*. Cambridge: Cambridge University Press, pp. 212–222.

Rosenstone, S. J. (1982). "Economic adversity and voter turnout." *American Journal of Political Science* 26:25–46.

Schank, R., and Abelson, R. P. (1977). *Scripts Plans Goals and Understanding*. Hillsdale, NJ: Lawrence Erlbaum.

Schlozman, K. L., and Verba, S. (1979). *Injury to Insult*. Cambridge: Harvard University Press.

Sears, D. O., and Lau, R. R. (1983). "Inducing apparently self-interested political preferences." *American Journal of Political Science* (in press).

Sears, D. O., Lau, R. R., Tyler, T. R., and Allen, H. M., Jr. (1980). "Self-interest vs. symbolic politics in policy attitudes and presidential voting." *American Political Science Review* 74:670–684.

Sears, D. O., Tyler, T. R., Citrin, J., Kinder, D. R. (1978). "Political system support and public response to the energy crisis." *American Journal of Political Science* 22:56–82.

Sigelman, L., and Tsai, T. (1981). "Personal finances and voting behavior." *American Politics Quarterly* 9:371–400.

Taylor, S. E., and Crocker, J. (1982). "Schematic bases of social information processing." In E. T. Higgens, C. A. Herman, and M. P. Zanna (eds.), *Social Cognition*. Hillsdale, N.J.: Lawrence Erlbaum.

Tufte, E. R. (1975). "Determinants of the outcomes of midterm congressional elections." *American Political Science Review* 69:812–826.

Tufte, E. R. (1978). *Political Control of the Economy*. Princeton: Princeton University Press.

Tversky, A., and Kahneman, D. (1973). "Availability: A heuristic for judging frequency and probability." *Cognitive Psychology* 5:207–232.

_____ "Causal schemata in judgments under uncertainty." (1978). In M. Fishbein (ed.), *Progress in Social Psychology*. Hillsdale, N.J.: Lawrence Erlbaum.

APPENDIX

MEASURES OF ECONOMIC DISCONTENT, MARCH, 1979, SURVEY RESEARCH CENTER SURVEY OF CONSUMERS*

Pocketbook Grievances

We are interested in how people are getting along these days. Would you say that you (and your family) are *better off* or *worse off* financially than you were a *year*

---

*"Don't know" responses average 1.4% across items, and never exceed 8%.

ago?

Better now	35.4%
Same	27.5
Worse now	37.1

Compared to how well you expected to do financially this past year, how well did you *actually* do? Would you say that you have done *better* than you expected, *not as well* as expected, or *about the same* as expected?

Better	27.1%
Same	56.6
Not as well	16.3

Now looking ahead—do you think that *a year from now* you (and your family living there) will be *better off* financially, or *worse off*, or just about the same as now?

Better	27.7%
Same	47.6
Worse	24.7

How about the next year or two—do you expect that your (family) income will go up *more* than prices will go up, stay *about the same*, or will be *less* than prices will go up?

Income more than prices	11.5%
Same	36.2
Income less than prices	52.4

During the past year or so, have you (or anyone in your household) lost a job or been laid off?

Yes   15.6%

Fallen behind in rent or house payments?

Yes   8.6%

Used savings or borrowed money to pay current bills?

Yes   40.1%

Put off medical or dental treatment because of the expense?

Yes   29.9%

Had family arguments about money problems?

Yes   26.5%

What about *not* having a job... is that something you *personally* are *very worried* about, *somewhat worried* about, or *not very worried* about?

Very worried	20.3%
Somewhat worried	14.7
Not very worried	65.1

Falling behind on current bills?

Very worried	20.5%
Somewhat worried	21.1
Not very worried	58.4

The cost of heating (and cooling) your home?

Very worried	20.8%
Somewhat worried	31.1
Not very worried	48.1

Your savings losing value because of inflation?

Very worried	29.0%
Somewhat worried	35.6
Not very worried	35.4

Having savings for retirement?

Very worried	29.0%
Somewhat worried	31.9
Not very worried	39.1

Sociotropic Judgments

Would you say that *at the present* time business conditions are better or worse than they were a year ago?

Better	36.6%
About the same	15.6
Worse	47.8

Now we would like to talk about the country as a whole. How do you think things in general are going? Would you say the country is in *excellent* shape, *good* shape, *only fair* shape, or *poor shape*?

Excellent	1.2%
Good	21.9
Only fair	56.8
Poor	20.1

What do you think are the most serious ways, if any, that life is getting worse in the United States?

Inflation	24.0%
Unemployment	5.0
Income	4.7
General economics	4.9
Morality	18.7
Government	10.1
None	10.7
Misc. others	21.9

Now, turning to business conditions in the country as a whole—do you think that during *the next 12 months* we'll have *good* times financially, or *bad* times, or what?

Good times	21.7%
Probably good	2.8
Good and bad	4.2
Probably bad	3.3
Bad times	68.0

And how about a year from now, do you expect that in the country as a whole, business conditions will be *better*, or *worse* than they are at present, or just *about the same*?

Better	10.5%
About the same	47.1
Worse	42.3

During *the next 12 months*, do you think that prices in general will go up, or go down, or stay where they are now?

Go up	
More than 10%	23.8%
Between 5% and 10%	49.0
Less than 5%	21.7
Stay the same	4.6
Go down	0.0

How about people *out of work* during the coming 12 months—do you think that there will be more *unemployment* than now, about the *same*, or *less*?

More unemployment	44.1%
About the same	46.7
Less unemployment	9.2

No one can know for sure, but what do you think will happen to *interest rates* for borrowing money during the next 12 months—will they go up, stay the same, or go down?

Go up	69.4%
Stay the same	22.8
Go down	7.9

7: Parties and Classes
in the Political Response
to Economic Conditions

M. Stephen Weatherford

A PUZZLE IN THREE PARTS

Since the publication some 10 years ago of the first research using modern statistical techniques to study the relationship between economic fluctuations and political outcomes (Goodhart and Bhansali, 1970; Kramer, 1971), we have seen a virtual torrent of findings on the topic. Researchers have attempted to explain both the vote and executive popularity; they have indexed economic conditions as averages for the population over time, for subgroups of the population, and in terms of both objective and subjective indicators of people's situations; and they have suggested a number of plausible processes linking conditions and political outcomes. Few generalizations can be drawn from this literature, however, beyond the rather vague conclusion that "the economy has served as a significant source of postwar electoral change" (Kernell and Hibbs, 1981; p. 49).

The earliest studies of political responses to economic conditions were motivated by highly simplified models that linked macroeconomic fluctuations directly to candidate choice (Kramer, 1971; Tufte, 1975; Wides, 1976; Klorman, 1978). Criticism of these models called into question such implicit assumptions as (1) the existence of clear party differences on the issue of economic management; (2) a high degree of control by an administration or a Congress over the macroeconomy; and (3) a fairly sophisticated level of political involvement on the part of voters in response to economic conditions (see especially, Stigler, 1973; cf. Arcelus and Meltzer, 1975; Rosenstone, 1982).

In what might be termed a second generation of models, researchers have addressed these criticisms in two ways. The first accepts the idea that there are few differences between the parties—both Democratic and Republican leaders are essentially Keynesian in approach. It also accepts and elaborates on the claim that government macroeconomic policy is flawed—not because government is powerless but because bad economic theory and lack of political courage dispose it toward chronically inflationary policies. Finally, it accepts the assertion that the public is unsophisticated about economic analysis, and that the voters' short memory and lack of foresight make stable, disciplined economic performance virtually impossible (Buchanan and Wagner, 1977; Brittain, 1977; Wagner, 1977). Starting with these premises, scholars have developed a fairly wide range of models of politico-economic interaction that show that officeholders' accountability to the voters leads them to take actions that consistently overheat the economy and result in politically induced cycles (Nordhaus, 1975; MacRae, 1977; Tufte, 1978; Keech, 1980).

The other line of scholarship accepts the findings that the public responds politically to economic conditions, but attempts to show that this fact is neither particularly surprising nor antidemocratic. This approach explains observed politico-economic interactions as, on the one hand, the expression of genuine economic interests and grievances by the public, and on the other, the attempt by partisan elected officials to secure office by enacting policies whose long-term trends and short-run trade-offs serve the interests of their supporters or potential supporters. Far from a simple "throw the rascals out" interpretation, this approach views politico-economic interactions as stemming from a (potentially complex) representational process that links a set of relatively stable, coherent, reality based interests in the public with governments that know the terms of their accountability. To make this case, it is necessary first to establish that party differences do exist, that governments can control the path of the economy, and that citizens can make reasonable evaluations of policy performance—and then to construct a more elaborate model of the process on a new foundation.

Two types of argument are offered against the assumption that the Republicans and the Democrats are alternative management teams pursuing the same economic policies. First, Page (1978) and others (e.g., Pomper, 1968) show that the platforms, pronouncements, and enacted policies of the two parties are clearly distinguishable on issues of macro-economic management. While party differences on noneconomic issues may have diminished, and while the demographic profiles of the parties' adherents have become more similar since the New Deal (Ladd and Hadley, 1978; Petrocik, 1981), party positions on economic goals and preferred policy instruments show persistent differences.

Second, Hibbs (1977) and Frey and his colleagues (Lau and Frey, 1971; Frey, 1978; Frey and Schneider, 1979, 1981) look not to the parties' intentions but to policy outcomes, and their research shows that alternations in party control of government produce predictable differences in rates of unemployment and inflation. The Democrats guide administrations in which unemployment falls (and inflation generally rises) (Hibbs, 1975; Hibbs and Vasilatos, 1981), while the Republicans lower the rate of inflation (generally with accompanying increases in unemployment). Hibbs's analysis is also directed at the second assumption of the first generation models, for it shows that the time path of the economy *can* be influenced in politically predictable ways by the partisan policies of the administration in power—and hence, by inference, that governments are justly held accountable by voters for the country's overall economic health.

The third assumption, about the level of public responsiveness to economic conditions, is a perhaps disingenuous shorthand for a large set of subsidiary issues. These include numerous aspects of the social psychology of political decision making (Kinder and Kiewiet, 1979; Kinder, 1981; Kinder and Mebane, 1981), though the bulk of policy oriented research has focused on only two broad issues: the role of socioeconomic classes and the role of political parties. Class is important because macroeconomic recession falls most heavily on lower- and working-class groups, while inflation is generally thought to inconvenience middle- and upper-class groups disproportionately. Political parties are important for two reasons. First, party loyalty is the major source of stability in aggregate voting patterns over a series of elections. Second, parties are the primary articulators of the political relevance of economic events, and party identification provides voters with important cues about which policies are most likely to serve their interests.

The balance of this chapter is divided into two parts. The first reviews the way in which party effects are conceptualized in models of the popular response to economic issues. This section draws on several recent studies of partisanship and politico-economic interaction to determine how alternative conceptions of the party role affect the ability of analytical models to estimate correctly the political consequences of economic conditions and class structure. The second section takes up the question of how class effects can best be assessed. It distinguishes two lines of thought in the empirical literature on socioeconomic class. Following recent sociological contributions to the theory of class structure, it formulates a conception of occupational divisions which reveals their political interests more transparently than earlier approaches. It then describes a set of operational procedures for sorting occupations into these class categories, and concludes by enumerating several research questions that this classification makes accessible.

PARTY IN A MODEL OF POPULAR RESPONSES TO ECONOMIC FLUCTUATIONS

Having established that the public does indeed respond to short-term economic fluctuation, scholars in the field must now distinguish among several partially overlapping and partially contradictory explanations. Some political sociologists suggest that public reactions to short-term economic policy are the specific manifestation of the "democratic class struggle" that characterizes advanced societies. Indeed, if recessions and severe inflations are seen as conditions that challenge the smooth operation of bourgeois capitalist economies—and hence as crises that illuminate and question their political underpinnings—then an under-standing of popular opinion on the issue of economic management contributes not merely to electoral analysis but also to understanding the historical interplay between class inequality and political accountability (Castells, 1980; Skocpol, 1981).

Class interests do not operate on political outcomes in a vacuum, however. Their impact may be especially weak in the American political system, where class organizations are weak, class animosities quiescent, and both parties and candidates typically contest political office as if issues were compartmentalized, ideology unpatriotic, and ambiguity the path to success (Page 1976; Shepsle, 1972; Page and Brody, 1972). Political behaviorists who have surveyed these facts, along with the well-substantiated role of party loyalty in conditioning perceptions of candidates and issues, suggest an alternative explanation. They say the question is not how economic fluctuations impact on class interests, but rather how they affect the party coalitions that support the government and the out-party. Class interests may impact directly on this process when people first take on a party affiliation, or during a critical period when party loyalties are in flux and realignment is a possibility. But during more normal times, the proximate, and primary, explanation for partisan opinions and votes is party loyalty (Converse, 1975).

The two lines of argument do not disagree about the long-term alignment of class and party loyalties: both point to the New Deal party system as embodying a rough but serviceable representation of class interests within an essentially consensual polity. What they disagree about is the impact of class on short-term electoral fluctuations. If party coalitions represent long-term alignments of class and party, and if a short-term conflict of class interests coincides with this alignment, then logic and parsimony dictate that any analysis of class effects on a given election outcome take account of the influence of party. It is conven-tional, that is, for public opinion analysts to assume that, in the short run (2–4 years), party identification is stable and exogenous, while issues and candidates fluctuate. This notion is encapsulated in the normal-vote approach to explaining election outcomes. Numerous survey-based stud-ies of the politico-economic linkage show that the inclusion of a party term reduces the independent effect of class nearly to statistical insig-nificance (Fiorina, 1978; Kinder, 1981; Kinder and Kiewiet, 1979). In an earlier paper on voting during the 1958 and 1960 recessions (Weatherford, 1978), I show that class and party affiliation vary together, but that, even controlling for party, class identification conditions candidate choice. While the spirit of that earlier paper is consistent with the argument that class inequalities in the personal impacts of recession produce differing levels of political responsiveness, the effects of class are small and can be explained as the result of unusually severe recessionary conditions. In more normal times, class differences may well be fully encapsulated in the party term.

If a model that excludes party is specified, the covariation of party with class will ensure that the class term will carry a large portion of the explanatory variance. This approach seems theoretically unjustified, however, because for many (perhaps most) citizens, a party identification that was initially adopted on the basis of class interests cues voting behavior in subsequent elections where class issues are either irrelevant or disregarded (Converse, 1966, 1975; Goldberg, 1966). This argument defeats the claim that current party identification is fully endogenous to the vote model; it shows that some term must be included in vote and popularity functions to indicate the role of party as a "standing decision" for most citizens. Although it does not show that class interests are irrelevant to the political response to short-term economic fluctuations, in practical statistical terms it does force the analyst to suppose that class operates primarily through long-standing party affiliation.

That party is not endogenous does not mean that current party identification should be regarded as a predetermined variable. Treating party as fully exogenous is also mistaken, for that approach unjustifiably inflates the causal role of party identification and depresses the importance of short-term class interests. This point can be made empirically, by showing that short-term changes in partisan feeling are a response to economic fluctuations. Work by Brody (1977) and, more elegantly, by Fiorina (1981b) confirms this supposition. Again, however, the conclusion should not be taken to extremes. Party affiliation is still largely stable and exogenous with regard to the vote, because the observed year-to-year fluctuations are small and usually involve only changes in intensity of affiliation rather than switches from one party to the other.

These reflections make it possible to illuminate two opposite errors in earlier research, and to explain an apparent contradiction between individual-level and aggregate-level findings on popular reactions to economic fluctuations.

The first type of mistake is typified by models that emulate the normal-vote approach to assessing the impact of economic issues on candidate choice. Such a model might, for instance, regress an indicator of short-term economic conditions (personal or national, objectively measured or subjectively perceived, or some combination of these), along with the conventional seven-step index of party identification, an indicator of class position, and possibly measures of other issue preferences, against the vote. The consistent finding of such models is that the effect of economic conditions and of class position is small—much smaller than would be predicted by simple extrapolation of the early aggregate-level studies (Fiorina, 1978; Wides, 1976; Klorman, 1978; Kinder and Kiewiet, 1979; Weatherford, 1978). Although the passage from aggregate findings to individual relationships is not necessarily straightforward (Kramer, 1980), the solidly individualistic nature of the hypothesized mechanism that motivates our expectations at both levels of aggregation makes these findings both surprising and suspect. The argument advanced above suggests that it is the party term that produces this pattern of estimates, by overcontrolling for the effects of both economic conditions and social status, and by correspondingly exaggerating the effect of party affiliation. A more appropriate design will be outlined in this chapter.

The second type of error occurs in models, usually those analyzing aggregate time-series data, which omit a measure of partisanship altogether, but include indicators of class and of the economy's recent performance. The argument advanced above would lead us to expect these models to show relatively strong effects of the economy and of class position on the dependent variable (popularity or vote), and they do (Schneider, 1978; Hibbs and Vasilatos, 1981). This argument also suggests certain expectations for several of the other parameter estimates of models taking this approach. First, terms that index variables related to party will pick up some of the effect of the omitted party term. Hence, in time series designs where each administration is allocated a separate intercept, the parameters for these terms should be slightly inflated. Second, the time decay or lag parameter should show that economic (and other) issues affect candidate choice long after they have faded from the mass media and from the memories of survey respondents (cf. Kramer,

1971; Popkin et al., 1971). The reason the estimated time decay parameter turns out to be so large, of course, is that the model omits party identification, which, as a cumulative index of past issue positions (Fiorina, 1978), would integrate such medium- and long-term issue effects.

These symptoms appear, for example, in an analysis by Hibbs and his colleagues (Hibbs et al., 1980) of presidential popularity among occupational and party groups. The findings of this paper, which represents separate analyses of presidential popularity, first among blue-collar, white-collar, and non-labor-force groups, and second among Democrats, Republicans, and independents, appear to contradict the results of earlier survey-based research. Unfortunately, Hibbs's findings are suggestive rather than definitive estimates of class and party effects. The primary weakness of his analysis is that both models are misspecified—the model of occupational status effects because it omits party, and the model of partisan effects because it omits class. The error here is one Brody and Page (1972) illuminated in the issue-voting literature a decade ago: separate parallel analyses merely repartition the same variance in the vote. Unless the independent variables are orthogonal, such analyses give no indication of the unique effects of one variable controlling for the other, or of the joint effects of all the variables together. The resulting estimated parameters are systematically misleading for both class and party—the more so because the correlation between the two indicates a theoretically important set of relationships.

This flaw in the analysis may also explain a counterintuitive pattern of coefficients on which Hibbs does not remark. Inflation is generally considered to be a symbolic issue of the sort that lends itself to partisan posturing, but since unemployment and fluctuations in real income have a more personal impact, the ease of reality testing inhibits partisan manipulation of these issues. This would lead us to suppose that coefficients among partisan groups would exceed those among class groupings for inflation, but that the opposite would be true for unemployment and changes in real income. But Hibbs's Tables 1 and 2 show just the opposite. Party coefficients generally exceed class coefficients for unemployment and income growth, and generally trail class coefficients for inflation.

Hibbs's analysis does provide information about historical fluctuations in the time series of executive support from 1960 to 1979, and it describes the relations between popularity and occupational status, and popularity and partisanship. But it does not produce valid estimates of the joint effects of these independent variables or of other components of the model (i.e., indicators of economic conditions) whose effects on popularity are conditioned by class and party. Other aggregate-level studies that include a party term (e.g., see Bloom and Price, 1975), or that test class and party separately with a different algebraic formulation of the mechanism that produces political responses to economic fluctuations (e.g., see Kernell and Hibbs, 1981), show that party effects generally exceed those of class. Again, as with the first sort of error, the treatment of the party term would account for this pattern of contradictory results.

Thus the role of partisan affiliation in explaining popular political responses to economic fluctuations is obviously substantial. Still, we are left with a dilemma. If party is neither endogenous nor exogenous, how can its effects be taken into account? This dilemma can be resolved by clearly specifying what effect party is expected to have, and by formulating an indicator of that effect. Of greatest importance is the fact that the dilemma hinges on statements about current party identification. One side argues that current party identification is stable from one election to the next; while the other points out that economic fluctuations produce some interelection shifts in affiliation. The appropriate analytical strategy is to index party identification in a manner that includes its stable component but excludes any short-term fluctuations that may be caused by economic events.

There are two ways to accomplish this strategy. One is to use a lagged indicator of party affiliation (this requires longitudinal panel data on the same individuals, which can readily be gathered through aggregate time-series studies). The other is to construct a suitable instrumental variable for party identification. Both approaches have been tried in individual-level research. Fiorina (1981, 1977) uses party lagged one electoral period; Kiewiet (1981) uses recalled vote in the previous election; and Weatherford (1980) uses the instrumental-variable approach. In all these studies, the effects of short-term economic conditions and, where included, of class are larger than those of individual-level studies that use current party identification as the control variable, and smaller than those of aggregate studies that exclude party.

SOCIOECONOMIC CLASS AND THE POLITICAL RESPONSE TO ECONOMIC FLUCTUATIONS

Numerous economic and sociological studies show that the effects of economic cycles, particularly on lower- and working-class people, are deep and widespread. Some short-term political responses to these conditions merely solidify established partisan tendencies, and thus are rightly absorbed into the party term. But, especially since the class-based alignment of the party system is fading with each passing generation, it seems reasonable to expect stronger short-term effects of class differences than have yet been uncovered. If one accepts the findings of individual-level research, one is compelled to explain why objective economic problems do not give rise to political demands. Most of the numerous studies that take this tack focus on the American tendency to view the personal and the political as two separate worlds (Lane, 1962; Brody and Sniderman, 1977; Sniderman and Brody, 1977; Kinder and Kiewiet, 1979).

These findings seem to me genuinely counterintuitive, and while I am convinced by Lane and others that class effects in the United States should be small compared to other advanced societies, I do think the miniscule estimates of existing research indicate some weakness in the analysis. The remainder of this chapter elaborates the foundation for this judgment and proposes an alternative conceptualization of class interests which should give researchers a better empirical purchase on the phenomenon.

Both common sense observation and numerous empirical studies verify that there are persistent inequalities among subgroups in the population in terms of vulnerability to economic misfortune. In general, the same groups that suffer particularly severe personal economic disruption during recessions also make below-average gains during periods of general economic growth (Gramlich, 1974; Blinder and Esaki, 1978; Thurow, 1965, 1969, 1975; Mirer, 1974). This fact, after all, is one of the defining aspects of the class structure, for socioeconomic class not only subsumes static cross-sectional inequalities but also connotes a cluster of skills and opportunities that give the notion of "life chances" an important dynamic component (Weber, 1947; Parkin, 1971; Giddens, 1973).

Class position helps to explain the pattern and dynamic incidence of short-term personal economic fluctuations, and hence is critical to an understanding of objective economic interests. But in the United States class consciousness and class-based organizations contribute very little to the politicization of these interests. Castells puts the point nicely in noting that "what distinguishes the American working class from other working classes is not its historical class interests, but its weak class organizational capacities" (1980, p. 160). This point not only helps to explain the centrism of American parties but also underlines our ignorance about how class effects operate during those frequent periods when the state of the economy does become a political issue. Where particular interests are potential rather than actual sources of partisan conflict, our ability to locate subgroup differences in political interest—and hence to extract their strategic implications—depends on how theory illuminates certain interest groupings and deemphasizes others. Virtually all studies of the political response to short-term economic fluctuations either ignore the possibility of class effects altogether, or else employ a concept of class whose theoretical basis is unconsidered or merely implicit. In the balance of this chapter, I discuss the concept of social stratification and its political implications in order to formulate a theoretically valid operational interpretation of class categories.

SOCIAL STRATIFICATION AND ECONOMIC CLASS

Studies of political behavior and attitudes frequently use the concept of socioeconomic stratification as if it were virtually identical to the division of the population into classes. This obscures a distinction that, at least in theory, is of critical importance (Ossowski, 1963).

One side of the distinction is the status model of stratification, which envisions society as a continuum along which individuals can be ranked. The graduations along this continuum are so small, and the mobility between ranks so high, that social groupings are transitory and the fact of belonging to any particular one has little significance for individuals (Blau and Duncan, 1967). This approach has been the dominant tradition in quantitative sociological studies of stratification, and its assumptions are shared by the human-capital perspective on education and occupational attainment in economics (Becker, 1965; Mincer, 1974). It assumes a relatively open, individualistic competition for places, and a distribution of education and skills in a stratification system without sharp breaks or discontinuities. This is the approach implicitly adopted by political scientists whose analyses involve forming an index of socioeconomic status (SES), either by amalgamating scores on occupational prestige, income, and education, or by simply ranking occupations as if they were imperfect discontinuous indicators of a continuous underlying distribution.

There is no question that such an approach measures an important type of social stratification, but the narrow focus on education and prestige ignores the other side of the distinction: the more conflictual aspects of stratification that arise from the hierarchical organization of work. The two major theoretical sources of this notion of stratification are Marx's emphasis on ownership of the means of production, and Dahrendorf's on the exercise of authority in the workplace. This approach to social stratification rests on the assumption that relations of production are primary in two senses. Individuals occupy particular positions to which certain interests and orientations are appropriate. And it is by virtue of occupying such positions that people differ in numerous "consumption side" characteristics such as prestige and income. Both Marx and Dahrendorf emphasize that the resulting system of stratification is characterized by relatively few, clearly bounded subgroups whose membership is relatively stable over time and that, consequently, take on stable and predictable identities as groupings of social, economic, and political interests.

The two sides of this distinction are not mutually exclusive analytical approaches. Rather they are two different processes by which people are sorted into social positions. Both processes occur in advanced societies, and the fact that they are both theoretically and empirically distinct means that an examination of the social and political implications of one does not necessarily dispose of the other as a live explanatory hypothesis (cf. Wright and Perrone, 1977; Robinson and Kelley, 1979; Vanneman,

1980). In some societies, the primary forces of stratification produce a relatively continuous distribution of statuses; while in others, different primary stratifying mechanisms, a different organization of production, or a different historical tradition result in a greater degree of class distinctiveness. Moreover, some areas of life—for instance, consumption expenditures out of income—lend themselves naturally to an interpretation in terms of a continuum, while others—for instance, labor relations —are typified by more clearly bounded group interests.

AN OPERATIONAL INTERPRETATION OF CLASS CATEGORIES

In this section, a brief explication of Marx's and Dahrendorf's concepts of class is undertaken, a synthesis of them is outlined,[1] and a set of procedures is described for developing an interpretation of class categories that combines the insights of both theorists.

Marx defines classes in modern society on the basis of two criteria: ownership of the means of production, and employment of labor power. These criteria distinguish one class from another within the dominant sector, in which production follows the capitalist mode. It is reasonable to expand Marx's criterion of ownership to include control of the means of production, so that capitalists are grouped with managing directors, who do not own but exercise effective direction over their firms (Baran and Sweezy, 1966; Zeitlin, 1974; Balibar, 1970). At the other end of the continuum, workers do not own the means of production, and instead of employing others, sell their own labor power. Existing along with these two classes, but distinguished from them particularly because of the type of production its members engage in, is the *petite bourgeoisie*. The petite bourgeoisie owns the means of production but does not purchase labor power. Therefore, the relations of production in which the petite bourgeoisie engages do not follow the capitalist mode of large organization, with its high degree of specialization and task differentiation. Rather, the petite bourgeoisie engages in what Marx called "small commodity production," whose primary distinction from capitalist production is the absence of surplus value appropriated through the exploitation of the workers by the owner of the means of production. Marx's criteria for distinguishing classes from one another are objective, and these classes necessarily have conflicting interests because of the exploitative nature of production relations. Marx's distinction between a "class in itself" and a "class for itself" makes clear, however, the contingent nature of class members' realization (consciousness) of their common interests in opposition to the interests of other classes (Marx, 1852/1972).

Unlike Marx, who emphasized ownership, Dahrendorf conceived of classes as based on authority relations. Those in a position to supervise others (i.e., to exercise authority), regardless of whether they are in turn answerable to higher supervisors, are members of the command class. Those who are subject to the authority of others but who supervise no one themselves belong to the "obey" class (Lopreato, 1968). A small category neither supervises nor answers to others: these persons are classless. (Dahrendorf's "classless" group and Marx's petite bourgeoisie are identical.) As with Marx, class relations for Dahrendorf take on an inherently conflictual nature, since the authority relations of the status quo benefit some and disadvantage others. But whether these interests are consciously perceived and acted upon is an open question (Dahrendorf, 1959, pp. 174–179).[2]

Dahrendorf's introduction of variations in authority provides a theoretically sound method for elaborating Marx's theory at its weakest point —its inability to account for the presence of important subgroups between the bourgeoisie and the proletariat. At the same time, the unwieldy heterogeneity of Dahrendorf's command class can be categorized according to variations in control over the means of production and the labor power of others. Robinson and Kelley (1979) summarize the empirical differences between Marx and Dahrendorf in this respect as follows:

Marx, focusing on the top of the organizational hierarchy, asks whether someone is at the very top or is, instead, subject to a boss's control. Dahrendorf, focusing on the bottom of the organizational hierarchy, asks whether someone is at the very bottom, with no authority whatsoever, or has, instead, at least one subordinate.... The result is that Marx misses what is for Dahrendorf the key class boundary, while Dahrendorf misses what is for Marx the key boundary.

Used together, the two theories provide grounds for inferring the economic interests of two pairs of contradictory positions: one located between capitalists and workers within the capitalist organization of production; and the other sharing the characteristics of capitalist and petit bourgeois modes of production.

Within the capitalist mode of production, there is a great array of positions between capitalists and workers.[3] The occupants of these positions do not exercise determinative control over investment resources or over what is produced, but they have more or less authority over how the production process is carried out and over the work of subordinates. Wright (1978, 1979) notes that there is a hierarchical relationship between these two forms of authority, in the sense that control over the physical means of production (the way in which raw material and capital are used together in the productive process) sets limits on the control of labor power within production. This logical ordering in terms of control is the key to distinguishing two segments of the intermediate position between workers and capitalists.

The first class location—the one closer to the bourgeoisie—consists of top managers, middle managers, and "technocrats." In general, managers play little part in the ownership of capital resources, although at the upper levels they may take some role in investment decisions. Middle managers and technocrats are in a more clearly contradictory position, since it contains both bourgeois and proletarian elements. Middle managers supervise part of the production process, and they have authority not only over their own immediate subordinates but also over members of the hierarchy who direct the labor process. At the same time, their authority is circumscribed within the corporate organization. Unlike foremen and supervisors below them, or capitalists or managing directors above them, middle managers genuinely have a foot in each camp: there is no class pole to which they are primarily drawn. Braverman's description of this contradictory location within capitalist production is apt:

The old middle class occupied its position by virtue of its position outside the polar class structure; it possessed the attributes of neither capitalist nor worker; it played no direct role in the capital accumulation process, whether on the one side or the other. This "new middle class," by contrast, occupies its intermediate position not because it is outside the process of increasing capital, but because, as part of that process, it takes its characteristics from both sides. Not only does it receive its petty share of the prerogatives and rewards of capital, but it also bears the mark of the proletarian condition. (1974, p. 467)

The other intermediate class within capitalist production comprises low-level managers, supervisors, and foremen. Occupants of these positions exercise authority over the activities of the workers under them, but have little or no control over the physical process of production. The extent to which this class location is truly contradictory depends on the overall organization of the workplace. In some plants, foremen are little more than disseminators of orders from above, while in others, they exercise more independent authority and discretion (Giddens, 1973; Dunkerley, 1975).

There remain two other intermediate class positions, contradictory locations between the petite bourgeoisie and other classes. These locations are contradictory not because they contain elements of two polar classes within a single mode of production but rather because they involve characteristics of different modes of production. The petit bourgeois differs from the capitalist in that he employs no labor, and hence appropriates no surplus value; he differs from the proletarian in the autonomy he is able to exercise in decisions about production. It is the occupation of positions between these two criteria that defines the remaining contradictory locations.

The first of these positions between the petite bourgeoisie and the capitalist class is that of small employers. If the distinctive feature of petit bourgeois production is the absence of exploitation, then the situation changes immediately when the first worker is hired. As the number of employees increases, the amount of surplus product contributed by the petit bourgeois employer himself shrinks to a smaller and smaller proportion of the total. This is the sort of incremental quantitative distinction that at some point (presumably when the portion of surplus value produced by employees first exceeds that of the employer) amounts to a qualitative difference: the petit bourgeois small employer then becomes a small capitalist. The overall organization of enterprise in the economy, as well as the types of policy proposed by political competitors, will determine whether the occupants of this contradictory location tend to resemble the petite bourgeoisie or capitalists in their political opinions.[4]

The final class grouping, the contradictory location between the petite bourgeoisie and the proletariat, comprises "semiautonomous employees" (Wright and Perrone, 1977). This subgroup is best described in terms of the distinction between conception and execution made by Marxist writers on the labor process. This contrast is meant to capture the degree of control over the means of production, as in Braverman's description of the historical development of capitalism in terms of the progressive removal of control over the design process from the hands of the direct producer of goods. It is this process that continuously proletarianizes the petite bourgeoisie. Originally, the petit bourgeois producer was the only one who combined conception—the choice of what to produce (along with some control over how to go about making it)—and execution in one economic actor. Within the capitalist enterprise, however, there are categories of employees who exercise some degree of control over their conditions of work and the process of production. The contrast between the engineer and the draftsman suggested by Wright (1979, Ch. 2) is illuminating. While the engineer typically is told what projects to work on, he has some discretion in designing and specifying the product itself. The role of the draftsman is to elaborate the engineer's specifications: he has essentially no discretion in determining the content of what is produced. Both these occupations require much skill and training, but they differ in degree of autonomy, with engineers classified as semiautonomous employees and draftsmen generally grouped with the working class.

As with the definition of other intermediate locations in the class structure, this one is unavoidably somewhat ambiguous. Just as quibbles can be raised over how many employees are necessary to change a small employer into a capitalist, the notion of relative autonomy invites questions about how much is enough (or too much) to justify classification in this category. Extreme bounds are relatively easy to state, but a precise definition of the border must be hedged. Still, it is possible to define these class locations quite rigorously in theoretical terms, and the few misclassifications that may occur in empirical situations should be distributed about evenly across categories.

The best estimate of the size of these class groupings is based on the University of Michigan's 1969 Survey of Working Conditions, a study which contains information about employment and authority patterns in the workplace and about the degree of autonomy workers perceive themselves as having. Figure 1, which is a schematic depiction of the structure of class positions described in this chapter, gives estimates of the size of each class grouping.

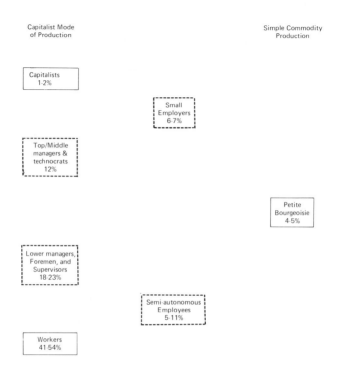

FIG. 1.   Class categories: "contradictory locations" and the fundamental Marxian classes.

Source: Adapted from Wright (1978, p. 63). Estimates of sizes of class groupings derived from ISR (1969).

METHODS OF CLASSIFICATION

Political scientists interested in examining class differences in political attitudes have traditionally been frustrated by the limitations of available data. There are good surveys which cover virtually all the dependent variables of political interest, but they measure social status by methods that make the unambiguous assignment of class position very difficult. A more serious deficiency is that the major electoral data sets include precise and reliable measures of occupational prestige, education, and income (the primary components of the continuous-status model of stratification), but ambiguous or unreliable measures of socioeconomic class. Thus the content of available data sets has led many researchers to suppose that elaborate and careful quantitative analysis of the continuous-status model amounts to an adequate test for the political impact of class or of stratification in general. Other researchers have been sympathetic to the difference between the two major conceptions of stratification, but they have had little choice but to base their measures of class on self-identification items. While such measures are often useful indicators, provided there is objective validating information, the difficulty of assessing their reliability otherwise limits their usefulness.[5]

Conversely, a number of recent sociological and economic studies have gathered a great deal of valuable data about working conditions, workplace autonomy, corporate authority structures, and job satisfaction (Institute for Social Research, 1969, 1972, 1973; National Opinion Research Corporation, 1972–1976; Tannenbaum et al., 1974), but without any concern for political behavior. Consequently, both their timing with respect to electoral and other political events and their content severely circumscribe their usefulness for political analysis.

One of the advantageous results of several recent studies of stratification which have utilized these data, however, is the enhancement of our understanding of the relationship between conventional measures of occupational position, which focus on prestige rankings, and the sorting of occupations into class locations (Hodge and Treiman, 1968; Wright, 1976; Wright and Perrone, 1977; Robinson and Kelley, 1979; Kalleberg and Griffen, 1978, 1980; Kohn and Schooler 1969; Spaeth, 1979; Stolzenberg, 1975). In the remainder of this chapter, I shall build on the results of this research to develop an empirical classification of occupations within the structure of class positions outlined above. This classification will then be available for investigating political responses to inflation and unemployment.

Some preliminary empirical work with this classification scheme has used the 1972–1976 American panel survey (Weatherford, 1982). These data are well suited to the purpose of studying politico-economic interaction since they span a period during which the state of the economy was a salient issue, and they contain a relatively rich set of indicators of class and occupational position. In addition to the usual Census Bureau classification of occupations and the Duncan ranking of occupational prestige, the 1974 survey includes the ISR's Political Behavior Classification of occupations. This categorizing scheme, which distinguishes nearly twice as many observed occupations among sampled respondents as either of the other two codes, gives precision to the occupational classification and fosters its efficient use in tandem with other data sources. While the procedures described below are adaptable to less precise occupational classifications, the properties of the resulting class categories may be slightly attenuated from the empirical results achieved with this particular data set.

In sorting occupations into class groupings, I have used information from the surveys themselves and from other sources, notably the Dictionary of Occupational Titles (U.S. Department of Labor, 1977) and the Census Bureau's reports on measures of the characteristics of workers in various occupations (U.S. Bureau of the Census, 1973). Since neither of these sources has received much attention from political scientists, a brief summary of their contents may be helpful.

Perhaps the major source of occupational data is the U.S. Bureau of the Census, whose publication entitled "Occupational Characteristics" tabulates data from the decennial census, showing selected characteristics of workers in about 500 occupations (U.S. Bureau of the Census, 1973). Though it is an invaluable source of information about workers themselves, it is not as appropriate for our purposes as a data source that describes the content of the jobs these workers do—for it is to the occupations themselves (and their relations to other positions in the production process) that theories of class structure point.

The Department of Labor publishes such a directory, the *Dictionary of Occupational Titles (DOT)*, which is primarily intended to guide the work of the U.S. Employment Service in matching job applicants with jobs (U.S. Department of Labor, 1977). Since the publication of the third edition of the *DOT* in 1965, sociologists and economists have made varied uses of these data to investigate the operation of the labor market, the distribution of income, and numerous topics related to social stratification (Eckhaus, 1964; Berg, 1970; Scoville, 1972; Lucas, 1974; Stolzenberg, 1975; Kalleberg and Griffen, 1978, 1980; Cullen and Novick, 1979; Spenner, 1980). The current edition of the *DOT* contains descriptions of some 12,000 occupations, each of which is characterized in terms of the complexity and physical demands of the work, the environment in which it is performed, and the training and aptitudes required of workers in the occupation. Unlike most other sources of information about occupations, which use worker self-reports, data in the *DOT* are the result of extensive direct information on jobs and their performances (U.S. Department of Labor 1972, 1977; Miller et al., 1980; Cain and Treiman, 1981).

The *DOT* is the main source of supplementary data for classifying occupations in the research reported here. In the *DOT*, each occupation is assigned a nine-digit code. The first three digits correspond to the Census Bureau's detailed classification, and they sort occupations in a fashion similar to the political behavior codes used in the 1974 Center for Political Studies (CPS) survey. These codes classify occupations by the technology involved, the industry, and the resulting product or service. The next three digits, which are the most useful for supplementing data for secondary analyses, classify tasks by their complexity in terms of data, people, and things. While the "people" dimension is somewhat arbitrarily arranged, the dimensions for "data" and "things" are Guttman scales ranging from complex tasks to simple ones. For instance, tasks range from "synthesizing" to "copying" data, from "setting up" to "feeding–offbearing" in relation to things, and from "mentoring" to "taking instructions–helping" people (U.S. Department of Labor 1977, p. 1365ff). The last three digits serve only to provide each occupational title a distinct code in the classification. Finally, each occupation is also scored on some 41 other characteristics, including the training needed for assuming the job, and measures of aptitude, temperament, interests, physical demands, and working conditions. These indicators are discussed, both substantively and in terms of measurement reliability, elsewhere (Kohn, 1969; Scoville, 1972; Spenner, 1973, 1980; Temme, 1975; Miller et al., 1980).

In research to date, I have coded occupations into classes based almost exclusively on the nine-digit code in the *DOT*. The next stage of the research will refine these codes by including information from Census Bureau publications and from the *DOT*'s additional indicators.

The actual classification of occupations proceeds in stages in the following way. First, it is ascertained whether the respondent is self-employed. If the respondent is self-employed, then the size of the business enterprise (from income or sales data included in the survey) and the industry can be used to classify the respondent as a capitalist, a petit bourgeois, or as occupying the contradictory location between these two categories. Some few respondents report that they work both for themselves and for others; these are generally classified either as petit bourgeois or as semiautonomous employees, depending on the occupation.

The lack of detailed information about the job and conditions of work for each respondent presents the most problems in classifying those who are employed by others. In the abstract, these workers fall into three categories, which can be distinguished fairly clearly as ideal types: middle managers and technocrats; lower-level managers and supervisors; and workers. Membership in the first group is generally unambiguous, since most of the job titles in this category indicate management responsibilities. However, some respondents classified as technocrats might arguably be better coded as semiautonomous employees. Although the number of these cases is small, it is unfortunate that there are no detailed data on the corporate hierarchy into which each respondent fits. In the second and third categories, lower-level managers and supervisors and ordinary workers, respectively, there are also relatively few ambiguous cases, since occupational titles generally provide enough information to allow classification according to the extent of supervisorial responsibility. In questionable cases (specifically, skilled and craft workers who may have limited authority over small workgroups, but whose occupational title gives no grounds for inferring this), I have classified the position as that of a worker rather than a supervisor. Again, the number of cases is small, and preliminary tests assessing the possible impact of altering the classification of these and other questionable cases indicates that it would be negligible.

Empirical work based on the formulation of class categories similar to this one has related class to income distribution (Wright, 1979; Robinson and Kelley, 1979) to various aspects of job satisfaction and occupational attainment (Kalleberg and Griffen, 1978, 1980), and to ideological self-identification (Robinson and Kelley, 1979). The consistent result of this research is that class structure contributes to the researcher's ability to explain a number of important social phenomena, even when other conventional variables like prestige and education are included in the model.

In the matter of politically relevant class feeling, however, and especially in predicting the effect of class on political responses to short-term economic fluctuations, the issue is not how a social scientist might allocate causal force among the various components of a complex global variable like socioeconomic class. Rather, the issue is how people in the mass public perceive the political interests of their position in the occupational hierarchy. Occupational prestige and the Marx–Dahrendorf class categories are not separate variables which might operate jointly to shape some political attitude; they are the operational indicators of two alternative hypotheses about political cognition—that is, class consciousness (cf. Kohn, 1969). The empirical puzzle is: do people predominantly view themselves as occupying slots in a continuously graded, individualistic hierarchy of positions; or do they think of politico-economic choices as bearing on interests which they share with a large number of similar others, interests which are naturally opposed to those of other classes? Note that this is not a question about stratification in general, but about the way in which economic inequality takes on political meaning. As consumers of cars, or clothes, or restaurant dinners, people might well picture the social world as a smoothly graded prestige ranking. The thrust of the theory I describe in this chapter is that when it comes to issues of political economy (principally macroeconomic management, but also such issues such as job training, minimum wage, and public employment programs), citizens see economic interests as characterizing particular groups of similarly situated people rather than as distinctive for each person.

Several preliminary empirical issues are joined in another report on this research (Weatherford, 1982), where it is shown that, compared to a matching measure of occupational prestige, the Marx–Dahrendorf class categories account for more of the variance in party identification and in public attitudes on inflation and unemployment. But numerous questions remain about how precisely these class categories operate and about their relation to sociologists' more conventional measures of occupational ranking. Does each separate category have a distinctive causal impact on political attitudes, or does this theoretical grouping into seven categories collapse into fewer, larger groups when its political impact is gauged? Much of the attractiveness of two- and three-class models of society arises from their economy, and the results of several theoretical and empirical studies support the expectation of fewer distinct classes (Parkin, 1971; Hamilton, 1972; Giddens, 1973). Do these categories vary along an underlying unidimensional continuum, and consequently have linear effects on political attitudes; or is the category space best described by multiple dimensions? The work of Wright (1979) and of Robinson and Kelley (1979) on income determination shows that class effects are predominantly linear and monotonic on income, but since political attitudes and electoral choice are more complex and multifaceted phenomena than levels of income, the implications of this research are largely indeterminant.

Precisely how does class affect political thinking in the American polity? Does it contribute to the politicization of personal problems? To the perception of party differences? To the strength of partisanship and the intensity of issue preferences? As with the treatment of partisanship, the theoretical orientation toward class may facilitate or inhibit the researcher's ability to understand the political effects of economic events. It will be the task of later research to elaborate and test the explanatory power of this conceptualization.

CONCLUSIONS

I have argued in this chapter that the empirical analysis of the political effects of short-term economic fluctuations requires not only dependable measures of economic conditions, but also an appropriate conceptualization of the roles of classes and parties.

The factor of political party is critical because parties have the potential for aggregating numerous inchoate economic grievances into electoral blocs, and then of organizing and simplifying competition between the government and the opposition over programmatic economic policies. Political behaviorists have become accustomed over the last three decades to thinking of partisanship as a predetermined component in models of the vote. When, by the late 1970s, the work of several researchers showed that people's party identification responds in predictable ways to short-term political and economic events, the authors of some aggregate studies inferred that the factor of political party, being determined by the same factors that determine the vote or ratings of executive popularity, should be omitted from such models. Despite its patterned short-term fluctuations, however, partisanship remains a quite stable political cue for most citizens. Recent contributions to analyses of the vote have experimented with alternative techniques for separating the stable from the varying components of party affiliation, and it is anticipated that future models of politico-economic interaction will integrate this work.

Class is the other master variable in the proper understanding of economic policymaking in the context of electoral accountability. The class structure maps the incidence of the personal impacts of macroeconomic cycles as well as the patterned distribution of economic interests. Moreover, the degree to which people are conscious of common class membership may help to explain why they make (or fail to make) these economic interests politically relevant.

As in economics and sociology, the treatment of stratification in political science has encompassed two traditions of research. The one, derived from Marx and extended by Dahrendorf, focuses on the physical and social relations of production, and emphasizes the discontinuous pattern of inequality and the consequent conflict that results from the hierarchical organization of work. The status tradition emphasizes open and competitive acquisition of training and occupational skills, and culminates in the Blau–Duncan paradigm of status attainment, and in the approach to social inequality that views stratification as a continuously distributed control variable in political analysis. Researchers working within each tradition have largely ignored the other tradition and have tended to infer that their findings are conclusive about stratification in general. The second part of this chapter described a reformulated concept of class categories which attempts to capture the process through which socioeconomic inequality might have political effects.

Over the last 10 years, the work of Kramer, Nordhaus, Lindbeck, MacRae, Keech, Monroe, and others has considerably advanced our understanding of the way in which government economic policy is conditioned by the timing of elections. Frey and (especially) Hibbs and others have mapped the role of ideology and the way in which the class-based party coalitions produce patterns, not only in the timing of growth spurts, but also in the distribution of the costs and benefits of policies located at different points along the Phillips curve, which charts the trade-off between unemployment and changes in the rate of inflation. These studies have been motivated by imputations of preferences and interests to the public. Though these imputed preferences are based on common sense, they find little support in the literature of political behavior.

The next task for researchers in political economy is to explain how the traditions of aggregate historical research and individual cross-sectional research fit together. This chapter, by focusing on party and class—two critical components of theoretical formulations in both these traditions—has attempted to contribute to the achievement of that task.

NOTES

1. This synthesis relies on the work of Parkin (1971) and Giddens (1973) among theoretical sources, and on that of Robinson and Kelley (1979) and, especially that of Wright (1978, 1979) and Wright and Perrone (1977) among empirical studies. More general critical commentaries on the class theories of Marx and Dahrendorf are found in Wright (1980); Hazelrigg (1972); Turner (1973); and Weingart (1969).

2. Dahrendorf asserts that these two authority classes are universal—that is, they occur in all associations from families to corporations to political parties. Because of this claim, the theory has frequently been criticized for being too broad (Giddens, 1973), but Dahrendorf generally regarded production relations as occupying the primary place among all authority relations (Dahrendorf, 1959, p. 142).

3. The resulting arrangement of class categories follows Wright (1978), although I disagree with his argument that the theoretical warrant for this conceptualization can be found in Marx. Other theoretical approaches to elaborating the Marxist classification are found in the studies of Poulantzas (1973, 1975); Carchedi (1975, 1977); Cutler et al. (1977); and Ehrenreich and Ehrenreich (1977). Approaches more strongly influenced by Weber include those of Parkin (1971) and Giddens (1973).

4. Marx illuminates the nature of the contradictory class location of small employers with an historical example:

A certain stage of capitalist production necessitates that the capitalist be able to devote the whole of the time during which he functions as a capitalist to the appropriation and, therefore, to the control of the labor power of others, and to the selling of the products of labor. The guilds of the Middle Ages, therefore, tried to prevent by force the transformation of the master of a trade into a capitalist by limiting the number of laborers that could be employed by one master within a very small maximum. (Marx, 1867, pp. 308–309)

5. Two classic studies done in the early years of the political behavior movement have probably received too little attention in this respect. Both Converse (1957) and Eulau (1962) analyze the psychological meaning of class identification, and Eulau's work elaborates the connections between objective and subjective indicators. See Weatherford (1976) for a summary of this literature.

REFERENCES

Arcelus, F., and A. Meltzer (1975). "The Effects of Aggregate Economic Variables on Congressional Elections." *American Political Science Review* 69:1232–1239.

Balibar, E. (1970). "The Basic Concepts of Historical Materialism." In A. Althusser, and E. Balibar (eds.), B. Brewster (trans.), *Reading Capital.* London: New Left Books, pp. 199–308.

Baran, P., and P. Sweezy (1966). *Monopoly Capital.* New York: Monthly Review Press.

Becker, G. (1965). *Human Capital: A Theoretical and Empirical Analysis with Special Reference to Education.* New York: National Bureau of Economic Research.

Berg, I. (1970). *Education and Jobs: The Great Training Robbery.* New York: Praeger.

Blau, P., and O. Duncan (1967). *The American Occupational Structure.* New York: John Wiley & Sons.

Blinder, A. S., and H. Y. Esaki (1978). "Macroeconomic Activity and Income Distribution in the United States." *Review of Economics and Statistics* XX:604–609.

Bloom, H., and D. Price (1975). "Comment." *American Political Science Review* 69:1240–1254.

Braverman, H. (1974). *Labor and Monopoly Capital: The Degredation of Work in The Twentieth Century.* New York: Monthly Review Press.

Brittain, S. (1977). *The Economic Consequences of Democracy.* London: Temple Smith.

Brody, R. (1977). "Stability and Change in Party Identification: Presidential to

Off-Years." Presented at the Annual Meeting of the American Political
Science Association.

_____, and B. I. Page (1972). "Comment: The Assessment of Policy Voting."
American Political Science Review 66:450–458.

_____, and P. M. Sniderman (1977). "From Life-Space to Polling Place: The
Relevance of Personal Concerns for Voting Behavior." *British Journal of
Political Science* 7:337–360.

Buchanan, J. M., and R. Wagner (1977). *Democracy in Deficit: The Political
Legacy of Lord Keynes*. New York: Academic Press.

Cain, P., and D. Treiman (1981). "The *Dictionary of Occupational Titles* as a
Source of Occupational Data." *American Sociological Review* 46:253–278.

Carchedi, G. (1975). "On the Economic Identification of the New Middle Class."
Economics and Society 4(1):1–86.

_____(1977). *On Economic Identification of Social Classes*. London: Routledge.

Castells, M. (1980). *The Economic Crisis and American Society*. Princeton:
Princeton University Press.

Converse, P. (1957). "The Shifting Role of Class in American Politics." In E.
Maccoby, et al. (eds.), *Readings in Social Psychology*. New York: Holt, pp.
388–399.

_____(1966). "The Concept of the Normal Vote." In A. Campbell, et al. (eds.),
Elections and the Political Order. New York: John Wiley & Sons, pp. 9–39.

_____(1975). "Public Opinion and Voting Behavior." In F. I. Greenstein, and
N. W. Polsby (eds.), *The Handbook of Political Science*. Reading, MA:
Addison-Wesley, pp. 75–169.

Cullen, J., and S. Novick (1979). "The Davis–Moore Theory of Stratification: A
Further Examination and Extension." *American Journal of Sociology*
84:1424–1437.

Cutler, A., B. Hindess, P. Hirst, and A. Hussain (1977). *Marx's* Capital *and
Capitalism Today*. London: Routledge.

Dahrendorf, R. (1967). *Conflict After Class*. London: Longmans Green.

Dunkerley, D. (1975). *The Foreman*. London: Routledge.

Eckhaus, R. (1964). "Economic Criteria for Education and Training." *Review of
Economics and Statistics* 46:181–188.

Ehrenreich, B., and J. Ehrenreich (1977). "The Professional-Managerial Class."
In P. Walker (ed.), *Between Labor and Capital*. Boston: South End Press,
1979, pp. 5–48.

Eulau, H. (1962). *Class and Party in the Eisenhower Years*. New York: Free Press.

Fiorina, M. P. (1977). "An Outline for a Model of Party Choice." *American
Journal of Political Science* 21:601–625.

_____(1978). "Economic Retrospective Voting in American National Elections."
American Journal of Political Science 22:426–443.

_____(1981a). *Retrospective Voting in American Politics*. New Haven: Yale
University Press.

_____ (1981b). "Short- and Long-Term Effects of Economic Conditions on Individual Voting Decisions." In D. A. Hibbs, and H. Fassbender (eds.), In *Contemporary Political Economy*. Amsterdam, North-Holland, pp. 73–100.

Frey, B. (1978). *Modern Political Economy*. Oxford: Martin Robertson.

_____, and F. Schneider (1979). "An Econometric Model with an Endogenous Government Sector." *Public Choice* 34:29–44.

_____, and F. Schneider (1981). "Recent Research on Empirical Politico-Economic Models." In D. A. Hibbs, and H. Fassbender (eds.), *Contemporary Political Economy*. Amsterdam: North-Holland, pp. 11–30.

Giddens, A. (1973). *The Class Structure of the Advanced Societies*. New York: Harper & Row.

Goldberg, A. S. (1966). "Discerning a Causal Pattern Among Data on Voting Behavior." *American Political Science Review* 60:913–922.

Goodhart, C. A. E., and R. J. Bhansali (1970). "Political Economy." *Political Studies* 18:43–106.

Gramlich, E. M. (1974). "The Distributional Consequences of Higher Unemployment." *Brookings Papers on Economic Activity* 2:293–341.

Hamilton, R. (1972). *Class and Politics in the United States*. New York: John Wiley & Sons.

Hazelrigg, L. (1972). "Class, Property and Authority: Dahrendorf's Critique of Marx's Theory of Class." *Social Forces* 50:473–487.

Hibbs, D. A. (1975). *Economic Interest and the Politics of Marcoeconomic Policy*. Cambridge, MA: Center for International Studies, Massachusetts Institute of Technology.

_____ (1977). "Political Parties and Macroeconomic Policy." *American Political Science Review* 71:1468–1487.

_____, with the assistance of R. D. Rivers and N. Vasilatos (1980). "The Dynamics of Political Support for American Presidents among Occupation and Partisan Groups." Cambridge, MA: Harvard University Department of Government.

_____, and N. Vasilatos (1981). "Macroeconomic Performance and Mass Public Support in the United States and Great Britain." In D. A. Hibbs and H. Fassbender (eds.), *Contemporary Political Economy*. Amsterdam: North-Holland, pp. 31–48.

_____ (1979). "The Mass Public and Macroeconomic Performance: The Dynamics of Public Opinion Toward Unemployment and Inflation." *American Journal of Political Science* 23:705–731.

Hodge, R., and D. Treiman (1968). "Class Identification in the United States." *American Journal of Sociology* 73:535–547.

Institute for Social Research (1969). *Codebook for the Survey of Working Conditions*. Ann Arbor, MI: Institute for Social Research.

_____ (1972). *Codebook for the Panel Study of Income Dynamics (Vol. 1): Study Design, Procedures, and Available Data*. Ann Arbor, MI: Institute for Social

Research.
_____ (1973). *Codebook for the Quality of Employment Survey*. Ann Arbor, MI: Institute for Social Research.

Kalleberg, A., and L. Griffen (1978). "Positional Sources of Inequality in Job Satisfaction." *Sociology of Work and Occupations* 5:371–401.

_____ (1980). "Class, Occupation, and Inequality in Job Rewards." *American Journal of Sociology* 85:731–768.

Keech, W. F. (1980). "Elections and Macroeconomic Policy Optimization." *American Journal of Political Science* 24:345–367.

Kernell, S. (1978). "Explaining Presidential Popularity." *American Political Science Review* 72:506–522.

_____, and D. A. Hibbs (1981). "A Critical Threshold Model of Presidential Popularity." In D. A. Hibbs, and H. Fassbender (eds.), *Contemporary Political Economy*. Amsterdam: North-Holland, pp. 43–72.

Kiewiet, D. R. (1981). "Policy-Oriented Voting in Response to Economic Issues." *American Political Science Review* 75:448–459.

Kinder, D. (1981). "Presidents, Prosperity, and Public Opinion." *Public Opinion Quarterly* 45:1–21.

_____, and W. R. Mebane, Jr. (1983). "Politics and Economics in Everyday Life." In K. Monroe (ed.), *The Political Process and Economic Change*. New York: Agathon Press, pp. 141–180 (this volume).

_____, and D. R. Kiewiet (1979). "Economic Discontents and Political Behavior." *American Journal of Political Science* 23:495–527.

Klorman, R. (1978). "Trend in Personal Finances and the Vote." *Public Opinion Quarterly* 42:31–48.

Kohn, M. (1969). *Class and Conformity: A Study of Values*. Homewood, IL: Dorsey.

_____, and C. Schooler (1969). "Class, Occupation and Orientation." *American Sociological Review* 34:659–678.

Kramer, G. (1971). "Short-Term Fluctuations in U.S. Voting Behavior, 1896–1964." *American Political Science Review* 65:131–145.

_____ (1980). "Aggregate Data Versus Survey Findings on the Effects of Economic Conditions on Voting Behavior." Yale University and Caltech. (Mimeographed)

Ladd, E. C., and C. Hadley (1978). *Transformations of The American Party System* (2nd ed.). New York: Norton.

Lane, R. E. (1962). *Political Ideology*. New York: Free Press.

Lau, L. J., and B. Frey (1971). "Ideology, Public Approval, and Government Behavior." *Public Choice* 10:20–40.

Lopreato, J. (1968). "Authority Relations and Class Conflict." *Social Forces* 47:70–79.

Lucas, R. (1974). "The Distribution of Job Characteristics." *Review of Economics and Statistics* 56:530–540.

MacRae, C. D. (1977). "A Political Model of the Business Cycle." *Journal of*

Political Economy 85:239–263.

Marx, K. (1972). "The Eighteenth Brumaire of Louis Bonaparte." In R. Tucker (ed.), *The Marx–Engels Reader*. New York: Norton. (Originally published, 1852.)

――――― (1967). *Capital* (Vol. 1). New York: Modern Library. (Originally published, 1867.)

Miller, A., D. Treiman, P. Cain, and P. Roos, (eds.) (1980). *Work, Jobs, and Occupations: A Critical Review of The* Dictionary of Occupational Titles. Washington, D.C.: National Academy Press.

Mincer, J. (1974). *Schooling, Experience and Earnings*. New York: Columbia University Press.

Mirer, T. (1974). "Aspects of the Variability of Family Income." In J. Morgan (ed.), *Five Thousand American Families—Patterns of Economic Progress* (Vol. 2). Ann Arbor, MI: Survey Research Center, pp. 201–212.

Monroe, K. R. (1983). *Presidential Popularity and the Economy*. New York: Praeger (forthcoming).

National Opinion Research Corporation (1972–1976). *Codebook for the General Society Survey*. Chicago: National Opinion Research Corporation.

Nordhaus, W. D. (1975). "The Political Business Cycle." *Review of Economic Studies* 42:169–189.

Ossowski, S. (1963). *Class Structure in the Social Consciousness*. London: Routledge.

Page, B. I. (1976). "The Theory of Political Ambiguity." *American Political Science Review* 70:742–752.

――――― (1978). *Choices and Echoes in Presidential Elections*. Chicago: University of Chicago Press.

――――― , and R. A. Brody (1972). "Policy Voting and the Electoral Process: The Vietnam War Issue." *American Political Science Review* 66:979–995.

Parkin, F. (1971). *Class Inequality and Political Order*. New York: Praeger.

Petrocik, J. R. (1981). *Party Coalitions: Realignments and the Decline of the New Deal Party System*. Chicago: University of Chicago Press.

Pomper, G. M. (1968). *Elections in America: Control and Influence in Democratic Politics*. New York: Dodd-Mead.

Popkin, S., et al. (1971). "Comment: What Have You Done For Me Lately?" *American Political Science Review* 70:779–805.

Poulantzas, N. (1973). *Political Power and Social Class*. London: Routledge.

――――― (1975). *Classes in Contemporary Capitalism*. London: New Left Books.

Robinson, R., and J. Kelley (1979). "Class as Conceived by Marx and Dahrendorf: Effects on Income Inequality and Politics in the United States and Great Britain." *American Sociological Review* 44:38–58.

Rosenstone, S. J. (1982). "Economic Adversity and Voter Turnout." *American Journal of Political Science*, 26:25–46.

Schneider, F. (1978). "Different (Income) Classes and Presidential Popularity: An Empirical Analysis." *Munich Social Science Review* 2:53–69.

Scoville, J. (1972). *Manpower and Occupational Analysis: Concepts and Measurements*. Lexington, MA: Lexington.

Shepsle, K. A. (1972). "The Strategy of Ambiguity: Uncertainty and Electoral Competition." *American Political Science Review* 66:555–568.

Skocpol, T. (1981). "Political Response to Capitalist Crisis: Neo-Marxist Theories of the State and the Case of the New Deal." *Politics and Society* 10:155–201.

Sniderman, P. M., and R. A. Brody (1977). "Coping: The Ethic of Self-Reliance." *American Journal of Political Science* 60:913–922.

Spaeth, J. (1979). "Vertical Differentiation Among Occupations." *American Sociological Review* 44:746–762.

Spenner, G. (1973). "Temporal Changes in Work Content." *American Sociological Review* 44:968–975.

_____ (1980). "Occupational Characteristics and Classification Systems: New Uses of the *Dictionary of Occupational Titles* in Social Research." *Sociological Methods and Research* 9:239–264.

Stigler, G. (1973). "General Economic Conditions and National Elections." *American Economic Review* 64:160–167.

Stolzenberg, R. (1975). "Occupations, Labor Markets and the Process of Wage Attainment." *American Sociological Review* 40:645–666.

Tannenbaum, P. et al. (1974). *Hierarchy in Organization*. San Francisco: Jossey-Bass.

Temme, L. (1975). *Occupation: Meaning and Measures*. Washington, D.C.: Bureau of Social Research.

Thurow, L. C. (1965). "The Changing Structure of Unemployment: An Econometric Study." *Review of Economics and Statistics* 47:137–149.

_____ (1969). "Analyzing the American Income Distribution." *American Economic Review* 5:261–269.

_____ (1975). *Generating Inequality: Mechanisms of Distribution in the U.S. Economy*. New York: Basic Books.

Tufte, E. (1975). "Determinants of the Outcome of Midterm Congressional Elections." *American Political Science Review* 69:812–826.

_____ (1978). *Political Control of the Economy*. Princeton, N.J.: Princeton University Press.

Turner, J. (1973). "From Utopia to Where? A Strategy for Reformulating the Dahrendorf Conflict Model." *Social Forces* 52:236–244.

United States Bureau of the Census (1973). *United States Census of Population: 1970*. Subject Report PC (2)-7A, "Occupational Characteristics." Washington, D.C.: U.S. Government Printing Office.

United States Department of Labor (1972). *Handbook for Analyzing Jobs*. Washington, D.C.: U.S. Government Printing Office.

_____ (1977). *Dictionary of Occupational Titles* (4th ed.). Washington, D.C.: U.S. Government Printing Office.

Vanneman, R. D. (1980). "U.S. and British Perceptions of Class." *American Journal of Sociology* 85(4):769–790.

Wagner, R. E. (1977). "Economic Manipulation for Fun and Profit." *Kyklos* 30:395–410.

Weatherford, M. S. (1976). "Economic Sources of Political Behavior: Class and Class Identification in American Politics." Ph.D. dissertation, Stanford University.

_____ (1978). "Economic Conditions and Electoral Outcomes: Class Differences in the Political Response to Recession." *American Journal of Political Science* 22:917–938.

_____ (1980). "Alternative Sources of Politico-Economic Demands: Carter Policies and the 1978 Congressional Elections." Presented at Annual Meeting of the American Political Science Association, Washington D.C.

_____ (1982). "Recession and Social Classes: Economic Impacts and Political Opinions." *Political Behavior* 4:7–31.

Weber, M. (1947). *The Theory of Social and Economic Organization*. New York: Oxford University Press.

Weingart, P. (1969). "Beyond Parsons? A Critique of Ralf Dahrendorf's Conflict Theory." *Social Forces* 48:151–165.

Wides, J. (1976). "Self-Perceived Economic Change and Political Orientations: A Preliminary Exploration." *American Politics Quarterly* 4:395–412.

Wright, E. (1976). "Class Boundaries in Advanced Capitalism." *New Left Review* 98:3–41.

_____ (1978). *Class, Crisis and the State*. London: New Left Books.

_____ (1979). *Class Structure and Income Determination*. New York: Academic Press.

_____ (1980). "Varieties of Marxist Conceptions of Class Structure." *Politics and Society* 9:323–370.

_____ , and L. Perrone (1977). "Marxist Class Categories and Income Inequality." *American Sociological Review* 42:32–55.

Zeitlin, M. (1974). "Corporate Ownership and Control: The Large Corporation and the Capitalist Class." *American Journal of Sociology* 79:1073–1119.

8: Economic Expectations, Economic Uncertainty, and Presidential Popularity

Kristen R. Monroe and Maurice D. Levi

The influence of economic conditions on voting and presidential popularity has been an important concern of political scientists and economists for the last 50 years.[1] Beginning with Kramer's (1971) work, there has been much rigorous statistical analysis of the political consequences of objectively measured aggregate economic conditions.[2] Recent research has extended systematic analysis to the measurement of the political impact of more subjective, individual perceptions of economic reality, with particular attention paid to the distinctions made between individual and overall economic well-being.[3] Much of this recent work has analyzed survey responses to explicit questions measuring economic attitudes using data collected by polling centers such as the Gallup, the Harris, or the University of Michigan's Survey Research Center. While some questions on expectations of future economic conditions do exist in these surveys, such questions have only recently been utilized to test for the political importance of economic expectations, perhaps because of the lack of a long time series collected at regular intervals. The few works in this area have concluded that the gap between the individual's expectations of future economic conditions and actual economic reality has a tremendous impact on political support.[4]

The present chapter considers the importance of economic expectations for mass public support for American presidents from 1950 to 1975. It moves analysis beyond a simple consideration of the political impact of economic expectations, however, to also include an analysis of the political importance of uncertainty over future economic events. In particular, short-term fluctuations in the Gallup Poll indicators of presidential popularity are explained through measurements of economic expectations and uncertainty about key economic events collected since 1946 by Joseph Livingston. These data are analyzed in a standard multivariate statistical analysis to determine the political importance of the gap between actual and expected inflation, the gap between actual and expected economic growth, uncertainty about inflation, and uncertainty about economic growth. Two additional variables are also included to avoid specification error; the first measures military involvement in Korea and Vietnam, and the second measures public shifts in attitudes toward the president resulting both from political activity around elections and from the honeymoon phenomenon following inaugurations.

By considering both the degree to which presidential popularity responds to the difference between actual and expected economic experience and the degree to which presidential popularity responds simply to uncertainty concerning economic conditions, we can test two alternative theories of short-term political-economic interaction. The first theory is the traditional theory of a revolution of rising expectations; this theory argues that political change is affected not so much by actual economic conditions as by the gap between actual and expected economic conditions. The second theory stresses the political consequences of uncertainty concerning future economic conditions; rather than arguing that the popularity of political incumbents rises and falls when the economy performs better or worse than expected, it suggests that popularity rises when there is a certainty about the economic future and falls when there is uncertainty. While both of these theories emphasize economic expectations in explaining political events, the two theories accentuate political psychologies which suggest quite different choices for policymakers who must face reelection.

This chapter consists of four parts. First, we present a brief discussion of the theoretical framework underlying the analysis; second, a discussion of the logic behind the expectations and uncertainty hypotheses; and third, a description of the model, variables, and data employed in the analysis. Finally, we present the empirical findings and some concluding remarks.

THEORETICAL FRAMEWORK

We can contrast our two theoretical approaches through the use of the following hypotheses, referred to for simplicity's sake as the expectations hypothesis and the uncertainty hypothesis. The expectations hypothesis suggests that public support for political incumbents is influenced not so much by actual economic conditions as by the gap between actual and anticipated economic reality. If this hypothesis is correct, political support will increase when the economy is better than had been expected, even if objectively conditions remain poor or actually deteriorate. Conversely, the expectations hypothesis suggests that political support will decline when economic conditions are worse than had been expected, even though the economy remains prosperous or genuinely improves. The classic example of this expectations hypothesis is De Tocqueville's analysis of the French revolution, a revolution which occurred in a France more prosperous than before but one whose rate of growth had slowed, leading expectations to outpace economic reality and resulting in frustrations culminating in revolt.

In contrast to this, the uncertainty hypothesis stresses the psychological dislocation from uncertainty about the economic future, an uncertainty which has negative political consequences that are independent of public reaction to the gap between actual and expected economic conditions. Thus, the uncertainty hypothesis emphasizes the public's need for certainty and predictability, rather than public pleasure at doing better than had been anticipated or displeasure at doing worse than had been expected. This hypothesis explains situations in which support for a president decreases because of an uncertain economic climate, despite the fact that this uncertainty resulted in the occurrence of better than expected economic conditions.

These theoretical approaches must rely on two disparate bodies of work: (1) general social science theories concerning the political consequences of violent political changes, primarily violent changes, resulting from frustrated economic expectations; and (2) much narrower, technical economic work which measures economic responses to uncertainty or frustrations concerning economic growth.

The historical literature concerning the political consequences of rising economic expectations begins with De Tocqueville (1840). Since then, many analysts have discussed historical situations in which political support was withdrawn from a regime not because economic conditions deteriorated, but rather because conditions failed to rise as quickly as past growth led the populace to expect (see, for example, Davies, 1962, 1969; and Gurr, 1970). Recent analysts have refined the measurement techniques and applied the psychological concept of a revolution of rising expectations to less violent regime changes or to microlevel survey data. The most significant analyses of public opinion responses indicating the importance of economic expectations for more routinized expressions of support for political incumbents in representative democracies are Alt's important work on England and the analysis of American public opinion by Hibbs and by Kuklinski and West (Alt, 1979; Hibbs, 1981; Kuklinski and West, 1981). These works suggest that although it may be difficult to operationalize and measure expectations systematically, the usefulness of attempting to develop such indicators is well worth the effort since the expectations factor is often crucial.[5]

THE EXPECTATIONS AND UNCERTAINTY HYPOTHESES

The relevant work on economic responses to uncertainty and frustrations concerning economic growth is more technical and less well known to political science. An accurate summary can be presented most simply within the context of a discussion of the logic behind the hypothesized political impact of economic expectations and uncertainty. We begin by assuming that people are satisfied when events turn out better than they had expected and are dissatisfied when events turn out to be worse than expected. The political consequences of this economic satisfaction/dissatisfaction then will be reflected in presidential popularity. This can be expressed in the following way:

$$P_t - P_{t-1} = \beta_0 + \beta_1(M_{t-1} - M^*_{t-1}) + \beta_2(\dot{Y}_{t-1} - \dot{Y}^*_{t-1}) + e \quad (1)$$

where P_t is the percent approving of the president in the opinion polls taken at the end of t, M_{t-1} is the inflation from $t-1$ to t (e.g., between any April and October), $\dot{Y}_{t-1}$ is the rate of real growth from $t-1$ to t, and M^*_{t-1} and $\dot{Y}^*_{t-1}$ are the expected rates of inflation and growth for the same period, $t-1$ to t, these expectations being held at the end of $t-1$. e is the regular regression error term.

In Eq. (1), we would expect β_1 to be negative. If the public does express its dissatisfaction politically, then presidential popularity should fall when inflation is faster than people anticipated. Similarly, we would expect β_2 to be positive since popularity should increase when economic growth exceeds earlier expectations. Of course, if economic events turn out exactly as had been anticipated in advance, then actual and expected values coincide, and there would be no political consequences and therefore no change in presidential popularity in Eq. (1).

The variable we have used for inflation in Eq. (1), $(M_{t-1} - M^*_{t-1})$, is best known as "unanticipated inflation." It is important to note that the formulation in (1) differs from having variations in political fortunes depend on variations in actual inflation (i.e., $M_{t-1} - M_{t-2}$). The formulation we have employed measures both unanticipated change ($M_{t-1} - M^*_{t-1}$) and the anticipated change ($M_{t-1} - M^*_{t-2}$). What relation (1) comes down to, then, is the assumption that anticipated changes in inflation are less likely to affect satisfaction than are unanticipated changes. The unanticipated changes thus should have greater political impact.

Although we shall provide evidence on both the formulation that uses just anticipated inflation and the formulation that includes anticipated changes in inflation, we should take a further conceptual look at our implicit assumption in (1) before actually testing our estimating equation. Some economists might theoretically argue that we should find little or no political impact from either unanticipated or anticipated changes in inflation because of the distributional aspects of inflation. The logic behind this leads us into the technical economic literature discussing the social costs and benefits of inflation. We will see that it is very important to consider the distributional effects of inflation, since the net aggregate effect suggests no clear political impact of errors in predicting past or current inflation. Uncertainty about future inflation, however, is disquieting enough to have a negative political impact of its own.

Inflation: Costs of Anticipated and Unanticipated Inflation

To the extent that inflation is anticipated, all nominally expressed contracts are likely to be adjusted such that there are none who gain and none who lose. There are, however, two routes through which there might be losses from anticipated inflation. The first of these routes is that whereby higher inflation means higher interest rates and thereby a reduced stock of real cash balances. With the cost of providing these balances being less than the service return, a welfare loss is incurred.[6] The second route is that whereby the income tax burden, in a progressive tax structure without indexed tax brackets, rises with actual inflation.

Although we have little empirical evidence of how powerful a political force either anticipated or unanticipated inflation will be, we would conjecture that the effects of anticipated inflation will be overshadowed by the potentially large dislocations from unanticipated inflation. It is well known that those people who contract for a fixed nominal income and fail to account for the inflation which will materialize will lose from this unanticipated inflation. It is also well known that creditors, the holders of nominally expressed private, public, and corporate debt, will also lose by failing to contract for compensation for unanticipated inflation.

But what of the other side of these losses? Those who agree to pay the fixed incomes, the real value of which is eroded by unanticipated inflation, will make a gain that equals the losses by receivers of the fixed incomes. Furthermore, those who issue the debt that leads to losses for the holders of that debt, will make offsetting gains. (One example concerns the many homeowners who agree to private fixed-interest mortgages and fare very well from unanticipated inflation.)

In addition to this, however, are the losses made by the holders of both public and corporate debt. These losses potentially will be offset by gains made by both taxpayers and corporate shareholders. These offsets, although discussed *inter alia* by Kessel and Alchian (1962), are perhaps a little less obvious and require a further word of explanation. Particularly since the government is by far the largest debtor, it might therefore be thought that unanticipated inflation would induce losses for all direct and indirect holders of that debt—a very large number of people. Since there is a chance that gains made by the government might be perceived to reduce the future tax burden, however, taxpayers might capitalize a gain precisely equal to the losses of the holders of the debt, namely, the bond holders. With taxpayers possibly perceiving gains that offset bond holders' losses, any aggregate effect becomes ambiguous.[7] Our overall conclusion, therefore, is that the distributional aspects of inflation leave the political impact of even unanticipated inflation extremely unclear.

The Political Impact of Economic Growth

We assume that the political response to economic growth will differ from that of inflation, where we had to consider the distributional effects of unanticipated inflation. We therefore hypothesized that an increase in the growth rate of industrial production above that expected to occur should cause nothing but economic and political satisfaction. The only possible disadvantage from such growth in industrial production would be an inflationary effect, and that impact, of course, would already be allowed for in our partial regression coefficients. We thus hypothesize that there should be an unambiguous gain in presidential popularity associated with industrial growth in excess of expectations. There should be no losers from real economic gains that would reduce the political influence of this variable.

Whether there are gains in popularity from the anticipated change in growth as well as from the unanticipated growth remains a key empirical issue. We might think on *a priori* grounds that merely keeping to the course along which industrial production has been heading would not induce much of a change in public opinion. Nevertheless, the issue of whether the politically relevant variable is unanticipated growth or actual growth (which contains the anticipated component as well) is an empirical question. We will see that the results seem to favor limiting our predictors to the unanticipated component.

We have argued that unanticipated inflation should result in gains that tend to be offset by losses, thereby suggesting that we should expect little

political impact from past unanticipated inflation. We also need, however, to consider the potential political consequences of uncertainty. This
uncertainty can have a negative political effect if we assume that there is
general risk aversion among the political public.[8] In other words, when
no one knows in advance if they will be gainers or losers from inflation,
even if they are as likely to gain as to lose from an inflationary
performance that differs from what they had anticipated, there still may
be residual political consequences which are negative simply because
people do not like living with uncertainty. This suggests that increasing
uncertainty should have an unambiguous depressing effect on political
popularity, quite apart from past errors in predicting inflation and even
apart from the expected course of future inflation. Indeed, there is no
necessary link between the rate of future inflation which is expected and
the degree of uncertainty with which these expectations are held. (For
example, the belief that inflation will be low could be held with a high
degree of uncertainty about the possible accuracy of this belief.)

MODEL, DATA, AND VARIABLE CONSTRUCTION

Taking the above as our theoretical framework, we developed a model
which explains fluctuations in presidential popularity through the gap
between actual and expected inflation, the gap between actual and
expected economic growth, the uncertainty about inflation, and the
uncertainty over economic growth. Two political variables, one measuring national involvement in the Korean and Vietnam wars and another
measuring the political shifts occurring around presidential elections and
inaugurations, were also included in the model to avoid specification
error. This gives the following model:

$$DPS = a + GAPINF + GAPGROW + UNCERINF$$
$$+ UNCERGROW + WARS + ELECADMIN + e$$

where DPS is the change in support for the incumbent president as
measured by responses to the Gallup Poll, GAPINF is the gap between
actual and expected inflation, GAPGROW is the gap between actual and
unexpected economic growth, UNCERINF is uncertainty concerning

future inflation, UNCERGROW is uncertainty concerning future growth, WARS is a measure of U.S. involvement in the Korean and Vietnam wars, ELECADMIN is a measure of political activity surrounding presidential elections and inaugurations, a is a constant, and e is an error term.

These variables were operationalized and constructed in the following way. To allow for the political importance of political popularity, we analyzed changes in presidential popularity ($P_t - P_{t-1}$) rather than levels in popularity (P_t). This allows for instances of similar economic situations occurring for presidents whose popularity fluctuates around quite different means. (Eisenhower is one example of a president who enjoyed consistently high popular support regardless of the economic situation.) Data on presidential popularity come from the Gallup estimates of public approval of the president taken in April and October. The change in presidential popularity thus is the shift in presidential approval between these two periods. (These two periods were chosen to correspond with the times when Livingston collected his data on expectations and uncertainty.)[9]

Measures of actual inflation come from the consumer price index traditionally used by economic and political analysts. We calculated the price shifts between April and October, in annual percentage terms, to correspond with the Livingston data.

We measured actual economic growth using data on the change in the industrial production index, rather than unemployment or income, first because this one measure is closely correlated with both unemployment and income,[10] and second because it should better detect national well-being rather than individual economic situations, something which work by Kinder and his colleagues suggests is the relevant political variable.[11]

Expectations of future inflation and economic growth come from survey responses by leading businessmen and economists on their expectations of 6-month and 12-month future inflation and economic growth. These data were collected by Joseph Livingston and were recoded by Carlson in 1977 (see Carlson, 1977).[12] The Livingston data provide a long time series of survey answers measuring expected inflation and economic growth. If the expectations hypothesis is valid, then the expectations of economic growth should affect presidential popularity, with the gap between actual and expected inflation and actual and expected growth having a positive influence on popularity.

To arrive at measures of uncertainty over inflation and growth we utilized the standard deviation from the mean expectations across respondents. The standard deviation can be employed as a measure of uncertainty since the more uncertainty there is about the future, the more divergent will be the experts' expectations and the more dispersed around the mean will be the responses of different forecasters. Carlson had already calculated this standard deviation across respondents' forecasts of indicators of inflation, and his measures were taken as an index of uncertainty on inflation. If the uncertainty hypothesis is valid this measure should have a negative effect on presidential popularity. Following the above logic, we calculated an index of uncertainty about real economic growth by similarly estimating the standard deviation across respondents' forecasts of growth in industrial production. These calculations were computed from data supplied directly to us by Livingston. Again if the uncertainty hypothesis is valid, this measure of uncertainty over economic growth should have a negative influence on popularity.

Because we know from much previous work that presidential popularity also responds to involvement in wars, a variable on U.S. military involvement was included to avoid specification error. This variable was coded +1 whenever the U.S. was involved in a foreign war and 0 when there was no substantial involvement. Relying on histories, chronologies, and Mueller's summary, we thus assigned a +1 to the period between October 1950 and October 1953. This period begins after the North Korean attack in June precipitated U.S. aid and ends with the armistice in July 1953 and the prisoner exchange, ending in January 1954. After this period, the variable was coded 0 until April 1965, as the first U.S. bombing of North Vietnam occurred in February, the first marines landed in March, and the first major demonstrations against the war took place in Washington, D.C., in April. The war variable remained +1 through April 1975, when the last troops left Vietnam on April 29th and the Communists took Saigon on April 30th. Thereafter it remained 0. Earlier work in this area suggests that although we know that public response to both the Korean and Vietnamese wars gradually declined, the modelling of this public reaction to wars is tricky. Responses to these wars shifted—both towards and against the war, depending on the group

—as the wars progressed. According to Mueller, this shift occurred for divergent reasons: perhaps because increased propaganda encouraged increased support, perhaps because public unawareness of military involvement diminished as increased casualties caused resentment among many at the high cost in human life, and perhaps because others felt the prior investment in human lives so great that it was imperative for the nation to persevere and win.[13] Given this complex pattern of public responses, especially to the Vietnam war, we might expect to find that the overall political effect of the wars in our time-series analysis will be neutral; nevertheless, it is necessary to include such a variable to avoid specification error, which will distort the political impact of the economic variables that are our central interest here.

A second proxy variable was designed to detect both the political activity which occurs around an election and the shift in public affections following a change in administration, either because of the traditional honeymoon period enjoyed by a newly elected president or because of a rallying around a president who inherited the office under tragic circumstances. There is much work suggesting the importance of including such proxy variables. Informed political observation supports Mueller's more systematic work on a coalition of minorities; both underline the importance of modelling in the kind of political fence mending which occurs around an election as presidential candidates and political parties attempt to piece together a winning coalition. Stimson's work drew attention to the political benefit to the president of a honeymoon period, the time of high ratings traditionally enjoyed by a newly elected president as he is given a chance by a hopeful public. Finally, Mueller's rally variable, developed to predict public rallying behind an incumbent president during an international crisis, can be extended to the kind of domestic crises the country experienced when Kennedy was assassinated and when Nixon resigned, both national traumas which caused the public to rally around the new president in more intense fashion than is usually the case. Several different versions of this combined election-honeymoon-domestic rally variable were constructed; the version which proved most useful was the predictor which was set equal to +1 every April or October after a presidential inauguration resulting because of an election, death, or resignation. (The only inauguration resulting from a death was Johnson's first term. The only inauguration as a result of a resignation was Ford's.)[14] This variable should have a positive effect on popularity as all these activities draw people towards the president.

FINDINGS

Analysis of this model suggests that uncertainty over change in prices, the gap between actual and expected growth, and the activity occurring around the time of presidential elections and inaugurations are statistically significant influences on presidential popularity (See Table 1). The R^2 suggests that we have explained 49% of the total variance. Analysis of the residuals (D.W. = 1.996) suggests there is no serial correlation of the error terms.

The signs for all of our significant predictors are as hypothesized. The war variable has no significant effect, suggesting that earlier positive feelings toward the war policy may have been cancelled out by later antipathy for the policy. Were we more interested in the shifts in popularity resulting from wars, we might attempt to disentangle the shifting impact of this predictor. Since our interest in it was primarily as a means to avoid specification error, however, analysis rests at this point.

Our findings are similar with regard to the predictor designed to measure the shifting public response to a president because of change in administration due to an election, death, or resignation and the emotional outpouring of support as a result of the rally or honeymoon phenomena. This highly significant variable could have been broken down into its component parts to determine which aspect of it is more

TABLE 1. Predictors of Presidential Popularity

	GAP-INF	GAP-GROW	UNCER-INF	UNCER-GRO	WAR	HNSAD-MIN
Beta	− .66	.40	− 10.47	.95	1.51	14.44
SE	.83	.19	3.49	.97	2.81	3.94
$R^2 = .49$						
$DW = 2.00$						
$N = 43$						

significant politically. This has been done elsewhere before, however (see Kernell, 1978; Monroe, 1978), and it is not central to our theoretical concerns here. Thus, we note its political significance and its statistical importance in our model and move on to our more central theoretical findings.

What is central to our theoretical concerns are the different findings about uncertainty and expectations of inflation and growth. The findings here are both quite remarkable and highly significant for public policy. The gap between expected and actual inflation is not significant, suggesting that the satisfaction of those who gain is offset by the dissatisfaction of those who lose from inflation. What does seem to disturb people is the tremendous uncertainty concerning future inflation. And this uncertainty carries great political costs for the incumbent president (beta = -10.47). There is an extremely important policy implication from this: the public might well prefer a policy on inflation which is steady and predictable, albeit not the most advantageous to many people, to the kind of frenetic stop-go/contraction-expansion we have seen so much over the last 20 years, both in the U.S. and in Great Britain. It suggests that incumbents who manipulate the economy for political purposes, as the political business cycle theorists have suggested is widely the case, will incur serious political liabilities. The finding that uncertainty over future prices carries political costs for incumbents suggests that voters are not economic gamblers so much as they are risk-adverters who crave more certainty in this volatile policy area.

Interestingly enough, this finding is not replicated with growth. Here the gap between actual and expected growth is the key predictor. When growth proceeds faster than expected, public pleasure is reflected in increased popularity for the president. Uncertainty about growth is not crucial. (Remember that we allowed for the fact that industrial production increased fairly regularly throughout this period, so we are actually analyzing public response to the rate of growth.)

Taken as a whole, then, our analysis suggests several important findings. First, economic expectations do have political significance, although the psychological process by which economic expectations are translated into political response is more complex than earlier analysts have realized. The evidence here suggests that the gap between the expected and the actual growth rate was politically significant. In other instances where the long-term pattern of change in economic fluctuations is more erratic, as was the case with inflation in the late 1960s and 1970s, then the public seems to be troubled merely by the uncertainty. Public uneasiness over the government's inability to control prices appears to offset any pleasure at doing better than had been expected in the inflation gamble. While we do not wish to minimize the importance of this finding in any way, it is necessary to recall that the rich microlevel literature in psychoanalysis underlines the human need for certainty. And the literature on decision making draws our attention to critical differences between risk-averters and risk-takers. Making the link between the micro and macrolevel phenomena in this area will be pursued in future work.

At the policy level, the findings presented here underscore the public's desire for more consistent policies on inflation, policies which will result in a steadier pattern of price fluctuations. The political football which inflationary policy has become between Republican and Democratic administrations appears to have resulted in political costs to all presidential incumbents. A less political approach might be advised, not just for the economic good of the country, but also for the political fortunes of future presidents.

NOTES

1. Barnhart's (1925) work on rainfall and voting for the Populist Party is the first systematic analysis of voting, and Clark's (1948) analysis of Gallup poll data is the first analysis of popularity data.

2. See Monroe (1979) for a review of the literature on voting and Sigelman (1979) for a review on the work on presidential popularity.

3. See, for example, Fiorina (1978), Kiewiet and Kinder (1978), Kinder and Kiewiet (1979), Klorman (1978), Shapiro and Conforto (1980), Weatherford (1977), and Wides (1976).

4. See De Tocqueville (1840), Hibbs (1981), and Alt (1979).

5. See Alt (1979), especially Chapter 4, or Carlson and Parkin (1975), on the technical difficulties involved in measuring expectations.

6. See Bailey (1956), Kessel and Alchian (1962), or Friedman (1969).

7. The emphasis on distributional effects of inflation on government debt is in the spirit of Meltzer (1951). Although evidence by Kessel (1960), De Alessi (1964), Broussalian (1961), and Reilly (1975) suggests business is not a net debtor, we need to consider the case here and to work through the potential political implications. If business is a net debtor, then losses incurred by the corporate bond holders might be perceived as a gain for the shareholders of business. The profits available for distribution will rise as the real burden of corporate debt is reduced. Again we are left with numerical distribution problems of gainers versus losers. Certainly, we are left wondering how we could have any clear-cut political effect from inflation. We will argue below that there is a clear-cut political effect from inflation, but that its political impact comes from different reasons. We will also compare results when unanticipated inflation and actual changes in inflation are used. See Hibbs (1977) for an interesting discussion of inflation's political implications.

8. The assumption on public risk aversion is a cornerstone in the vast literature on portfolio theory.

9. Livingston's data have been used extensively by economists, but have only recently entered the political science lexicon. For examples using the wage-response and price rationality problems, see Turnovsky (1970), Turnovsky and Wachter, (1972), Pesando (1975), and Carlson (1977). For examples of their usage in the estimation of the Fisher equation, see Gibson (1972), Lahiri (1976), and Levi and Makin (1979). For a detailed description of the Livingston survey data, see Gibson (1972) or Carlson (1977).

10. A problem with many of the earlier estimates of the short-term political impact of growth arises from the fact that real growth has, up until now, been the norm, with few periods of no growth or regression of income. To us, this suggests the value of expressing changes in presidential popularity in terms of the difference between actual growth and expected growth, rather than in terms of mere changes in income levels, as most earlier analysts have done. Surely, continued growth at old rates should not necessarily have strong political benefit. Stigler (1973) has convincingly argued why unemployment is not likely to have important short-term political consequences on voting. Monroe (1978) has reached the same conclusion on the basis of empirical tests using presidential popularity data. We therefore chose to use anticipated change in the industrial production as the measure of success at achieving general economic growth and we use no separate measure of the fraction employed.

11. See the Kinder and Mebane chapter in this book for a discussion of the sociotropic voter argument and a summary of the literature in this area.

12. See Carlson (1977) or Turnovsky (1970) for more details on these data. One potential drawback involved in using these data centers on the fact that forecasts are made by an economic elite, while popularity data come from a mass survey of ordinary citizens. This may mar our findings somewhat; to the degree that

businessmen are representative of the Gallup respondents, however, this draw-back is minimized.

13. Mueller's work on public support for the Korean and Vietnamese wars finds a similar temporal response to both wars, that of gradually declining support, although the opposition to the war in Vietnam was more vocal. (See Mueller, 1973, especially Chapter 3, pages 42–3 and 62, and Chapter 5, for a discussion of important group differences in responses to wars. Also see Mueller (1970) for a full description of the rally phenomenon, wars, and presidential popularity dating back to Truman.)

14. A separate Watergate variable was included in one test of the model but was not significant.

REFERENCES

Alt, J. (1979). *The Politics of Economic Decline.* Cambridge: Cambridge University Press.
Baily, M. J. (1956). "The Welfare Cost of Inflationary Finance." *Journal of Political Economy,* 66(April):93–110.
Broussalian, J. V. (1961). "Unanticipated Inflation: A Test of Debtor-Creditor Hypothesis." Unpublished Ph.D. dissertation, University of California, Los Angeles.
Carlson, J. A. (1977). "A Study of Price Forecasts." *Annals of Economic Social Measurement* 6(Winter):27–56.
Carlson, J. A., and Parkin, M. (1975). "Inflation Expectations." *Economica* 42:123–138.
Davies, J. C. (1969). "The J-Curve of Rising and Declining Satisfactions as a Cause of Some Great Revolutions and a Contained Rebellion." In H. D. Grahm and T. R. Gurr (eds.), *Violence in America: Historical and Comparative Perspectives.* Washington, D.C.: National Commission on the Causes and Prevention of Violence.
_____ (1962). "Towards a Theory of Revolution." *American Sociological Review,* 27(February):5–19.
De Alessi, L. (1964). "Do Business Firms Gain from Inflation?" *Journal of Business,* 37(April):162–166.
De Tocqueville, A. (1840). *The Old Regime and the French Revolution.* New York: Harper.
Downs, A. (1957). *An Economic Theory of Democracy.* New York: Harper & Row.
Fiorina, M. P. (1978). "Economic Retrospective Voting in American Elections: A Micro-Analysis." *American Journal of Political Science,* 22(2):426–443.
Friedman, M. (1969). *The Optimum Quantity of Money and Other Essays,*

Chicago, Aldine.

Gibson, W. E. (1972). "Interest Rates and Inflationary Expectations: New Evidence." *American Economic Review* 62(December):854–865.

Gurr, T. R. (1971). *Why Men Rebel*. Princeton, N.J.: Princeton University Press.

Hibbs, D. A., Jr. (1977). "Political Parties and Macroeconomic Policy" *American Political Science Review*, 71(3):1467–1487.

_____ (1978). "Why are U.S. Policy Makers so Tolerant of Unemployment and Intolerant of Inflation?" Paper prepared for the Brookings Project on the Politics and Sociology of Global Inflation and Unemployment.

_____ (1981). "Public Reactions to the Growth of Taxation and Government Expenditure." *World Politics* 23(3):413–435.

Kernell, S. (1978). "Explaining Presidential Popularity." *The American Political Science Review* 72(2):506–522.

Kessel, R. A., and Alchian, A. A. (1962). "Effects of Inflation." *Journal of Political Economy*, 70(December):521–537.

Kiewiet, D. R., and Kinder, D. R. (1978). "Political Consequences of Economic Consensus—Personal and Collective." Paper presented at the Annual Meeting of the American Political Science Association, New York: August 31–September 3, 1978.

Kinder, D. R., and Kiewiet, D. R. (1979). "Economic Discontent and Political Behavior: The Role of Personal Grievances and Collective Economic Judgments in Congressional Voting." *The American Journal of Political Science* 23(3):495–527.

Klorman, R. (1978). "Trend in Personal Finances and the Vote." *The Public Opinion Quarterly*, 42(1):31–48.

Kramer, G. (1971). "Short-Term Fluctuations in U.S. Voting Behavior, 1896–1964." American Political Science Review, 65(1):131–143.

Kuklinski, J., and West, D. M. (1981). "Economic Expectations and Voting Behavior in the United States House and Senate Elections." *The American Political Science Review* 75(2):436–447.

Lahiri, K. (1976). "Inflationary Expectations: Their Formation and Interest Rate Effects." *American Economic Review* 66(March):124–131.

Levi, M. D., and Makin, J. H. (1979). "Fisher, Phillips, Friedman and the Measured Impact of Inflation on Interest." *Journal of Finance* 34(March):35–52.

Metzler, L. A. (1951). "Wealth, Saving and the Rate of Interest." *Journal of Political Economy* 59(April):93–116.

Monroe, K. R. (1978). "Economic Influences on Presidential Popularity." *The Public Opinion Quarterly* 42(3):360–369.

_____ (1979). "Econometric Analysis of Electoral Behavior: A Critical Review." *Political Behavior*, 1(2):137–174.

Mueller, J. (1970). "Presidential Popularity from Truman to Johnson" *The American Political Science Review* 64(1):18–34.

_____ (1973). *War, Presidents and Public Opinion*. New York: Wiley.

Pesando, J. (1975). "A Note on the Rationality of the Livingston Price Expectations." *Journal of Political Economy* 83(August):849–858.

Reilly, F. (1975). "Companies and Common Stock as Inflation Hedges." *The Bulletin*, New York University.

Sigelman, L. (1979). "The Dynamics of Presidential Support: An Overview of Research." *Presidential Studies Quarterly* 9:206–216.

Shapiro, R. Y., and Conforto, B. M. (1980). "Presidential Performance, the Economy, and the Public's Evaluation of Economic Conditions" *Journal of Politics* 65:49–67.

Stigler, G. (1973). "General Economic Conditions and National Elections." *American Economic Review* 63(May):160–167.

Turnovsky, S. J. (1970). "Some Empirical Evidence on the Formation of Price Expectations." *Journal of American Statistical Association*, 65(December):1441–1454.

_____ and Wachter, M. L. (1972). "A Test of the Expectations Hypothesis Using Directly Observed Wage and Price Expectations." *Review of Economics and Statistics*. 54(February):47–54.

Weatherford, M. S. (1977). "Economic Conditions and Electoral Outcomes: Class Differences in the Political Response to Recession." *The American Journal of Political Science* 22(4):917–938.

Wides, J. W. (1976). "Self-Perceived Economic Change and Political Orientations: A Preliminary Exploration." *American Politics Quarterly*, 4(3):395–411.

INDEX